MOVIE
MASTERMIND

Ronald Bergan & Robyn Karney

Photographs Supplied by Joel W. Finler

WHO?
Are these stars

Portland House
New York.

Acknowledgements

My heartfelt thanks are due to the team of compilers who, although under pressure, brought so much enthusiasm as well as skill to this book. A special thank you to Bernard Hrusa-Marlow for giving so much time and care to the gargantuan task of checking the manuscript for accuracy. To my editorial assistant, Tammy Collins, who in addition to bringing her eagle eye to bear on the proceedings, typed her way through the mess of papers at record speed, gratitude must be recorded; as it must to Max Loppert, Gilbert Adair and Clive Hirschhorn for their immensely helpful comments and their encouragement and to Linda Lucas for invaluable assistance.

Robyn Karney
General Editor

Chief compiler	Ronald Bergan
Picture questions and photographs supplied by	Joel W. Finler
Special contributors	Robin Cross
	Tom Vallance
Research	Bernard Hrusa-Marlow
Design	Rick Fawcett/Dark Design

WHERE?
Are these films located

1986 edition published by Portland House, distributed by Crown Publishers, Inc by arrangement with Octopus Books Limited

ISBN 0 517 61358 1

Printed in Hong Kong

Jacket Photography:
Front: The Kobal Collection, Joel Finler.
Back: Joel Finler.

Contents

Something for Everyone

You don't have to be a film fanatic or a movie buff to have fun with a quiz. This chapter is designed to encourage you to enjoy this book. If you think it's too easy, don't worry – they get harder and harder.

1   Often a physical action or mannerism or a disaster befalling a character becomes a permanent memory of a particular film. In which well-known films did

a Katharine Hepburn fall into a Venetian canal?

b Jack Lemmon strain spaghetti through a tennis racket?

c Fred Astaire dance on the walls and ceiling of his hotel room?

d Paul Henreid set the fashion for lighting one's lover's cigarette simultaneously with one's own?

e Charles Laughton swing from the bells of a cathedral?

f Paul Newman eat fifty hardboiled eggs?

g Cary Grant flee across a field pursued by a crop-duster?

h Diane Keaton beat a man at tennis?

i Freddie Bartholomew fall overboard an ocean liner?

j Grace Kelly sing?

2   Test your general knowledge of movies and stars with this mixed bag of questions:

a On the life of which famous star was the movie MOMMIE DEAREST based and who wrote the book?

b Who or what was E.T. and what do the letters stand for? Who directed the movie?

c What did Eddie Fisher, Mike Todd, Michael Wilding and Richard Burton have in common?

d Can you name the first James Bond film?

e Which well-known American actor expressed his disapproval of the Oscar by turning it down when he won it, and for what film was he given it? (The answer required is not Marlon Brando, who behaved in a similar fashion)

f What was Sophie's choice in the film of that name?

g In what famous comedy are the last words spoken 'Nobody's perfect', and who said them to whom?

h Which film told the real-life story of boxer Jake La Motta and who played the part?

i Who were KRAMER VS KRAMER?

j 8½ purports to be an autobiographical film by which film director?

3   Literature has always been a rich source of inspiration to the cinema. Can you name the writers of the plays or novels from which the following films were made?

a HENRY V

b LOST HORIZON

c GREAT EXPECTATIONS

d OF HUMAN BONDAGE

e WAR AND PEACE

f A MAN FOR ALL SEASONS

g MYRA BRECKINRIDGE

h A STREETCAR NAMED DESIRE

i WUTHERING HEIGHTS

j THE DAY OF THE JACKAL

4   Movie Buffs see film titles everywhere, even in a letter written while on vacation. There are 42 titles to be found in the letter below:

Dear Ruth

Having wonderful time at the Holiday Inn, Casablanca. Arrived at the airport in Morocco at 12 o'clock, high noon on Friday the 13th and took a taxi to the hotel. Tipped the taxi driver 8½ dollars. What robbery! We have a room at the top with a rear window facing the sea – not at all like 10 Sunset Boulevard. We met a woman on the beach from Nashville, Tennessee, who's been coming here since the summer of '42. She keeps us a place in the sun every day. For night life there is plenty of dancing. In the dark one can hear the lovers kissing. The rocky landscape is lovely to look at, but I miss the reds and browns of the autumn leaves in New York. New York is where I want to live. We'll be coming home before October 1984, in time for Halloween. Regards to Wilson.

Sincerely yours

John and Mary

5   Born Frances Gumm, she became a star at 16 in a famous musical. By what name do we know her, what was the film, and who wrote the famous children's book on which it was based? Can you name Miss Gumm's now famous daughter, and that daughter's musically well-known half-sister?

Here is a classic scene from a very famous and enduring film, set during a war. Which war was it? You can almost certainly name the film and recognise the two stars – who are they? – but can you name the other two actors pictured here, and say what the relationship is between the woman and the two men not in uniform? The leading man owned a bar in the film. Who played the bar's resident pianist, and what was the song that he made famous?

---

6   The following pairs of film stars share a surname but are not necessarily related. Provide the surname in each case, and say which *are* related and how:

a Roy, Ginger
b Nastassia, Klaus
c Vivien, Janet
d Gene, Grace
e Peter, Jane
f Buster, Diane
g Robert, Elizabeth
h Jeff, Beau
i Tony, Jamie Lee
j Dick, Eleanor

7   Famous film studios are often identified only by their initials. What do the following stand for?

a WB
b MGM
c RKO
d UA
e U-I

8   In certain films the name of a place remains as alive in the memory as the stars and characters. With which films do you associate these places?

a Shangri-la
b Manderly
c Xanadu (1940)
d Krypton
e Tara

9   Identify the form of transport represented by each of the following:

a THE TITFIELD THUNDERBOLT
b THE BLUE MAX
c CHITTY CHITTY BANG BANG
d THE AFRICAN QUEEN
e BLUE THUNDER

10 What was the main locale of the following films?
a MERRY CHRISTMAS, MR LAWRENCE
b THEY SHOOT HORSES, DON'T THEY?
c THE GREATEST SHOW ON EARTH
d THE GREAT ESCAPE
e THE CHINA SYNDROME
f THE BRIDGE ON THE RIVER KWAI
g JAWS
h VICTORY AT ENTEBBE
i CALIFORNIA SUITE
j MIDNIGHT EXPRESS

The still shows a scene from one of the most famous epic films of all time. What is it? Name the two stars pictured here, as well as the characters they played. Who was the leading man, and who directed the picture? Can you name the writer of the novel on which the film was based, and do you know who the leading lady's real-life husband was at the time? During which war did the story take place, and which city was the setting for its most spectacular scene of destruction?

11 Ten famous film directors are listed below, with the wrong first names attached to the well-known surnames. Can you unscramble them?
a François Antonioni
b Alfred Lean
c Ingmar Herzog
d David Spielberg
e Werner Bergman
f Jean-Luc Truffaut
g Martin Hitchcock
h Michelangelo Godard
i Steven Lang
j Fritz Scorsese

12 Many movies have named one or more of the four seasons in their titles. In what season would you meet the following pairs?
a Katharine Hepburn and Peter O'Toole
b Katharine Hepburn and Elizabeth Taylor
c Paul Scofield and Vanessa Redgrave
d Ingrid Bergman and Liv Ullmann
e Cliff Richard and Ron Moody
f Mickey Rooney and Gloria de Haven
g Anna Neagle and Michael Wilding
h Jennifer O'Neill and Gary Grimes
i Judy Garland and Gene Kelly
j Alan Alda and Sandy Dennis

13 What do the following names or titles in each group have in common?
a Cary Grant, Elizabeth Taylor, Bob Hope
b THE EMPIRE STRIKES BACK
A SHOT IN THE DARK
INDIANA JONES AND THE TEMPLE OF DOOM
c Carole Lombard, Leslie Howard, Audie Murphy
d THE BIRDS
JAMAICA INN
DON'T LOOK NOW
e Peter Sellers, Ben Kingsley, Richard Burton

14 Which stars have acquired the following nicknames:
a The Sex Kitten?
b The King?
c The Duke?
d The Pelvis?
e America's Sweetheart?
f The 'It' Girl?
g The Platinum Blonde?
h The Sweater Girl?
i The Oomph Girl?
j The Man Of A Thousand Faces?

15 A number of directors have also been actors, or have made appearances in their own or other's films. Which directors played roles in the following, and say whether they were their own or not? If not, name the director of the movie:
a TOOTSIE
b CHARIOTS OF FIRE
c THE THIRD MAN
d EATING RAOUL
e SAINT JACK
f CLOSE ENCOUNTERS OF THE THIRD KIND
g CHINATOWN
h TAXI DRIVER
i HUSBANDS
j STALAG 17

16 The cinema is often called 'the seventh art'. Which of the other six arts were the subjects of the films below?
a TURNING POINT
b THE HORSE'S MOUTH
c THE FOUNTAINHEAD
d BELOVED INFIDEL
e THE COMPETITION

17 The cinema is also considered the baby of the arts. Can you name the 'Baby' films that featured
a Mia Farrow
b Bette Davis
c Lee Remick
d Katharine Hepburn
e Carroll Baker

18 Who played the royalty in the following films:
a THE KING AND I?
b THE KING OF MARVIN GARDENS?
c KING CREOLE?
d KING KONG?
e KING RAT?
f A KING IN NEW YORK?
g THE DUCHESS AND THE DIRTWATER FOX?
h QUEEN CHRISTINA?
i THE PRINCE AND THE SHOWGIRL?
j QUEEN BEE?

19 Fill in the missing numbers – some titles use figures, some words:
a ...A SPACE ODYSSEY
b ...DAYS AT PEKING
c ...MOTELS
d ...WOMEN
e ...FOR THE ROAD
f ...EASY PIECES
g THE...STEPS
h ...SQUADRON
i ...ANGRY MEN
j THE...BLOWS

Jack Lemmon and Sissy Spacek, but what is their relationship, where are they, and why are they together? Give the title of the film, and name the director. What nationality is he and what was the film which first made him famous? Spacek was nominated for the Best Actress Oscar for this film (1982) but didn't get it. Who did and what for? However, she *did* get the Oscar in 1980. What was the film, and name the real-life character she portrayed in it.

All Singin'All Dancin'

The Hollywood musical has long been one of the most popular forms of screen entertainment. Memorable scores and great performances have combined with a high standard of production skills to create a unique art form.

1 Three immortal musical partnerships: Fred Astaire and Ginger Rogers, Judy Garland and Mickey Rooney, Jeanette MacDonald and Nelson Eddy. Match the films below to the correct song and attach them to the appropriate partnership:

A NEW MOON
B SHALL WE DANCE?
C THE GAY DIVORCEE
D BABES IN ARMS
E FOLLOW THE FLEET
F NAUGHTY MARIETTA
G WORDS AND MUSIC
H STRIKE UP THE BAND
I MAYTIME
J GIRL CRAZY
K SWINGTIME
L BITTER SWEET

a 'Ah, Sweet Mystery of Life'
b 'Night and Day'
c 'Love's Old Sweet Song'
d 'Lover Come Back to Me'
e 'Our Love Affair'
f 'Let's Face the Music and Dance'
g 'Let's Call the Whole Thing Off'
h 'How About You?'
i 'The Way You Look Tonight'
j 'I'll See You Again'
k 'I Wish I Were in Love Again'
l 'Could You Use Me?'

2 It's well-known that stars are not always cast in a musical because of their vocal ability! Sometimes they battle through the songs, more often than not they are skilfully dubbed. Can you say which of the following were dubbed and by whom?
a Audrey Hepburn in FUNNY FACE
b Rita Hayworth in PAL JOEY
c Ann Blyth in THE STUDENT PRINCE
d Harry Belafonte in CARMEN JONES
e Vanessa Redgrave in CAMELOT
f Natalie Wood in WEST SIDE STORY
g Twiggy in THE BOY FRIEND
h Albert Finney in ANNIE
i Leslie Caron in GIGI
j Deborah Kerr in THE KING AND I

3 Several musicals have featured a prim heroine who melts under the influence of romance and music. Identify the films and players:
a A repressed Salvation Army lass spends an evening in Havana with a gambler, becomes tipsy and falls in love.
b A Russian emissary, who regards love as purely a chemical reaction, succumbs to the charms of Paris and a Hollywood musical producer.
c A farmgirl, at first hostile to the theatrical troupe using her farm to rehearse and stage a new show, falls in love with the producer and reveals a great talent for song and dance.
d A prim Salvation Army lass dresses glamorously and visits a nightclub in order to convince the playboy she loves that she is not too good for him.
e A straitlaced dean of a music academy, upset by the remarks of a trumpet player she meets on a train, alters her entire appearance and becomes sought after by both the trumpeter and a crooner.

4 The following unlikely candidates have all appeared in a musical or musicals. Name the film(s) in each case:
a Burt Reynolds
b Lee Marvin
c Rod Steiger
d Marlon Brando
e Walter Matthau
f William Holden
g Liv Ullmann
h Hedy Lamarr
i Ernest Borgnine
j Karl Malden

No doubt you can identify the film from which this very well-known still is taken, as well as the stars illustrated? But do you know who was originally chosen to play the male lead, was prevented from doing so by injury and suggested the fellow on the left above? Who wrote the score of the film, who choreographed the dance numbers, and who was the director?

5 Many musicals have drawn their inspiration from a previously successful non-musical. As Julie Harris playing Sally Bowles in I AM A CAMERA is to Liza Minnelli in the same role in CABARET, so are the following to each other. Name the films:
a Janet Gaynor/Leslie Caron
b Jean Gabin/Tony Martin
c Giulietta Masina/Shirley MacLaine
d Shirley Booth/Barbra Streisand
e Greta Garbo/Cyd Charisse
f Wilfred Lawson/Stanley Holloway
g Irene Dunne/Deborah Kerr
h Eva Dahlbeck/Elizabeth Taylor
i Robert Donat/Peter O'Toole
j Norma Shearer/Natalie Wood

6 The 1950s saw a rash of musical remakes of classic comedies of the 1930s. Name the titles of the musical versions of the following films and the players who were the musical counterparts of the performers mentioned:
a NINOTCHKA; Greta Garbo, Melvyn Douglas
b THE WOMEN; Norma Shearer, Joan Crawford, Rosalind Russell
c BACHELOR MOTHER; Ginger Rogers, David Niven
d IT HAPPENED ONE NIGHT; Claudette Colbert, Clark Gable
e TOM, DICK AND HARRY; Ginger Rogers, George Murphy, Burgess Meredith

7 A pot-pourri of quickies:
a Which debonair British musical star of the 1930s co-starred with Fred Astaire in THE BAND WAGON (1953)?
b Of which of his accomplished dancing partners did Fred Astaire remark: 'When you've danced with her you stay danced with'?
c Two of her major hits were IN OLD CHICAGO and ALEXANDER'S RAGTIME BAND and she played the title role in LILLIAN RUSSELL. Who is she?
d The 1929 musical BROADWAY was remade in 1942 and starred one of Hollywood's most famous tough guys, purporting to play himself. Name him.
e What film made a star of John Travolta and in which musical movie did he appear the following year?
f Who built a stairway to paradise in a famous MGM musical starring Gene Kelly and Leslie Caron?
g In what film did Elvis Presley make his screen debut? And in which year?
h In which films did Betty Hutton play real-life personalities Texas Guinan, Pearl White, Blossom Seeley and Annie Oakley?
i What later Academy Award winner played the small role of Zelda in SINGIN' IN THE RAIN? For which film did she win the Oscar?
j In which film did Marge and Gower Champion dance with an elephant?

8 Identify the actor or actress who created each of the following roles, as well as the musical in which the character featured:
a Nicky Arnstein
b Lina Lamont
c Tony Manero
d Captain Von Trapp
e Madame Crematon

9 The 1962 version of Rodgers and Hammerstein's STATE FAIR featured Pat Boone and Pamela Tiffin as the brother and sister who find romance at the fair, Ann-Margret and Bobby Darin as their romantic partners, and Alice Faye and Tom Ewell as their parents. Who played these roles in the classic 1945 version?

The one-and-only Marilyn Monroe, of course, performing the outstanding number from her last musical. Can you name the film and the song she performed in this sequence? Who was the film's director, Marilyn's continental leading man, and the British singer who formed the third part of a triangle? Who were the three guest stars hired in the film to teach the leading man the art of comedy, song and dance?

A highlight from one of the best musical films of the 1950s. The gentleman on the left is Fred Astaire, but can you name his playmates, the title of the film, and the song being performed? Who directed the film, and what were the other two musicals he had previously made, also starring Astaire? Who was Fred's leading lady in this one, and to which tune did they perform a memorably romantic *pas-de-deux* by lantern light in Central Park? The score consisted almost entirely of standards by which composing team?

10   Name the choreographer of, and the film in which a dance number
a Begins with two halves of a sketch coming together to form a backdrop
b Begins with a white speck becoming larger and larger to form a girl's face, which is finally seen in close-up
c Concerns itself with the subject of choreography
d Has three men dancing on dustbin lids
e Begins with the raising of a house and ends with its destruction

11   Who portrayed
a TWO SISTERS FROM BOSTON?
b THREE LITTLE GIRLS IN BLUE?
c TWO GIRLS AND A SAILOR?
d 100 MEN AND A GIRL
e FOUR JILLS IN A JEEP?

12   The theme of three servicemen at loose in the big city is a familiar one to musical fans. Who played
a The three sailors in ON THE TOWN?
b The three soldiers in IT'S ALWAYS FAIR WEATHER?
c The three sailors in HIT THE DECK (1955)?
d The three sailors in THREE SAILORS AND A GIRL?
e The three sailors in SO THIS IS PARIS?

13   The 1942 musical THE FLEET'S IN told of a serviceman (William Holden) accepting a wager that he could date a cabaret star noted for her coldness. The same plot was used for a 1960 musical; what was its title and who played the serviceman and the dancer he wooed?

13

14   In which films were the following dances performed?
a 'The Continental'
b 'The Riviera'
c 'The Yam'
d 'The Carioca'
e 'The Tapioca'

15   In which films were the following songs introduced?
a 'The Lady in Red'
b 'The Lady in the Tutti-Frutti Hat'
c 'A Gal in Calico'
d 'The Gal With the Yaller Shoes'
e 'Lovely Lady in White'

16   When THE WIZARD OF OZ was remade as THE WIZ in 1978, Diana Ross inherited Judy Garland's role as Dorothy. Who played her companions the Scarecrow, the Tin Man and the Cowardly Lion, originally played by Ray Bolger, Jack Haley and Bert Lahr?

Part of a torrid number from one of the most under-rated musicals of the 1950s, directed by one of Hollywood's veteran craftsmen and featuring the songs of a renowned triple-threat composing team. Can you name the film, the director, the dancers pictured here (the lady was also the film's heroine), and the three composers whose lives the film depicted, plus who played them and who did the choreography?

17   Boy-girl song-and-dance duets have always been a staple of the musical, the most famous team undoubtedly being the brilliant Astaire and Rogers. Name the teams who performed the following routines, and the films in which they were featured:
a 'I'm Old Fashioned'
b 'Main Street'
c 'Polly Wolly Doodle'
d 'Why Can't You Behave?'
e 'You're The One That I Want'
f 'Kokomo, Indiana'
g 'Between You and Me'
h 'Like Monday Follows Sunday'
i 'Who's Got the Pain?'
j 'Rude, Crude and Unattractive'

18   Fred Astaire's best remembered dancing partner is Ginger Rogers, but who was his *first* dancing partner on screen, and in what film?

19   Hollywood's dance directors made an invaluable contribution to the musical film with their imaginative staging and fluid choreography. Match the choreographers with their films:
A Busby Berkeley
B Hermes Pan
C Robert Alton
D Eugene Loring
E Dave Gould
F George Balanchine
G Patricia Birch
H Onna White
I Bobby Connolly
J Nick Castle

a TOP HAT
b OLIVER!
c DAMES
d ROYAL WEDDING
e BORN TO DANCE
f SGT PEPPER'S LONELY HEARTS CLUB BAND
g BROADWAY MELODY OF 1940
h YOLANDA AND THE THIEF
i GOLDWYN FOLLIES
j EASTER PARADE

20   Who spoke the following memorable lines of dialogue, and in which musical films?
a 'If we bring a little joy into your humdrum lives, we know all our hard work ain't been in vain for nothin''
b On hearing a knock at the door: 'If it's the wolf, we'll eat it'
c 'I can see you now, with your cutlass in one hand and your . . . your compass in the other'
d 'I've taught everyone from Nijinsky to Mickey Rooney'
e 'Is McKinley still President?'

This still shows one of the electrifying dance routines from a musical of the 70s that not only proved a sensational box-office attraction but made its youthful leading man a superstar overnight. Doubtless you can name him and the film, but who is the leading lady pictured dancing with him here? Which pop group provided most of the soundtrack music, who directed the film, and what was the sequel?

21 Which musicals of the 1970s and 80s would you associate with
a Flower Power?
b A school of performing arts?
c Visitors from the planet of Transylvania?
d A dance director's heart attack?
e A rock parody of an old Lon Chaney horror classic?

22 The team of Rodgers and Hammerstein were responsible for the scores of several great Broadway successes which were eventually brought to the cinema screen. From the cast lists below, name the films:
a Julie Andrews, Christopher Plummer, Eleanor Parker
b Gordon MacRae, Shirley Jones, Rod Steiger
c Deborah Kerr, Yul Brynner, Rita Moreno
d Mitzi Gaynor, Rossano Brazzi, Juanita Hall
e Gordon MacRae, Shirley Jones, Barbara Ruick

23 Harold Arlen, during his long career as one of America's finest composers, worked with several lyricists. Who collaborated with him on the following films?
a A STAR IS BORN
b STAR SPANGLED RHYTHM
c CASBAH
d LET'S FALL IN LOVE
e MY BLUE HEAVEN

24 The following songs were introduced by stars making their debuts in feature films. Name the stars and the films in which they sang the songs:
a 'A Spoonful of Sugar'
b 'It's You Or No-one'
c 'Arthur Murray Taught Me Dancing in a Hurry'
d 'Dream Lover'
e 'Always a Lady'

25 Many a musical has been graced with the work of famous composer partnerships. Fill in the missing member of the following teams:
a Jerome Kern and ...?
b Mike Leiber and ...?
c Betty Comden and ...?
d Richard Rodgers and ...?
e Don Raye and ...?
f Tim Rice and ...?
g Bert Kalmar and ...?
h Al Dubin and ...?
i Buddy De Sylva, Lew Brown and ...?
j Arthur Schwartz and ...?

26 Richard M. and Robert B. Sherman, composers who won an Oscar with 'Chim Chim Cher-ree' from MARY POPPINS, their first film, went on to score several other family musicals. For which films did they compose the following songs?
a 'Gratifaction'
b 'A Rose Is Not a Rose'
c 'The Age of Not Believing'
d 'Fortuosity'
e 'Mother Earth and Father Time'

27 Who played the two 'little girls from Little Rock' in GENTLEMEN PREFER BLONDES?

28 Musicals have occasionally brought together some unlikely star combinations. In which films did the following co-star?
a Elvis Presley and Barbara Stanwyck
b Bing Crosby and Ingrid Bergman
c Carmen Miranda and Wallace Beery
d Neil Diamond and Sir Laurence Olivier
e Humphrey Bogart and Louise Fazenda

29 Two noted American comic-strips, 'Li'l Abner' and 'Little Orphan Annie' were turned into hit Broadway musicals, and thence into films. Who played the title roles in the film versions?

30 Bing Crosby and Frank Sinatra are undoubtedly the most famous film crooners of all time. Which one introduced each of the following songs and in which film?
a 'White Christmas'
b 'You're Sensational'
c 'My Kind of Town'
d 'Swinging on a Star'
e 'Adelaide'
f 'Moonlight Becomes You'
g 'I'm An Old Cowhand'
h 'Time After Time'
i 'I Couldn't Sleep a Wink Last Night'
j 'June in January'

31 Name the 1963 musical (from a Broadway hit) inspired by fan-worship of Elvis Presley and the hysteria caused by his induction into the Army.

The sizzling roof-top dance from one of the most acclaimed musicals of all time. What was the film's title, what number is being performed here, and who is the lady at the centre of attention. She won an Oscar for her performance – what other player in the film also won an Academy Award? Who wrote the songs, who were the *two* directors, and who was responsible for the Oscar-winning photography? Who played the leading roles of the star-crossed lovers?

32 The following are the real names of noted musical performers. Can you identify them?
a Harry Clifford Leek
b Lucille Collier
c Tommy Hicks
d Sophie Abuza
e Virginia Katherine McMath
f Suzanne Burce
g Alice Leppert
h Francesca Mitzi Marlene de Charney von Gerber
i Dino Crocetti
j Ethel Zimmerman

33 'I'm a Dreamer, Aren't We All?' was sung by one of the screen's first sweethearts in an early musical. What was its name, who was the star, and who was her co-star with whom she duetted 'If I Had A Talking Picture of You'?

34 Opera singers have traditionally met with limited success in attempts at Hollywood stardom, but that hasn't stopped them – or Hollywood – from trying. Match the opera stars below to the films in which they were featured:

A Grace Moore
B Lauritz Melchior
C Lily Pons
D Ezio Pinza
E Risë Stevens

a THE CHOCOLATE SOLDIER
b STRICTLY DISHONORABLE
c LUXURY LINER
d I DREAM TOO MUCH
e I'LL TAKE ROMANCE

35 Each group of musicals listed below was made by the same director. Name the director of each group:

a YANKEE DOODLE DANDY
  THIS IS THE ARMY
  NIGHT AND DAY
b THE SINGING FOOL
  FOOTLIGHT PARADE
  NAVY BLUES
c TIN PAN ALLEY
  MOON OVER MIAMI
  CONEY ISLAND
d LITTLE MISS BROADWAY
  DOWN ARGENTINE WAY
  THAT NIGHT IN RIO
e KID MILLIONS
  BORN TO DANCE
  ON THE AVENUE

36 In partnership with Gene Kelly, Stanley Donen directed two classic musicals, ON THE TOWN and SINGIN' IN THE RAIN. His career as a solo director, though varied, has included such gems as SEVEN BRIDES FOR SEVEN BROTHERS and FUNNY FACE. From your knowledge of his achievements, can you name

a His first film as sole director?
b The two films he co-directed with George Abbott?
c The film he directed which had a score by Frederick Loewe and Alan Jay Lerner?
d The film he co-directed with Kelly which featured a dance by Kelly on roller-skates?
e The MGM musical in which Donen appeared as chorus boy and dancer?

37 One of the most fondly remembered musical stars is Deanna Durbin, whose sweet soprano and engaging personality charmed audiences for a decade. In which of her films did she introduce the following songs:

a 'I Love To Whistle'
b 'Waltzing in the Clouds'
c 'Spring Will Be A Little Late This Year'
d 'Amapola'
e 'Beneath the Lights of Home'
f 'It's Raining Sunbeams'
g 'More and More'
h 'My Own'
i 'The Turntable Song'
j 'Say a Prayer For the Boys Over There'

38 In FOLIES BERGERE Maurice Chevalier played a dual role, thus confusing the wife (Merle Oberon) of one character and the girlfriend (Ann Sothern) of the other. This film was remade twice. What were the titles of the remakes and who played the three leading roles in each of them?

A sequence from what has come to be regarded as the most popular musical of all time. Its title should present no problem, but what *two* songs were used for this extended 'Broadway Ballet' number? What link is there between the film's producer and its score? Who are the two main players shown here, and in which film did they co-star set in the Scottish highlands? Who played the movie star whose voice was so decidedly wrong for talkies? Finally, who wrote the hilarious screenplay and what script did they write for Astaire, taking a similarly satirical look at the world of the theatre?

---

41   Nelson Eddy's name will always be linked with that of Jeanette MacDonald in the minds of film-goers, but who were his partners in the following films?
a ROSALIE
b BALALAIKA
c THE PHANTOM OF THE OPERA
d THE CHOCOLATE SOLDIER
e LET FREEDOM RING

42   James Cagney played legendary composer-entertainer George M. Cohan in two films – can you name them?

43 Busby Berkeley has long been acknowledged a genius of the early days of talking pictures, particularly for the staggering inventiveness he brought to the production numbers in the musicals on which he worked. Name the songs and films which featured the following:

a The exterior of a train splits in the middle to show the interior corridors and sleeping compartments

b Dozens of girls with look-a-like masks of the heroine form a gigantic jigsaw puzzle of her face

c Fifty-six grand pianos, with girls playing them, glide through a formation of patterns in waltz time

d Sixty violins glowing in the dark form into one enormous neon-lit violin

e With a background of white pillars and white ribbons, a hundred dancers appear to become thousands when reflected in an octagon of mirrors

44 The play 'Burlesque', filmed in 1929 as DANCE OF LIFE and in 1937 as SWING HIGH SWING LOW, became a musical vehicle for Betty Grable in 1948. What was the name of this version, who was Betty's Oscar-nominated co-star, and name the three other films she made with him?

This musical military routine was conceived by the most renowned choreographer of the 1930s, but for one of his less celebrated films. Who was he, what was the film, and what was the song being performed here? Who wrote the song, and what Academy Award-winning number had they written two years earlier for the same choreographer's memorable routine of a New York playgirl who meets a tragic end? Who directed the film illustrated, and who were the stars (a real-life married couple at the time)?

45 The original version of THE JAZZ SINGER was released in 1927 and secured the fortunes of a major film studio. Which studio was it, and what was the historical significance of the film? Who played the title role and what famous musical ingenue of the 1930s did this star later marry? Name two of the films she made with the famous choreographer Busby Berkeley.

46 Which famous jazz musicians appeared in the following films?
GOING PLACES
CABIN IN THE SKY
HIGH SOCIETY
HELLO DOLLY

Make 'Em Laugh

ABOVE and LEFT
Name the three 'ladies' in the stills. Give the reasons for their particular mode of dress. Which of the three
a Gets engaged to a millionaire?
b Makes unusual use of a horse?
c Imitates one of the other two?
Give the titles and directors of each film. In which movies did the following wear drag?
i) Peter Sellers ii) Alec Guinness iii) Robert Preston iv) George Sanders v) Jerry Lewis

RIGHT
The key to the door is also the key to the title of the film. Name it. Who's holding the key and why was it particularly important? Who played the man's boss and the elevator girl? The characters' names were F. Kubelik, C. C. Baxter and J. D. Sheldrake. Which was which?

ABOVE
Sunday morning in the park:
a Which park?
b What is the name of the game being played?
c Who are the two stars in the foreground?
d Name the film and its sequel
e Who wrote and directed both films?

RIGHT
An unmistakable figure in a typical scene of comic confusion:
a Name the film
b Name the character with the pipe and the actor-director who played him
c What is his relationship to the man under the sunshade in the film?
d In which film did he first play the character – and in which last?
e Which of his films won an Oscar?

ABOVE
What was the title of this very successful 1970s comedy, what does the title stand for and when was the action supposed to have taken place? Name the characters and the actors pictured. Which of the two characters was retained for the TV spin-off and who played him in it? What was the name of the character played by Sally Kellerman in the film?

ABOVE
Buster Keaton in a scene from one of his greatest films. What is it? What does the title refer to and what is Keaton's relationship to it? During what period is the film set?

LEFT
Identify the movie and the stars illustrated. Each was known for their witticisms. Which of the following belongs to whom?
a 'Beulah, peel me a grape'
b 'Some weasel took the cork out of my lunch'
c 'When I'm good I'm very good, but when I'm bad I'm better'
d 'If at first you don't succeed, try again. Then quit. No use being a damn fool about it'
e 'Whenever I'm caught between two evils, I take the one I've never tried'

RIGHT
The Marx Brothers, of course, but do you know:
a The real names of Groucho, Harpo, Chico and Zeppo?
b The name and date of their first feature film?
c Which studio brought them to screen fame and to which studio they subsequently moved?
d Which brother, at 82, gave a one-man stage show on Broadway?

ABOVE

This still shows Tracy and Hepburn in one of the many pictures they made together. Which one? Who is the actress in the centre and what is the relationship between the three characters? Tracy and Hepburn's first picture together underwent a revival in a different guise during the 70s. What was the picture and what new treatment did it receive? Can you name any of the other seven pictures they starred in together?

RIGHT and ABOVE RIGHT

Stills from two of Woody Allen's successes. Give their titles. Name the actress, the actor who plays her brother, and the four films in which she has appeared with Woody. Who are the two characters on either side of Woody in the other picture? Who played his leading lady? Can you name the three other films Allen has directed in black and white? Name the film which he directed but did not appear in and to whom did it pay homage?

FAR RIGHT

A scene from THE PINK PANTHER. To what does the title refer? Who are the stars in the still and what is their relationship in the film? What is the name of the character on the left? Who played The Phantom?

26

ABOVE
Name the movie and the astonished couple in the picture. What is the problem of the character on the left? What distinguished actor played a butler in the film and how was it a first for him? The actress illustrated had her first screen role in a British movie. What was it called and who was her director/co-star?

RIGHT
The title of the film is a famous catch-phrase. Whose catch-phrase? Give the film's title and name the two leads illustrated. What is the male character's profession? Where is the film set? Where does it end? Who directed it? What other film have the two stars made together?

ABOVE

Complete the following publicity advertisement for the movie illustrated: 'Ridin', Ropin', Wranglin', and all that Western bullshit pulled together by . . . in his new Comedy Classic . . ., brought to you by . . ., the people that gave you 'The Jazz Singer'. Who is the wide-eyed actor in the hat, and what was unusual about the character he played? What two roles were played by the director? What was the confusing name of the character played by Harvey Korman? Who played the Waco Kid and Lily von Shtupp?

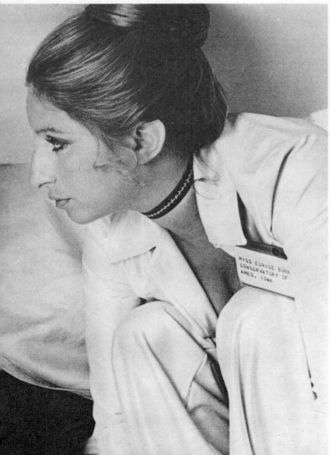

ABOVE LEFT
Who are the orientals pictured here? Name the film and the two stars missing from the still. What made this film different for the lady illustrated? What encore did Peter Sellers give in the film? Where was it filmed?

ABOVE
Although mostly associated with juvenile roles, this famous silent actress was also the producer of many of her own best known pictures. Can you name her, and the title of the film illustrated? It was remade in the 1960s by which famous husband-and-wife team?

LEFT
A scene from a comedy-horror picture directed by and starring the man on the right. Who is he and what is the film? Who is the girl? What was the real-life relationship between her and the man illustrated at the time the film was made? Name the other films in which the director gave himself a role.

RIGHT
The spitting image of Danny Kaye in one of his best comedies. What was it called? Why is he spitting? The answer lies in his confusion between drinking cups. Complete the following: 'The vessel with the . . .', 'The flagon with the . . .', 'The chalice from the . . .'.

31

Reach for the Stars

A An expert horseman since he was old enough to walk, this actor has become best known for westerns but in fact spent the greater part of his early film career as a handsome leading man of drawing-room comedy, drama and thrillers, working with such directors as Lubitsch, Wyler, Sturges and Hitchcock. Born in 1905, he started in films as an extra, landing his first good role in 1929:

a Who is he?

b In 1933 he made a film with the actress who has been his wife for over fifty years; the film concerned a possessive mother. What was it, who played the mother, and who was the actress he married in real life?

c In two of his 50s westerns, he played legendary sheriffs Bat Masterson and Wyatt Earp. What were the films?

d In 1943 he starred in a comedy concerning the housing shortage in wartime Washington. What was the film, who directed it, who was his leading lady and what was the name of the 1966 remake?

e His last film was a fine western co-starring another great western star in a fitting finale to both their careers. What was the film, who was the co-star and who was the film's director?

B Born into a celebrated London theatrical family, she started making her reputation with the Royal Shakespeare Company in the early 60s. Her striking appearance, coupled with genuine ability, made for a painless transition into films and, after playing the on-screen daughter of her real-life father in a minor 1958 film, she stepped into stardom in a comedy, directed by Karel Reisz and starring David Warner, in 1966. The same year found her working for Antonioni and Fred Zinneman. She married (and divorced) director Tony Richardson:

a Who is she?

b To whom did she bear a child out of wedlock?

c She appeared in a screen adaptation of a Chekhov play. What was it? Who directed the film?

d Surprisingly, she played the lead in the film version of a Broadway musical. What was it, and who was her co-star?

e For which film did she win an Oscar, who was her female co-star, and who wrote the memoir on which the film was based?

C Born in 1920, this good-looking and sensitive actor came from the New York stage to score a hit with critics and public with his first two films. Though he worked with several of Hollywood's finest directors, his film career was chequered due to his own moody, neurotic personality and a serious car accident. He died at the tragically early age of 45.

a Who is he?

b What were his first two films, and who directed them?

c What film was he making when he had the accident that broke his jaw? Who were his two leading ladies? And who composed the film's acclaimed background score?

d In 1951 he starred in the second screen version of a Theodore Dreiser novel. What was the film? Who directed it? And who played his role in the earlier version?

e His last film was shot in Germany. What was its name? Who directed it?

D One of England's most distinguished exports to Hollywood, this Scottish-born actress danced with the Sadlers Wells *corps de ballet* before turning to dramatic theatre. An impressive string of British film credits preceded an MGM contract, but she seemed doomed to colourless ladylike roles till the part of a promiscuous wife – and a sensational love scene in the surf – led to parts worthy of her talent:

a Who is she?

b What was the film with the surfside love scene, who directed it and who was her amorous co-star?

c She has been Oscar-nominated six times: for the film above, as well as for her roles as the doomed wife of a man ruthlessly ambitious for their son, a singing governess, a mother-dominated spinster, a nun marooned in the Pacific, and an Australian sheep-drover's wife. What were the films?

d In a notable British film, she played three different women in the central character's life over a period of 50 years. What was the film? Name the two men who wrote, produced and directed it, and who played the central character?

e She played another governess, this time a tormented and haunted one in a chilling psychological thriller. What was it, who directed it, and on what book was it based?

E The son of a Sicilian immigrant, he was born in New York's 'Hell's Kitchen' district which, in 1978, was the setting for a film he wrote, directed and starred in. After trying his hand at a variety of jobs – including being an usher at a Manhattan cinema and appearing nude in an off-Broadway play, he was given the lead (as a gangster) in a low-budget effort called THE LORDS OF FLATBUSH. Small parts in FAREWELL MY LOVELY and CAPONE followed, but it wasn't until 1976 that he found fame and fortune – as well as an Oscar for a film whose script he also wrote:

a Who is he?
b What was the name of the film with the 'Hell's Kitchen' background?
c In what film did he portray the rise and fall of a Union boss?
d In what film did he play a Vietnam veteran?
e He directed a film starring John Travolta. Name it.

F Called by Time Magazine '. . . . one of the most convincing character actors in Hollywood history', he has played Pope John XXIII, an effete mortician, a racketeer, a movie mogul, and, in Humphrey Bogart's last film, a crooked boxing promoter. And that's just for starters! After an inconsequential movie debut in 1951, he bulldozed his way to stardom playing Marlon Brando's older brother – a performance which won him an Oscar nomination. A second nomination followed his performance as a New York Jew haunted by his experiences at the hands of the Nazis:

a Who is he?
b In 1967 he finally received an Oscar. What was the film? What role did he play in it?
c One of his most abject failures was his role as a famous movie comedian. Who?
d In what film was he obsessed by John Philip Law?
e To what well-known British actress was he married for some years?

G The discovery of this glamorous blonde star, while sipping a soda in a Hollywood drug store, has become part of movie mythology. Throughout the 40s her name was the epitome of film glamour, and her career survived many marriages and a notorious murder scandal:

a Who is she?
b Her first major film role was as a murder victim – what was the film, and who was its director?
c As a dying showgirl she is inspired by hearing her old theme music to walk majestically down the steps of a theatre lobby, thus making one of the most famous staircase descents in cinema history. What was the film, and who played her two showgirl chums who met happier fates?
d Dressed in white, she made a memorable entrance in a classic *film noir* when she dropped her lipstick which rolled to her feet. What was the film. Who played her role in the 1981 remake?
e She won an Oscar nomination in 1957 for portraying a troubled mother in a superior adaptation of a best-selling novel. What was the film and who played her daughter?

H After training for a Broadway stage career with Stella Adler and Lee Strasberg, this New York born actor appeared in several off-Broadway productions before making an inauspicious movie debut in 1968. A 1970 Roger Corman film starring Shelley Winters didn't do much for him either, and it wasn't until 1973, when Martin Scorsese discovered him, that his career went into orbit. He won a Best Supporting Oscar for his next film, and was nominated for an Oscar for his work in a Michael Cimino-directed Vietnam war drama:

a Who is he?
b In what film did he play a saxophonist opposite Liza Minnelli?
c For what part in what film did he win his Best Supporting Actor Oscar?
d What was the name of the character he played in a film loosely based on the reign of Irving Thalberg? What was the name of the film?
e He distinguished himself in films directed by Martin Scorsese, in 1973, 1976 and 1982. Name them

I The son of a postal clerk, he was reared in New York's tough East Harlem and in his teens showed immense physical prowess in all forms of sport and athletics – including circus acrobatics. After trying his luck in circuses, vaudeville and nightclubs he made a stunning movie debut in 1946 in an effective *film noir* version of a Hemingway short story. A truly dazzling career followed, climaxed in 1981 with his performance in a Louis Malle-directed drama for which he won a British Academy (BAFTA) Award:

a Who is he?
b In which film did he tour Connecticut via the swimming pools of the rich?
c For what war drama did he win the New York Critics' Best Actor award in 1953?
d He appeared opposite Tony Curtis as a tough newspaper columnist. What was the film?
e One of his best films found him an authority on bird diseases. What was the film?

The Love Parade

Countless films promise a happily-ever-after life for the embracing couple at the fade-out but, as in life, love on the screen is sometimes unrequited or disappointed, manipulative or illusory.

1   Several of the most famous love stories of the screen have been filmed more than once. Each section below lists the leading men of separate versions of the same story. Name the films and the leading ladies:
a Charles Boyer/Cary Grant
b John Boles/Charles Boyer/John Gavin
c Douglass Montgomery/Robert Taylor/ John Kerr
d Leslie Howard/Laurence Harvey/Leonard Whiting
e Warren William/John Gavin

2   The following are the last lines of some memorable love stories. Who said them to whom, and in what films?
a 'Don't leave me – Marguerite, come back, come back'
b 'You've been a long way away. Thank you for coming back to me'
c 'That's the dumbest thing I ever heard'
d 'Maybe I'll live so long that I'll forget her. Maybe I'll die trying'
e 'It's alright. After all, I could have been the girl in the brown and white dress. Anybody could've'
f 'Shut up and deal'
g 'Don't let's ask for the moon – we have the stars'
h 'Hey, can I try on your yellow dress?'
i 'Years from now, when you talk of this – and you will – be kind'
j 'I lived a few weeks while you loved me. Goodbye, Dix'

3   The course of true love rarely runs smoothly when someone of royal blood falls for a mere commoner. Name the films in which
a Royal Audrey Hepburn loved commoner Gregory Peck
b Royal Deborah Kerr loved commoner Stewart Granger
c Royal Edmund Purdom loved commoner Ann Blyth
d Commoner Nelson Eddy loved royal Eleanor Powell
e Commoner Joan Blondell loved royal Fernand Gravet

4   Some of the screen's most memorable romances have been based on true characters. In the couplings below, the first name is that of the performer, the second that of the character *played* by their partner. Name the character played by the first, the performer of the second, and the film:
a Fredric March and Elizabeth Barrett
b Merle Oberon and Fredric Chopin
c Gregory Peck and Sheilah Graham
d James Brolin and Carole Lombard
e Anna Neagle and Charles II

5   'What a tangled web we weave when first we practise to deceive' could have frequently been the motto of Bette Davis, whose screen suffering was often caused, in part at least, by her characters' mendacity. In which film did she
a Lie to her cellist sweetheart about her relationship with a temperamental composer-conductor?
b Lie to her husband and her attorney that the man into whom she had emptied a revolver had tried to force his attentions upon her?
c Lie that she had loaned her car to the cook's son, thus getting him accused of a hit-and-run killing for which she is guilty?
d Pretend to be her dead twin sister, drowned in a boating accident, because she loves her sister's husband?
e Lie to her husband, returned after being thought dead, that the child born in his absence is hers, although in fact it is the result of the husband's previous union with a concert pianist?

This famous romance of the Foreign Legion was the first American film for a legendary German actress. Who is she, who is her leading man, and what is the film? It was directed by a man who made seven films in all with the actress – can you name him, and the other six films they made together (the first in Germany). This particular romance ended with the heroine becoming a camp follower of her legionnaire lover – her final action as she sets out to follow him across the desert has become part of cinema legend – what was it?

6　Sisterly love has caused many a sacrifice, but few can equal that of the 40s heroine who, having accidentally run over her sister's child, becomes pregnant herself (though she knows giving birth will kill her) in order to replace her sister's child. What was the film, and who played the sisters?

7　Four-handkerchief love stories frequently feature a heroine given only a short time left for life and happiness. Name the films described, and the actresses:

a　Realising that she has only a few hours left, she sends her doctor husband on his business so that she can die in dignified solitude (two answers)

b　Terminally ill, she takes a new boyfriend every month until one refuses to be treated casually and proposes

c　An actress with a heart ailment adopts a child and trains her to take her place after death, but the husband resents the child's attempts to duplicate his wife's actions (two answers)

d　A nightclub star tells her lover that she'll be waiting for him when he comes out of prison in five years, though she knows she has only two years to live

e　A dying mother tries to pave the way for her husband to marry the woman who loves him after her death

A railway parting in a classic British drama whose lovers' first and last meetings were at a railway station. What was the film, who played the lovers, and what incident led to their meeting? What was the name of the play from which the film was adapted, and who wrote it? What classical work was used as background music and what pianist played it on the soundtrack?

8　Who played 'I' in
a　I WAS A MALE WAR BRIDE?
b　I KNOW WHERE I'M GOING?
c　I LOVE MY . . . WIFE?
d　I MET HIM IN PARIS?
e　I TAKE THIS WOMAN?

9　Which romantic melodrama, filmed twice, has an intriguing climax where the hero, blinded in the war, memorises the whereabouts of everything in his room so that he can convince the heroine that he can still see, and thus that his rejection of her is genuine? Also, who played the blind hero?

10　In the glossy romantic melodrama WEEKEND AT THE WALDORF, who were the two star couples who found love during two days at the famed hotel?

11 The most romantic of fairytale heroines, Cinderella, has been adapted to the screen several times in various forms. Who, in each case, played the heroine in THE GLASS SLIPPER and THE SLIPPER AND THE ROSE? Which well-known comedian played the title role in a somewhat unusual version, and what was it called?

12 The spirit world has been responsible for some of the most touching, or funniest, romantic screen stories. Name the films described and the players of the parts in italics:

a A young *widow* buys a house on the English coast and, with the help of a deceased *sea captain*, who comes to love her, writes a best selling book

b When a *widower* marries again, the ghost of his *former wife* returns to taunt him, so he and his *wife* enlist the aid of a *spiritualist*

c An impecunious young *artist* meets a strange young *girl* in Central Park, and discovers that she is the ghost of a child drowned years before but now searching through eternity for someone to love her

d A *young man* with political ambitions is haunted by a 17th-century *witch* re-incarnated to avenge herself for the actions of the young man's ancestors. She falls in love with him, to the annoyance of the man's *fiancé* and the witch's *father*

e A *young man* living in an old London house finds the diaries of one of his ancestors, after which he is struck by lightning and transported back to the 18th century. Living the previous existence, he falls in love with a beautiful *cousin*, and on being transported back to the present learns that she died after the man she loved mysteriously disappeared (2 sets of answers)

13 The enduringly popular and passionate love stories by the Brontë sisters, Charlotte's 'Jane Eyre' and Emily's 'Wuthering Heights', have each been filmed three times. Can you name the two stars and the director of each of the six films?

14 Each of the following films featured a couple who were real-life husband and wife at the time. Can you name them?

a THE ILLUSTRATED MAN
b YOUNG BESS
c THE FOURPOSTER
d BUTTERFIELD 8
e THE PERFECT FURLOUGH (GB: STRICTLY FOR PLEASURE)
f FROM THE TERRACE
g SINCE YOU WENT AWAY
h THE MECHANIC
i IF A MAN ANSWERS
j THE RELUCTANT DEBUTANTE

15 A moving and popular Italian film featured a slow-witted heroine who was trained by the travelling player she adored to behave like an obedient pet. Distressed by the death of a friend, she whimpered like a dog for days and her man left her. What was the film, who directed it, and who played the heroine and the man she loved?

16 Several romantic heroines have been in the enviable position of having two or more eligible suitors to choose from. In the films below, who played the heroine, and who played the suitors (number of suitors in brackets)?

a BOOM TOWN (2)
b PITTSBURGH (2)
c THE BRIDE WORE RED (2)
d THE SEVENTH VEIL (3)
e THE AFFAIRS OF SUSAN (4)

17 The legendary lover Don Juan has been portrayed many times on screen. Who played the title role in

a DON JUAN (1926)?
b THE PRIVATE LIFE OF DON JUAN (1934)?
c THE ADVENTURES OF DON JUAN (1949)?
d THE LOVES OF DON JUAN (1948)?
e DON JUAN OR IF DON JUAN WAS A WOMAN (1973)?

The young stars of a 1970s box-office sensation. Who are they and what was the film? A phrase spoken by the leading man in the film became its advertising slogan – what was it? Who wrote the story and what was the name of the sequel?

18 The following advertising slogans were used to publicise five films of the 1940s which had ladies' names as their titles. What were they?
a *'Please* don't tell anyone what she did!'
b 'She had a lot to learn – but not about men!'
c 'The shadow of this woman darkened their love'
d 'She made a career out of love'
e 'A love story every woman would die a thousand deaths to live!'

19 Religion figures heavily in several screen dramas, and it usually means that the course of true love will not lead to a romantic finish. Name the films described below, and the stars who played the parts listed in italics:
a A young *nun* nursing in the Belgian Congo re-assesses her views after meeting an agnostic, but attractive, *doctor*
b A *marine* and a *nun* are trapped together on an island in the South Pacific during World War II, but though he falls in love with her she explains her dedication to her faith and their relationship remains platonic until they are rescued
c A love affair which blossoms in Rome during World War II is doomed, since the couple are, respectively a young *catholic priest* and a *postulant nun*
d A spinster *poetess*, estranged from her mother, falls in love with a *naval hero* who feels the war has left him unfit to fulfil his dream of becoming a priest; though she loves him, the poetess persuades him to try the church, while she effects a reconciliation with her mother
e A small-town *priest* is accused of the murder of a *nun* to whom he has been strongly attracted

20 Hollywood has frequently paired great figures of history for screen romances, often with little regard for accuracy. Who played the title roles in
a THE PRIVATE LIVES OF ELIZABETH AND ESSEX?
b SAMSON AND DELILAH?
c CAESAR AND CLEOPATRA?
d DAVID AND BATHSHEBA?
e SOLOMON AND SHEBA?

21 Who played the title roles in these entirely fictional romantic pairings:
a THE MAJOR AND THE MINOR?
b THE COWBOY AND THE LADY?
c HER HIGHNESS AND THE BELLBOY?
d EDWARD AND CAROLINE (EDOUARD ET CAROLINE)?
e MINNIE AND MOSCOWITZ?

26 Doris Day and Rock Hudson made three romantic comedies together. Can you name them?

23 'If I'd been a ranch they would have called me the Bar Nothing' is an oft-quoted line spoken by the titular heroine of one of the 40s' most torrid and celebrated mixtures of crime and passion. Can you name the film, the actress who played the title role, and the men who played her husband and her lover?

24 Heroines have sometimes been called upon to masquerade as members of the opposite sex in movies, a ploy which invariably leads to romantic complications. Name the actresses who wore male apparel, and the films in which they did so, from the descriptions below:
a A royal personage, in masculine hunting togs, is mistaken by the Spanish ambassador for a boy, and finds himself spending a night in an inn with him
b In order to study religion, a Jewish girl disguises herself as a boy and finds herself having to marry a girl
c A penniless entertainer disguises herself as a man in order to work as a female impersonator (3 sets of answers)
d A confidence trickster in Victorian England disguises herself as a boy to trick victims, then finds herself wooed by both males and females
e A would-be actress dresses as a boy in order to accompany a film-comedy director while he experiences life as a tramp

25 Parental self-sacrifice of one sort or another has been the lot of several screen heroines. Match the screen mothers below to their fictional off-spring and name the films:
A Bette Davis
B Susan Hayward
C Olivia DeHavilland
D Lana Turner
E Joan Crawford

a Ann Blyth
b Keir Dullea
c Jane Bryan
d John Lund
e Joey Heatherton

26 The first three-colour Technicolor film, made in 1935, was an adaptation of a classic novel with a tempestuous heroine. What was the film, who directed it and who played the heroine?

27 In a popular French film, he is a racing driver and widower, she a film continuity girl and widow. What is it called, who played the lovers, and in what fashionable resort does their affair take place? Who directed the film, and who composed its catchy theme music?

The irreplaceable Greta Garbo in what many consider her finest performance. What is the film, who is her young leading man and who was their director? The film required Garbo, as a courtesan, to give up the man she loves at the behest of his father and return to her vicious protector, the Baron de Varville. Who played the father and which of Hollywood's finest screen villains played the Baron?

---

28 Name the films with LOVE in the title which featured the following star combinations:
a Natalie Wood, Steve McQueen, Edie Adams
b Gary Cooper, Audrey Hepburn, Maurice Chevalier
c Jennifer Jones, William Holden, Isobel Elsom
d Jennifer Jones, Joseph Cotten, Ann Richards
e Greta Garbo, John Gilbert, George Fawcett
f Lana Turner, Cliff Robertson, Hugh O'Brian
g Maggie Smith, Timothy Bottoms, Charles Baxter
h Deborah Kerr, Clifford Evans, Mary Merrall
i Tyrone Power, Loretta Young, Don Ameche
j Paul Newman, Joanne Woodward, Thelma Ritter

29 The most famous screen lover in the early days of cinema was Rudolph Valentino. Two screen biographies have been made of his life, both titled VALENTINO. Who played Rudolph in each of them?

30 Loss of memory has cued much emotional drama on screen, but perhaps the best-remembered case occurs in the MGM film in which a happily married man loses his memory and later employs his unrecognised wife as his own secretary! What was the film, who were the two stars, and who wrote the novel on which the film was based?

31 Name the directors of the following groups of films – each group was made by one director:
a THE GOOD FAIRY
   DODSWORTH
   THE LETTER
b CAMILLE
   ZAZA
   TWO FACED WOMAN
c THE TRESPASSER
   THE FLAME WITHIN
   DARK VICTORY
d TOVARICH
   THE SISTERS
   ALL THIS AND HEAVEN TOO
e A STOLEN LIFE
   MY REPUTATION
   POSSESSED

32 In 1974 Robert Redford played the enigmatic Jay Gatsby, but F. Scott Fitzgerald's masterly book 'The Great Gatsby' had been filmed twice before, once as a silent. Who played Jay in the two previous versions?

Hollywood Scandal!

Scandalous incidents both fuelled Tinsel Town's publicity machine and led to strict censorship. Sometimes the stories of outrageous happenings are amusing, sometimes they encompass real tragedy.

1 Some of the most famous names in movies had the oddest phobias. Have you heard:
a Which MGM leading lady carried a bottle of strong disinfectant with her whenever she travelled, to swab down her hotel room?
b Which comedian could not bear to be confined in an elevator?
c Which Great Lover of the screen hated the 'phone so much that it caused him to stutter?
d Which movie mogul refused to touch used banknotes?
e Which star of ALEXANDER'S RAGTIME BAND was so jittery about dancing up a flight of stairs that she fainted dead away?

Liz Taylor is here being visited on the set of which film by her lucky husband No 4? Who is he and in what film did they co-star? Husband No 5 was already in the offing when this picture was taken. In what aptly titled film did they co-star in 1973 and, by the way, who was he?

2 Death has overtaken a number of stars in unexpectedly tragic fashion
a Which well-loved screen judge died of a heart attack while chasing a gang of youths who were throwing rocks at his house?
b Who died in a fire which started while she was watching one of her old movies on TV?
c Who wrote off his Porsche, and himself, in 1955?
d Which well-stacked leading lady literally lost her head while out for a spin in her Cadillac?
e Which beautiful star drowned tragically in 1982 while bathing off the yacht in which she and her husband were sailing? Who was her husband, and what was unusual about their marriage?

3 The Hollywood marriage-go-round provided the gossip columnists with a never-ending source of tit-bits for their avid readers
a Which tempestuous star sent her husband a Christmas present of a pair of boxing gloves with a card inscribed, 'Darling, so you can punch me if I leave you again'? Who was her fortunate husband?
b Which pair of celebrated lovers tried to avoid publicity by marrying in the First Episcopal Church, Kingman, Arizona?
c Which marriage of barely two weeks ended with this suicide note: 'Dearest Dear, Unfortunately this is the only way to make good the frightful wrong I have done you, and to wipe out my abject humiliation. I love you. Paul. PS You understand that last night was only a comedy'?
d Hollywood is full of much-married people. Name Joan Crawford's husbands. What did the last one do for a living?
e What do Joan Bennett, Hedy Lamarr and Myrna Loy have in common?

4 Which real figures, scandalous or connected with scandal, were played by
a Edward Arnold in 1937?
b Vivien Leigh in 1941?
c Richard Attenborough in 1971?
d Jean Paul Belmondo in 1974?
e Broderick Crawford in 1977?

Marilyn Monroe socialises during a break in the filming of her penultimate picture. With her are her husband, her co-stars and the wife of one of them. The breath of scandal touched her relationship with the married star. Identify all of them. What was the film, and who directed it? For which of Marilyn's films did husband No 2 write the screenplay? Husband No 1's talents lay in another direction. Who was he and what did he do?

---

5   Louella Parsons and Hedda Hopper were Hollywood's queen bee gossip columnists, fawned upon and feared in just about equal measure
a Why was Louella's husband so useful to her professionally?
b 'And . . . never looked lovelier' was a joky reference to Louella's column in a revue of the 30s. Of whom was Louella talking in such fulsome tones and why did they both owe so much to William Randolph Hearst?
c Louella could be extremely bitchy. In 1932 she wrote of a newcomer to Hollywood that she was 'fat, fair and I don't know how near forty'. Who was the object of her playful remarks?
d In which Billy Wilder film did Hedda Hopper appear as herself?
e Who sent Hedda a skunk as a Valentine gift?
f Hedda's son William was an actor. What was his most famous TV role?

6   Some stars have had a refreshingly frank view of themselves, often eagerly endorsed by their friends and acquaintances
a Who remarked of herself, 'I used to be Snow White, but I drifted'?
b Who claimed she had a reputation 'as pure as the driven slush'?
c About whom was it said, 'The son-in-law also rises'?
d Who was dubbed 'The Pink Powder Puff' and why?
e Which director remarked of which star that 'As a human being ——— is a very great actress'? What was the film they had just completed?

7   When the pressures or the heartbreak got too much, when the offers began to dry up or the profile started to sag, there was always suicide as a final way out:
a Who burned herself to death on a pyre made from her old publicity hand-outs?
b Who left a suicide note blaming it all on boredom?
c Whose body was found by boyfriend Rex Harrison?
d Who blew his head off while cleaning a gun after being supplanted by Richard Barthelmess as D. W. Griffith's favourite 'country boy'?
e Who shot his bride of barely three weeks, and then turned the gun on himself?

1884-21

8 In 1935 she won a subscription contest organised by a Communist newspaper and travelled to the USSR. Her first film was TOO MANY PARENTS. As far as she was concerned, she had at least one too many – her mother, who in 1944 committed her to a mental institution
a Who was she?
b What was her first big hit and who was her co-star?
c What was so ironic about the 1941 AMONG THE LIVING, in which she had a featured role?
d To whom was she married in her early, successful days?
e What was the title of her autobiography?

9 Only a suspicion of murder hung over the death of the star of the first film in the list below. But there was, alas, no doubt about the gruesome fates of others. Who were they?
a THE BOHEMIAN GIRL
b MATA HARI
c REBEL WITHOUT A CAUSE
d ZABRISKIE POINT
e VALLEY OF THE DOLLS

From which Lana Turner film is this still taken? Who is playing her daughter? In 1958, Lana was at the centre of a murder trial. Who was on trial and who was the victim? Where was the victim's body found? Why did the affair echo the plot of JOHNNY EAGER (1941)?

---

10 Drugs have cut short many a film career, and there have been some narrow escapes
a Which athletic leading man became hooked on morphine after straining his back while rescuing the victims of a train crash?
b She starred in THE WHITE MOTH but fatally burned her wings on a heroin overdose in 1926. Who was she?
c Which star was arrested on a marijuana rap in 1948? What happened to him? Who was the starlet arrested with him and what was the title of the exploitation quickie in which she starred after the trial?
d Who sang 'Sweet Marijuana' in the 1934 MURDER AT THE VANITIES?
e Who was detained by customs officers at Heathrow Airport in 1984 and later fined for possession of a small amount of marijuana?

11 Hollywood was famous for its hard drinkers

a Of whom was it said that when he travelled he needed three trunks – one for clothes and two for liquor?

b Whose luxury yacht was equipped with boxes of special earth in which to grow the mint for his favourite juleps?

c Which fast-talking character actor's career was nearly ruined when, after a drunken spree on location in Mexico, he urinated from a balcony on the Mexican flag. What was the film from which he was instantly fired?

d Which rugged leading man died from a fall after a solitary drinking bout?

e Whose house was known as 'Cirrhosis by the Sea', and who thought of the nickname?

12 Babies have occasionally thrown a spanner in the works of a star's career. Children have proved troublesome too

a In 1942 her mother and Louis B. Mayer arranged for the abortion of a child she desperately wanted. Who was she and to whom was she married at the time?

b Jean Renoir said of her that 'she is so honest she will always prefer scandal to a lie' when she gave birth to a famous director's illegitimate child. Who was she and who was the director? What was the film they were making together when they fell in love?

c Of which leading lady did Helen Hayes say that she 'tried to be all things to all people, but I just wish she hadn't tried to be a mother'?

13 A generous helping of breast has quickened many a filmgoer's pulse, and sent the censor rushing for his scissors

a Whose film debut was described by a Hollywood wag as 'The Sale of Two Titties'? What was the film and who was the producer/director?

b She romped naked through the woods in a Czech film of the 30s, but when she came to make a Hollywood biblical epic, Groucho Marx observed, 'I never see movies where the man's tits are bigger than the woman's'. Who was she, what was the title of the original topless epic and who was her well-endowed leading man in her biblical venture?

c In 1958 Tony Curtis loosened her Saxon blouse the better to enable her to row. Four years later a brassière manufacturer voted her the Golden Bust Award. Who was she?

d Whose creamy bosom, generously displayed in a 1945 British costumer, was covered up for American consumption?

e Which 'peaches and cream' English-born star and symbol of wholesome family entertainment bared her breasts in 1981 in a movie directed by her husband? Who is he and what is the film?

14 Censorship has produced some bizarre results:

a In 1939 the censor Joseph Breen wrote to the Hays Office, guardian of America's screen morals, 'We have withheld this line as profanity'. What was the line, in which film was it delivered, and by whom?

b In which film does this exchange take place? Leading man: 'Kind of a good omen – just one bed'. Leading Lady: 'Uh, Uh'. Leading man: 'You know what that means?' Leading Lady: 'Uh, Uh – it means you're going to sleep on the floor'.
Who were the stars?

c Why was Mervyn LeRoy banned for a time from the state of Georgia?

d Which film was the first boldly to display an uncovered female navel and whose navel was it?

e In which film was Vivien Leigh transformed from a prostitute to an adulteress by simply changing a single line?

15 Courtroom revelations could stop a star's career in its tracks. The lucky ones survived to skulk another day

a Who took her secretary to court for embezzlement and got more than she bargained for when her former employee took the witness stand?

b Whose steamy affair with George S. Kaufmann was consigned to a diary whose contents were read out at a divorce hearing?

c Which leading man's fans deserted him when a divorce case revealed that he had a wife and five children?

d Which celebrated yachtsman emerged unscathed from a charge of statutory rape? In which ironically titled film did he star shortly after his acquittal?

e Which studio chief recently caused an international business scandal – although an actual court case was avoided – by embezzling his company? Which studio was it, and who was the actor, the forgery of whose name on a cheque, led to the investigations?

f Which former protégée of Charlie Chaplin brought a paternity suit against him?

16 Some stars have fallen on hard times. Their careers in shreds, they were forced to take up humble employment in order to survive

a Who became a receptionist for a Los Angeles plastic surgeon?

b Who worked on a counter at Macy's department store?

c Who found employment as a cook and housekeeper in a Rhode Island rectory?

d Who drove a hansom cab in New York's Central Park?

e Who worked as a $50-a-week leg man for an agent?

17 Big stars are not always what they seem to be. Their characters can be very different to those which they cultivate on the screen, as can be their looks

a Who fainted at the sight of his own blood on the set of the 1939 BEAU GESTE?

b Whose head of hair jumped ship after a brief encounter with a set of electric curlers during the filming of REAP THE WILD WIND?

c Which child star was given a detachable latex nose bridge at the insistence of Louis B. Mayer?

d Who died of a heart attack in a hot saline bath while trying a drastic slimming course?

e Which great tough guy of the screen hung a small black crêpe on his front door when his pet Sealyham died, and then buried the departed pooch in an all-steel vault in his backyard?

18 Outrageous pets were just one way of raising the eyebrows of the more prudish folk in Hollywood

a Who always went sailing with a pet vulture named Maloney?

b Why dyed her pet chows to match her red hair?

c Who tended a menagerie of 75 budgerigars, each of which she claimed to know by name?

d Who owned a wolfhound named Trotsky?

e Who provided her poodle, Cliquot, with a custom-made jacket complete with heart-shaped pockets filled with Kleenex, 'in case he has to blow his nose'?

Silent comic Fatty Arbuckle's career was wrecked by one of the most notorious of Hollywood's scandals. With what crime was he charged after a party held on Labor Day 1921? Who was the starlet at the centre of the scandal? Later, the disgraced Arbuckle directed a number of films, under what assumed name?

19 Big stars can often be surprisingly temperamental on the set. Do you know:

a Why the camera crew told Wallace Beery to pick on someone his own size during the filming of SLAVE SHIP?

b Which star called for a mouthwash after kissing Erich von Stroheim, and in what film?

c Who said 'I love to play bitches and she helped me in the part'? Of whom was she talking and what was the film they were making at the time?

d Who said 'There's no one quite like Bill in the world . . . Thank God!'? To whom was she referring and what was the only film they made together?

e Who shouted in frustration during an endlessly protracted death scene, 'Die, goddammit, Spence! I wish to Christ you would!'? Who was the expiring star and what was the film?

f Who laid out Peter Lorre on the set of BACKGROUND TO DANGER after having cigarette smoke blown repeatedly in his face by his small co-star?

Reach for the Stars

A She studied with Ruth St Denis and Ted Shawn, but began her career in the Ziegfeld Follies. Her face was used as the model for the strip cartoon heroine, Dixie Dugan. She played a circus high diver fought over by Robert Armstrong and Victor McLaglen, and then went to Europe to make two masterpieces. Back in Hollywood she was reduced to making two-reelers with Fatty Arbuckle, and B-westerns. In the 70s an English critic imagined he had rediscovered her, but many years earlier the French had realised her true quality:

a Who is she?

b In which film did she ride the freight trains with Richard Arlen? Which classic comedy of the 40s placed its stars in the same situation, and who were they?

c In her most famous film she met her death at the hands of a celebrated murderer. What was the film, and who was the murderer?

d When she returned to Hollywood in 1930, Warners wanted her for PUBLIC ENEMY, but she turned down the part. Who got it?

e In 1938 she co-starred in a B-western with a former member of The Three Mesquiteers. Who was he?

B He started as a journalist but his sister eased his way into an acting career. In 1919 he and his brother were the toast of Broadway. A year later he accomplished, without make-up, a screen transformation which later took Fredric March and Spencer Tracy considerably longer. He married one of the silent screen's most beautiful leading ladies, but eventually ruined himself with alcohol:

a Who is he?

b In 1917 he played E. W. Hornung's gentleman burglar in RAFFLES THE AMATEUR CRACKSMAN. What other stars later played the role? In what other film did he play a gentleman thief?

c One of his best films, made in 1932, featured a stunning debut by a beautiful young actress. What was the film, and who was she?

d In what film was he played by Errol Flynn and on what book was it based?

e In his first talkie, he recited from one of his two most famous Shakespearean stage roles; in his last film, from the other. Which Shakespearean characters were they? And can you name the films?

C The daughter of a Spanish dancer, she performed as a child in the family vaudeville act, and made her first screen appearance using the family surname of Cansino. After some years playing Mexicans, Egyptians, half-breeds, etc., a Hollywood studio realised her potential, altered her hairline and dyed it red, and eventually capitalised on her fine dancing ability. Thus one of the screen's great 'love goddesses' emerged:

a Who is she?

b A major break came when Carole Landis refused to dye her hair red for the remake of an old Valentino hit, and the Technicolor role thus came her way. Name the film. Who played the Valentino part?

c She once stated that her proudest screen achievements were her dances with Fred Astaire. Can you name the two films she made with him?

d Her second husband was a controversial actor-director. Who was he, which film did they make together, and in what way did he drastically alter her appearance for the film?

e She will forever be associated with the film where she performed a number in which she tossed her hair over her face and peeled off long black gloves. Name the film, the song, her co-star and the film's director.

D Born Ella Geisman, she topped popularity polls in the late 40s with her refreshing personality and distinctively husky voice. She graduated from 'girl next door' roles to 'perfect wives' adeptly, could sing and dance as well as act, and had a long marriage to an actor who had made his mark in both musicals and thrillers:

a Who is she?

b Who was her husband, and what were the two films they starred in together?

c She played the wife of a dance-band leader in one of her most famous films. What was the film? Who was her leading man? And name the other two films she made with him

d In her first feature film she sang a song to a diminutive top star. What was the film, what was the song, and who was the star?

e In 1949 she triumphed as the most boyish of four sisters in a famous story. What was it? Who played the other sisters? And who played all four parts in the 1933 screen version of the same novel?

Torsos and Togas

The film epic is the cinematic equivalent of Grand Opera. A knowledge of history and the Bible might help you to answer the questions below, but a knowledge of Hollywood Babylon would probably be more useful.

1　'Give me a couple of pages of the Bible and I'll give you a picture,' Cecil B. DeMille once said:
a Of which of his films did he say, 'Credit is due to the Book of Judges not me'?
b In which film's prologue, over a shot of the Earth turning, does DeMille speak of the story as a symbol of 'man's unquenchable thirst for freedom'?
c Before turning to the Bible, DeMille had made a reputation as a director of risqué domestic comedies. This prompted his brother William to comment, 'Having attended to the under-clothes, bathrooms and matrimonial irregularities of his fellow citizens, he now began to consider their salvation'. What was his first Bible film in the 20s? Name two of his comedies of the early 20s that had references to the Book of Genesis in their titles
d Away from the Bible, to whom did DeMille say 'How would you like to play the wickedest woman in history?'? What was the role?
e What did the B in Cecil B. DeMille stand for?
f What was his first film spectacular?
g On which of his films did he ask the visiting D. W. Griffith to direct a scene?
h Whose was the voice of God in the sound version of THE TEN COMMANDMENTS?
i Which of his leading men took fright at a wind machine, prompting DeMille's comment that he was '100% yellow'. What was the film they were making at the time and why did it represent a notable first for DeMille?
j The Barnum of Hollywood, DeMille was, naturally, attracted to the circus, and treated a film about it in the same grandiose way as he did his Biblical epics. What was the film called, and who had his first major starring role in it?

2　Characters' names in many an epic have ranged from the absurd to the unpronounceable. Who played these roles and in which films?
a Rolfe, son of Krok
b Marcus Superbus
c Chrysagon
d Ftatateeta
e Sheik Ilderim

3　Epics take so long to plan and film that changes and replacements are a common occurrence
a Who was the famous innovative director originally chosen for CLEOPATRA (1962) and replaced after disagreements?
b In the same film, who were the actors originally chosen to play Caesar and Anthony, and who eventually filled the roles?
c Stanley Kubrick directed SPARTACUS, but who started the film and directed some of the early scenes?
d Who were the first choices for the director and title role in the 1925 BEN HUR and who replaced them after several hours of film had already been shot?
e Who assumed the role of Solomon in SOLOMON AND SHEBA (1959) after the star originally chosen for the role suddenly dropped out? Who was the first choice and what was the cause of his sudden departure? What was unusual about his replacement's performance?

4　Who played the title roles in the epics below?
a NICHOLAS AND ALEXANDRA
b IVAN THE TERRIBLE
c THE PRODIGAL
d THE STORY OF RUTH
e BARABBAS
f THE SCARLET EMPRESS
g BECKET
h MOHAMMED, MESSENGER OF GOD
i RASPUTIN AND THE EMPRESS
j MOSES

'This picture was conceived in a state of emergency, shot in confusion, and wound up in blind panic'. Thus spoke the director of CLEOPATRA starring Elizabeth Taylor. Who was he and what other film concerning Ancient Rome did he direct? Which famous film studio in what European city was largely used for CLEOPATRA, and what unfortunate Hollywood studio lost a fortune in backing the enterprise? And, by the way, who played Octavius Caesar?

14 The heavies in epics are inevitably consigned to a grisly fate. Horrible as their ends might be, they certainly display some amazing powers of cinematic invention. In which film was

a Ernest Borgnine forced to jump into a pit filled with wild dogs?
b Sidney Poitier crushed under a giant golden bell?
c Charles McGraw drowned in a giant vat of brown stew?
d Vincent Price throttled with his own whip?
e Joan Collins sealed up in a pyramid?

15 Greek history and mythology have been happily, if not always accurately, plundered by film-makers. Who played

a Odysseus in ULYSSES?
b Philip of Macedon in ALEXANDER THE GREAT?
c Archimedes in THE SIEGE OF SYRACUSE?
d Pheidippides in THE GIANT OF MARATHON?
e Hera in JASON AND THE ARGONAUTS?

Peter O'Toole heads into battle. Say whether the following statements are true or false:
a The film is KHARTOUM
b It was directed by Carol Reed
c Alec Guinness played Prince Faisal
d Anthony Burgess wrote the screenplay
e It was Omar Sharif's first role in English

---

16 Who played Napoleon Bonaparte in:
a WAR AND PEACE (1956)?
b WATERLOO?
c MARIE WALEWSKA?
d DESIREE (1954)?
e THE STORY OF MANKIND?

17 Who led the team of special effects wizards responsible for the more spectacular moments in
a THE TEN COMMANDMENTS (1956)?
b BEN HUR (1959)?
c THE LAST DAYS OF POMPEII (1935)?
d SAMSON AND DELILAH?
e JASON AND THE ARGONAUTS?

18 'I wake up inna middle of night, I say to myself, Whatsa greatest book ever wrote? The Bible! So I make a movie of the Bible! I hire the greatest director inna world to direct it':

a Who 'wake up inna middle of night'?
b Who was the greatest director 'inna world'?
c What was the title of the film?
d How much of the Bible was filmed?
e Who played Abraham, Noah, Sarah, Adam, Cain and the Angel of Death?

Here is a scene from one of Cecil B. DeMille's outrageous epics. Do you know the title and the three stars illustrated? Which Roman emperor was being portrayed by the actor on the left and who was the empress? In one famous scene, the empress invites her harlot friend to 'take off your clothes, get in here, and tell me all about it'. What was this royal Roman person engaged in doing at the time, and what was particularly special about it?

19 Match the couples below to their epics:
A Cary Grant and Sophia Loren
B Anthony Quinn and Sophia Loren
C Paul Newman and Pier Angeli
D Jack Palance and Anita Ekberg
E Farley Granger and Alida Valli
F Alain Delon and Claudia Cardinale
G Henri Vidal and Michele Morgan
H Jeff Chandler and Rita Gam
I Martin Potter and Capucine
J Christopher Plummer and Virginia McKenna

a ATTILA
b SENSO
c WATERLOO
d FELLINI'S SATYRICON
e THE PRIDE AND THE PASSION
f SIGN OF THE PAGAN
g THE LEOPARD
h THE SILVER CHALICE
i THE MONGOLS
j FABIOLA

20 Which actors played these Roman emperors in the following films:

a Marcus Aurelius in THE FALL OF THE ROMAN EMPIRE?

b Claudius in I, CLAUDIUS (the famous unfinished film)?

c Caligula in THE ROBE?

d Vespasian in THE ANTAGONISTS (aka MASADA)?

e Constantine in CONSTANTINE AND THE CROSS?

21 'There's a special excitement in playing a man who made a hole in history large enough to be remembered centuries after he died.' So said Charlton Heston, who is indelibly fixed in the public mind as an epic hero. Which parts did he play in:

a JULIUS CAESAR (1970)?

b THE BUCCANEER?

c THE GREATEST STORY EVER TOLD?

d THE AGONY AND THE ECSTASY?

e KHARTOUM?

'Against the might, the decadence, the awesome fury of Imperial Rome – One Man's heroic struggle and triumph!' Who was the eponymous hero and who (illustrated centre) portrayed him? The film was a remake (1959) of a very famous silent epic. Who was the evil Messala in each version and how did his fate, in each case, differ? Name the character far right, and the actress playing her. May McAvoy took her role in the silent version, and turned up again in this one – as what? Identify the other two actresses.

22 No epic is complete without a predatory vamp lusting after the clean-limbed hero. Who played

a Messalina in DEMETRIUS AND THE GLADIATORS?

b Cleopatra in SERPENT OF THE NILE?

c The lesbian queen with a penchant for cheetahs in SODOM AND GOMORRAH?

d Bathsheba in DAVID AND BATHSHEBA?

e The title role in the 1953 SALOME? How did the plot in this film differ from the Bible story?

The Way of the West

To most Americans, the pioneering era between 1850 and 1890 was their country's most exciting time. The Gold Rush, the Civil War and the Indians Wars all nourish the mythology of the Western.

1   Westerns generally reinforce the theory that it's a man's world where men are men and women are . . . nowhere. But there were quite a few ladies who held their own against the men. Can you name the actresses who portrayed:

a Calamity Jane in THE PLAINSMAN (1936), THE BADLANDS OF DAKOTA, THE PALEFACE, CALAMITY JANE AND SAM BASS, and CALAMITY JANE

b Belle Starr in BELLE STARR and MONTANA BELLE

c Annie Oakley in ANNIE OAKLEY and ANNIE GET YOUR GUN

d THE MAVERICK QUEEN and CATTLE QUEEN OF MONTANA

e Frenchy in DESTRY RIDES AGAIN

f Frenchie in THE LEGEND OF FRENCHIE KING

g Frenchy in DESTRY

h Vienna in JOHNNY GUITAR

i Ella in COMES A HORSEMAN

j CAT BALLOU

2   'A four-legged friend, a four-legged friend. He'll never let you down,' sang Roy Rogers. Match the faithful friends to their riders:

A Fritz
B Champion
C Trigger
D Topper
E White Flash
F Tony
G Tarzan
H Silver
I Silver
J Eagle's Wing

a William S. Hart
b Martin Sheen
c Buck Jones
d Tom Mix
e Gene Autry
f William 'Hopalong Cassidy' Boyd
g Tex Ritter
h Roy Rogers
i Clayton 'Lone Ranger' Moore
j Ken Maynard

3   In most westerns there was a simple choice between good and evil, heroes and villains. They usually faced each other in a showdown in what seemed the only street in town, in front of the only hotel and only saloon. Sort out the goodies from the baddies below:

a Henry Fonda and Charles Bronson in ONCE UPON A TIME IN THE WEST

b Joseph Cotten and Gregory Peck in DUEL IN THE SUN

c Henry Fonda and Kirk Douglas in THERE WAS A CROOKED MAN

d Henry Fonda and James Stewart in FIRECREEK

e Richard Widmark and Robert Taylor in THE LAW AND JACK WADE

4   Many western screenplays are slight variations on the same plot. However, there should be no doubt as to the titles of the stories summarized below. Name the movies:

a 'An ageing gunfighter learns he has cancer.' Who played the gunfighter and what was particularly poignant about the role?

b 'A brave sheriff faces outlaws alone on his wedding day.' Who played the sheriff, and who was his bride-to-be?

c 'A one-eyed US marshal helps a 14-year-old girl track down her father's killer.' Who played the marshal and the girl? What extra satisfaction did the actor get for the role?

d 'A thief is saved from a lynch mob by marrying a spinster.' Who played both roles and who directed the film?

e 'Two men, one fat and the other thin, help a girl rescue her gold mine from villains.' Who were the pair and what songs did they sing in it?

A moment from the showdown in Edward Dmytryk's WARLOCK (1959). To what does the title refer? Who is the actor with the gun? At whom is he shooting and does he survive? Who was the actor's father-in-law? For which two films did he win the Best Supporting Actor Oscar?

5 Some movie titles need elucidating. Could you explain the significance of the titles below, i.e. to what or to whom do they refer? Name the male stars, and the directors:

a THE OX-BOW INCIDENT
b HEAVEN'S GATE
c LITTLE BIG MAN
d WINCHESTER '73
e THE MISSOURI BREAKS
f UNION PACIFIC
g A BIG HAND FOR THE LITTLE LADY
h THE IRON HORSE
i THE WAR WAGON
j THE SEARCHERS

6 The West is 'a man's country'. Can you name the actors who portrayed the 'man' in the following films?

a THE MAN FROM LARAMIE
b MAN OF THE WEST
c MAN WITHOUT A STAR
d THE MAN WHO LOVED CAT DANCING
e THE MAN WHO SHOT LIBERTY VALANCE
f MAN IN THE SADDLE
g A MAN CALLED HORSE
h MAN WITH THE GUN
i A MAN OF THE EAST
j MAN WITH NO NAME

This is a scene from John Ford's classic western STAGECOACH about nine people making a coach trip through dangerous Indian territory. Can you identify the woman (far left) and the man standing? What sort of characters did they play? Can you name two other passengers missing from the picture, and the driver? Where were the action sequences shot? What is the name of the character played by John Wayne.

---

7 Critics have written of the 'purity of the western' as some speak dangerously of the 'purity of the race'. But the western is, to quote Polonius, 'tragical-comical-historical-pastoral' and – we could add – musical-satirical-fantastical. The next few posers are not concerned with the thoroughbreds of the genre, but with the bastards, hybrids and odd-balls. In which of these westerns would you find the following characters and who played them?

a A rabbi
b An elderly gay couple
c A gay Red Indian
d A Jewish Red Indian
e A black sheriff
f A Japanese samurai
g An English butler won in a poker game
h An English gentleman sheriff
i A man in granny drag
j A female marshal

8 In the majority of westerns, before and after John Ford's STAGECOACH (1939), Red Indians had no individual identity, being merely savage hordes descending on innocent settlers. But in the 50s, directors and writers began to feel their consciences pricking and tried to redress the balance. Even John Ford changed his attitude. 'They are a very dignified people – even when they are defeated. Of course, it's not very popular in the United States. The audience likes to see Indians killed. They don't consider them as human beings – with a great culture of their own – quite different from ours,' he commented. Match the actors who played Red Indians, half-breeds or adopted Indians, with the film titles:

A Rock Hudson
B Charlton Heston
C Elvis Presley
D Victor Mature
E Jeff Chandler
F Rod Steiger
G Robert Taylor
H Jeffrey Hunter
I Robert Forster
J Jack Palance

a WHITE FEATHER
b THE SAVAGE
c RUN OF THE ARROW
d ARROWHEAD
e THE STALKING MOON
f CHIEF CRAZY HORSE
g DEVIL'S DOORWAY
h TAZA, SON OF COCHISE
i FLAMING STAR
j BROKEN ARROW

9 Still in Indian territory. Many a dark-haired beauty has been almost literally roped into playing a squaw. Match the actress with the titles:

A Natalie Wood
B Rita Moreno
C Debra Paget
D Cyd Charisse
E Dolores Del Rio
F Anne Bancroft
G Elizabeth Threatt
H Susan Cabot
I Katy Jurado
J Katharine Ross

a THE BIG SKY
b THE SEARCHERS
c FORT VENGEANCE
d THE WILD NORTH
e TELL THEM WILLIE BOY IS HERE
f CHEYENNE AUTUMN
g THE RESTLESS BREED
h TOMAHAWK (GB: BATTLE OF POWDER RIVER)
i WHITE FEATHER
j ARROWHEAD

10 From the titles of three films in each case, can you identify the actor who donned cowboy hat and spurs? If you're still stuck then Question 11 will provide you with further clues:

a SADDLE TRAMP
  WICHITA
  RIDE THE HIGH COUNTRY
b COMANCHE STATION
  RIDE LONESOME
  THE TALL T
c THE MAN WHO SHOT LIBERTY VALANCE
  CANYON PASSAGE
  STAGECOACH
d VILLA RIDES
  CHATO'S LAND
  THE WHITE BUFFALO
e WALK THE PROUD LAND
  RIDE A CROOKED TRAIL
  THE CIMARRON KID
f THE FASTEST GUN ALIVE
  JUBAL
  COWBOY
g MONTE WALSH
  THE MAN WHO SHOT LIBERTY VALANCE
  THE COMANCHEROS

11 Here are further clues to help you track down the cowboys in Question 10:
a He also made movies for Alfred Hitchcock and Preston Sturges in the 40s
b He appeared in two Fred Astaire-Ginger Rogers musicals
c He lent his high, husky distinctive voice to a character in a Walt Disney film
d He appeared in movies from 1951 to 1954 under the surname Buchinski (or Buchinsky)
e He was the most decorated G.I. in World War II and played himself in a film of his war exploits
f He had an important role in SUPERMAN
g This actor won an Oscar for a dual role in a western

12 One of the most popular movies of the late 50s was the vast CinemaScope western THE BIG COUNTRY. Who directed it? Who played the hero and who were the two female leads? Who was the quick-tempered foreman, and which member of the cast won the Best Supporting performance Oscar? Who composed the famous score?

13 The following movies are remakes changed to a western setting. Name the original non-western film and its director:
a THE OUTRAGE
b THE FIEND WHO WALKED THE WEST
c COLORADO TERRITORY
d BROKEN LANCE
e THE MAGNIFICENT SEVEN

The theme of many Howard Hawks movies is the camaraderie of men who risk their lives. This is no exception.
a What is the title? RIO BRAVO, RIO LOBO, EL DORADO or EL CONDOR?
b Who played the sheriff and the gunfighter pictured? Who played their young hothead friend?
c The movie is a virtual remake of one of the other titles mentioned. Which one?
d Who played the sheriff, the gunfighter and the kid in the earlier movie?
e Which of the actors in the still stated: 'People think I have an interesting walk. Hell, I'm just trying to hold my gut in'?

14   Fill in the blanks:
The year . . . was a fruitful one for westerns. It produced 20th Century-Fox's JESSE JAMES, . . .'s STAGECOACH, Warner Bros.' DODGE CITY, . . .'s UNION PACIFIC and . . .'s DESTRY RIDES AGAIN. The following year, MGM released . . . , starring Spencer Tracy, Robert . . . , and Walter . . . . The director was King Vidor who shot the film on location in Oregon, although it was set in . . . . It tells of Major Robert Rogers, head of the Rangers, who protects the territories from ravaging . . . during the . . . century.

15   Folk hero Davy Crockett – congressman, bear-hunter, frontiersman – died in defence of the Alamo. Who played him in THE ALAMO? Who directed the film? Who starred in DAVY CROCKETT, INDIAN SCOUT (1950)? Walt Disney studios produced two films on Davy Crockett starring Fess Parker. What were their titles? Why was Fess Parker changed to Frank Parker when the films were shown in France?

16   In which westerns would you find the following unlikely stars?
a Audrey Hepburn
b Jon Voight
c Jeanne Moreau
d Stubby Kaye
e Hoagy Carmichael
f Mitzi Gaynor
g Shirley MacLaine
h Bobby Darin
i Bing Crosby
j Rita Hayworth

17   Many legends grew up out of the exploits of real-life people. Although historically inaccurate, westerns drew on these lives in their need for larger-than-life characters. The following questions relate to Hollywood's depiction of these legendary figures. Which of the films below were about Billy the Kid, Wild Bill Hickock, Wyatt Earp and Doc Holliday, and who played them?
a THE LEFT-HANDED GUN
b THE PLAINSMAN (1936)
c MY DARLING CLEMENTINE
d CALAMITY JANE
e GUNFIGHT AT THE O.K. CORRAL

18   Who played Jesse and Frank James (in that order) in:
a JESSE JAMES?
b KANSAS RAIDERS?
c THE LONG RIDERS?
d THE RETURN OF FRANK JAMES?
e THE RETURN OF JESSE JAMES?

19   Match the actors with the films in which they played Buffalo Bill:
A Charlton Heston
B James Ellison
C Paul Newman
D Louis Calhern
E Joel McRea

a BUFFALO BILL
b PONY EXPRESS
c ANNIE GET YOUR GUN
d BUFFALO BILL AND THE INDIANS
e THE PLAINSMAN (1936)

20 General Custer died with 224 soldiers at the Battle of the Little Bighorn, slaughtered by Indians. Hero or villain? Victim or oppressor? Custer has been portrayed in different ways. Match the actor with the film and say whether he was played sympathetically or not:

A Ronald Reagan
B John Miljan
C Errol Flynn
D Richard Mulligan
E Robert Shaw

a THE PLAINSMAN
b LITTLE BIG MAN
c SANTA FE TRAIL
d THEY DIED WITH THEIR BOOTS ON
e CUSTER OF THE WEST

21 The director John Ford raised the western to artistic status. His films are romantic visions of the Old West where men were men, defending the lives of women and children in the fort, community or homestead. He created a personal, recognizable world that is an essential part of American culture. Can you answer the following questions on the westerns of John Ford?

a In which of John Ford's westerns did the following co-star with his favourite actor and friend, John Wayne?
  i) William Holden
  ii) Maureen O'Hara
  iii) Jeffrey Hunter
  iv) Shirley Temple
  v) Vera Miles
b TWO RODE TOGETHER. Who were they?
c Which Wimbledon champion had a role in THE HORSE SOLDIERS?
d What was the name of John Ford's older brother who appeared in many of his brother's films?
e Who was the large character actor who appeared in innumerable Ford films, usually getting involved in a bar-room brawl? What is the name of his director son?

22 More good guys and bad guys, but this time can you name the films in which the following protagonists face each other? The first-named is the 'goody' in each case:
a Alan Ladd and Jack Palance
b James Stewart and Robert Ryan
c Clark Gable and Robert Ryan
d Marlon Brando and Karl Malden
e Gary Cooper and Karl Malden
f Gregory Peck and Skip Homeier
g Rock Hudson and Dean Martin
h Robert Mitchum and George Kennedy
i Clint Eastwood and Lee Van Cleef
j Yul Brynner and Eli Wallach

23 From the 15 names below select those that made up the MAGNIFICENT SEVEN and the members of THE WILD BUNCH, collecting them into two groups:
Warren Oates, Horst Buchholz, William Holden, Edmond O'Brien, James Coburn, Ben Johnson, Ernest Borgnine, Robert Vaughn, Lee Van Cleef, Charles Bronson, Robert Ryan, Jordan Christopher, Yul Brynner, Steve McQueen, Brad Dexter

24 Who played the title roles in the following films:
a McCABE AND MRS MILLER?
b ROOSTER COGBURN?
c THE OUTLAW JOSEY WALES?
d THE GOOD, THE BAD, AND THE UGLY?
e NEVADA SMITH?
f ALVAREZ KELLY?
g THE OUTLAW?
h THE BALLAD OF CABLE HOGUE?
i JEREMIAH JOHNSON?
j TELL THEM WILLIE BOY IS HERE?

This western was originally titled 'Woman With A Whip', but by what title is it known? Here is a clue to help you: 'There are 39 more than you can see'. Who is the lady in distress, and what was her occupation in the film? Who is holding her hostage, and who played the marshal?

A scene from an Indian epic, showing an English aristocrat in a rather uncomfortable position.
a **What is the title of the film?**
b **What is the name of its sequel?**
c **What Indian tribe was depicted?**
d **Which Dame played an Indian mother-in-law, and for what role in a famous Hitchcock film is she rather better known?**
e **Who is the leading actor, and in which western did he appear with Charlton Heston, James Coburn and Senta Berger?**

25   The western is generally so unsmiling in praise of the manly virtues that it has provided comedy with a theme against machismo and violence. Comedians are not known for their physical stature and by placing a weedy figure or a refined Easterner in a western situation, comic incongruity is created. Name the comedians and the comedy-westerns from the clues below:
a The comedians head west and take a train apart
b The comedian makes friends with a cow and stops a stampede by wearing a devil's costume
c The comedians head west with a prize bull. One of them is a pampered millionaire from New York who becomes a sheriff
d The comedians are travelling salesmen out west. As a result of a gunfight, one of them becomes guardian to Marjorie Main and her brood of kids
e The comedians, the landscape and the humour are unmistakably British

26   Ever since the early days of sound, songs have been an essential ingredient in a cowboy film. There is hardly a John Ford picture without a ballad. In the mid-30s, the singing cowboy became very popular in movies with more guitar-slinging than gun-slinging. In which westerns would you find the following Oscar-nominated songs? Say which of them won the award:
a 'Buttons and Bows'
b 'Secret Love'
c 'Raindrops Keep Fallin' on My Head'
d 'Ole Buttermilk Sky'
e 'The Green Leaves of Summer'
f 'Mule Train'
g 'Am I in Love?'
h 'Strange Are The Ways of Love'
i 'Do Not Forsake Me...'
j 'Marmalade, Molasses and Honey'

27   Naturally, the western has also been the subject of full-scale musicals. Name the western musicals in which the following ladies appeared:
a Jeanette MacDonald
b Rosemary Clooney
c Gloria Grahame
d Jean Seberg
e Bebe Daniels
f Ida Lupino
g Doris Day
h Judy Garland
i Betty Hutton
j Irene Dunne

28 Westerns have made place names such as Dodge City, Tombstone and Abilene Town known throughout the world. Test your geographical knowledge of the west by filling in the blanks in the titles in the first list with those of the second:

a SHOOTOUT AT ---
b DUEL AT ---
c 3.10 TO ---
d IN OLD ---
e BAD DAY AT ---
f --- ACROSS THE RIVER
g LAST TRAIN FROM ---
h ROUGH NIGHT IN ---
i GUNS OF FORT ---
j FORTY GUNS TO ---

1 YUMA
2 APACHE PASS
3 DIABLO
4 JERICHO
5 CALIFORNIA
6 GUNHILL
7 TEXAS
8 PETTICOAT
9 MEDICINE BEND
10 BLACK ROCK

'Red' Indians have not always been depicted as evil savages. In the 50s, there was a flood of pro-Indian films. This was one of the first to have an Indian hero at its centre.
a **What is the title of the film?**
b **Who is the 'Red Indian' actor?**
c **Who played his squaw?**
d **In what other film did he play a Red Indian?**
e **Who directed the film?**

29 What do the following westerns have in common?
a A FISTFUL OF DOLLARS
FOR A FEW DOLLARS MORE
HANG 'EM HIGH
b A FISTFUL OF DOLLARS
FOR A FEW DOLLARS MORE
DUCK YOU SUCKER!
c UNCONQUERED (1947)
THE SQUAW MAN
THE TRAIL OF THE LONESOME PINE (1916)
d GUNFIGHT AT THE O.K. CORRAL
THE ALAMO
HEAVEN'S GATE
e HEAVEN'S GATE
BRING ME THE HEAD OF ALFREDO GARCIA
PAT GARRETT AND BILLY THE KID
f UNCONQUERED (1947)
THE HANGING TREE
DISTANT DRUMS
g COMES A HORSEMAN
THE HIRED HAND
DRUMS ALONG THE MOHAWK
h PAT GARRETT AND BILLY THE KID
BUTCH CASSIDY AND THE SUNDANCE KID
THE LIFE AND TIMES OF JUDGE ROY BEAN

30 As a last roundup on westerns, here are a few maverick questions:
a Who said 'When you call me that, smile' and in what film?
b Name the John Ford western of 1948 which tells of three outlaws who find a baby in the desert on Christmas Day, and who played them?
c Which western co-starred Gary Cooper and Burt Lancaster? Who was the director?
d Alan Ladd and Richard Widmark both played Jim Bowie. What were the films?
e What actor made his debut in RED RIVER? Who was the director and who the co-star?
f Who played Johnny Guitar and in which film did he play Jim Bowie?
g What was unusual about the casting of THE LONG RIDERS (1980)?
h Children of movie stars sometimes follow in father's footsteps. Which offspring of famous western stars appeared in YOUNG GUNS OF TEXAS (1962) – three of them – and THE YOUNG LAND (1959) – one of them?
i Who starred in OUTLAND, and of which classic western was it a sci-fi remake?
j Who were the three directors of HOW THE WEST WAS WON? Which of the following stars did not appear in it – Debbie Reynolds, Spencer Tracy, Carroll Baker, Gregory Peck, Angie Dickinson, George Peppard?

Drama and Suspense

ABOVE
This photograph comes from the Best Picture Oscar winner of 1975. Can you name the film and the writer of the original novel on which it was based? Who is the star illustrated? What is the film's setting? Who was the major star who bought the rights to the novel and planned to act in and produce the film version during the 60s? What was his connection with the film as it was finally made? The actor seen here won the Oscar for Best Actor, but who won for Best Actress, Director and Screenplay Adaptation?

ABOVE RIGHT
This picture shows Elizabeth Taylor in a scene from a 1951 film. Name the movie, the actor seen with her here, and supply the name of the third co-star. This was the second screen adaptation of the same novel, filmed in 1931 under its own title. What was it, who wrote it, and who were the three stars then? Can you name the directors of both versions?

RIGHT
Three people in for 'a bumpy ride'. What is the film's title and who was its director? The actress on the left was a last minute replacement in the lead role. Who is she and who was originally meant to play the part? What was the name of the character she portrayed? The character's name featured in the cast list of a movie in the 70s. What was it? Can you name the actor on the right, the character's name and profession? Who is the up-and-coming starlet seen here with him? Who played the title role? Which of the cast won Oscars?

ABOVE

Identify the three stars seen here, in the midst of a family quarrel, from a work by Tennessee Williams. Which two were in the original Broadway stage production, and who directed it on both stage and screen? What are the characters' names and what is the relationship between them? By the way, what's the film called?

RIGHT

Enemies face to face. Can you name:
a The film, and the author of the book on which it was based?
b The director?
c The actor being restrained and his supercilious captor?
d The country in which the scene takes place?
e The female star and an earlier film with a similar theme in which she appeared?

ABOVE
Elizabeth Taylor and Richard Burton in a dramatic moment from one of the many films they have made together. How many? Which one is this, and who wrote the original play on which it was based? Who directed the film, and who were the co-stars? How many Oscars each have Taylor and Burton won, and for what films?

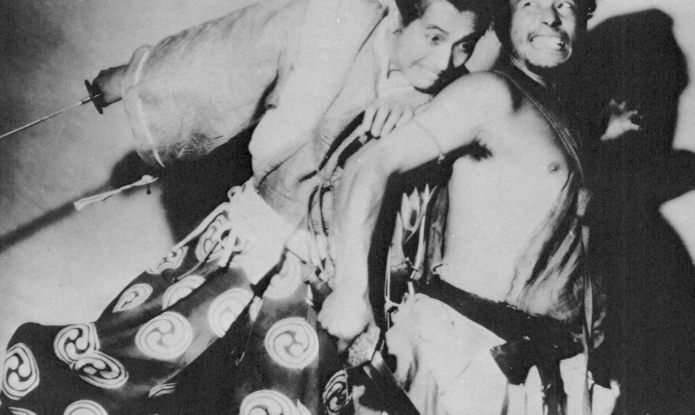

ABOVE LEFT
The title of this film is evident from the still – or is it? What is the name of the little boy who played the leading role and who was the author of the original novel on which the film was based? The film's director is best known for his adaptations of novels for the screen. Who is he and can you name the films he made from the works of the following authors: a) Heinrich von Kleist b) Heinrich Böll c) Robert Musil d) Marcel Proust. The director's wife often collaborates with him on the scripts of his films and is a film director in her own right. Can you name her?

LEFT
This is a scene from a film which questions the nature of truth in a particular way. In what way and what is the film's title? Who directed it and who is the actor on the right? What characters are the two actors portraying? The female lead made an American film with Marlon Brando. Who was she and what was the film?

ABOVE
Do you recognise the three stars seen here in a film adaptation of a novel of the same name? What is it and who wrote it? In what country did its events take place, and who played the leading female role? The star in the centre appeared in another film by the same author, and set in a similar part of the world. What was it? Unusually, the author in question actually appeared in a brief cameo in a French film of the 70s. Do you know which one?

67

ABOVE LEFT
This political thriller was based on true events.
What was its title? Can you name the two real-
life reporters played here by Dustin Hoffman
and Robert Redford, as well as the newspaper
they worked for? Who won an Oscar for his performance as their editor and what was the
editor's name? A porno film title figured in the
story. What was the title and to whom did it
refer?

LEFT
a What was the subject of conflict between these
two people and in what movie?
b The movie won Oscars for Best Actor, Best
Director and Best Supporting Actress. Name
the winners
c The director began his film career as a
scriptwriter. Which of these films did he co-
script:
i) BONNIE AND CLYDE? ii) WHAT'S UP
DOC? iii) SUPERMAN?
d The first film of the actor pictured here was:
i) THE GRADUATE? ii) THE TIGER MAKES
OUT? iii) ME NATALIE?

ABOVE
What is the relationship between the title of this
film and the female character pictured here?
Who is the actress? Where is the scene taking
place and at approximately what time of day?
Name the film's director and say in what language the film was made. What other pictures
did he make with this actress?

ABOVE
Name the two actresses here, the film, and the director. What is the relationship between the two characters? In an attempt to broaden the appeal of his films, the director cast the following stars in three pictures during the 70s: Elliott Gould, David Carradine and Ingrid Bergman. Can you name the pictures and the female co-stars in each?

RIGHT
The lady frolicking in the fountain was a famous sex symbol of the 50s and early 60s. Who is she? The still comes from the biggest box-office success of any foreign language picture in the USA up to the time of its release. Name the film, its setting and its director. Can you name two other films the director made with the star illustrated? Name the director's actress wife, and how many films have they made together?

70

Reach for the Stars

A Though she recently turned down the lead in the Broadway version of Tom Stoppard's play 'The Real Thing', her career is doing splendidly all the same, thanks to the likes of John Fowles and William Styron both of whom have recently provided her with two of the meatiest roles any actress could want. Before entering movies, she appeared in a number of Broadway plays, including Tennessee Williams's '27 Wagons Full of Cotton' for which she was nominated for a Tony:

a Who is she?

b What was her first film and who were its stars?

c In what Woody Allen film did she appear?

d What was the TV series for which she won an Emmy Award?

e John Fowles wrote the novel, but who wrote the screenplay and what was the film called? Who was the leading man?

B After appearing in two successful British films at the beginning of the 60s, one of which starred Laurence Olivier and the other Hayley Mills, this handsome, RADA-trained, Derbyshire-born actor received star billing in a film based on a novel by Stan Barstow. Starry appearances in the West End and on Broadway have further enhanced his prestigious career as, indeed, have his more recent television appearances in plays by Terence Rattigan and Alan Bennett:

a Who is he?

b For what film was he nominated for an Oscar, and who directed it?

c Who was his female co-star in FAR FROM THE MADDING CROWD? Who directed it? Who wrote the novel from which it came?

d In what film did he have a spastic daughter? Who played the child's mother?

e Philippe de Broca directed him in this French comedy set in a lunatic asylum. What was it?

C Born in Toronto, she began her career as 'Baby Gladys Smith'. She was a Belasco actress before she was spotted in a line of extras by D. W. Griffith. Her first starring role teamed her with an alcoholic matinée idol whom she later married. She stopped the traffic when she visited Moscow with her second husband, and later co-starred

with him in a Shakespeare adaptation. They were divorced in 1935 and he died four years later. She survived to become Hollywood's most famous recluse:

a Who is she?

b Which of her roles was repeated by Hayley Mills?

c In her autobiography, she claimed that in the 1912 FRIENDS she was involved in an important technical innovation. What was it?

d A famous 1921 role of hers was repeated by Freddie Bartholomew. What was it?

e What was the name of the house in which she lived from the 20s to her death?

D It was as a glamour girl of sorts that this star made it into films in 1943 via Summer Stock, nightclubs and Broadway, but her latent abilities as a serious actress were not recognised until 1948 when she played a waitress strangled by Ronald Colman. She has since won two Oscars and in 1972 was nominated for a third. She has been married three times. Her second marriage was to a well-known Italian actor, and her third to Anthony Franciosa. She has appeared in a Broadway musical about the Marx Brothers, which flopped:

a Who is she?

b What were her Oscar-nominated films?

c What was her real name, and who was her glamorous second husband?

d In what film did she appear as Lenny Baker's archetypal Jewish mother?

e She played a half-breed with Tab Hunter in this one. What was it called?

E A walking definition of the suave, modern-day urban male, he was born in Fontana Liri, Italy, of indigent peasant stock in 1923. His highly successful film career began in 1947, but it wasn't until he was chosen by Federico Fellini to appear in a controversial account of Rome's Via Veneto set that he became an international star, equally at home in comedy and drama:

a Who is he?

b In what film did he play a priest? Who was his co-star, and what role did she play?

c In what film did he play a jaded NATO officer romantically involved with Virna Lisi?

d In LA NOTTE he was trapped in a loveless marriage. Who played his wife and who directed?

e He appeared in a film in which four men eat themselves to death. What was it called?

71

Childhood Memories

Child stars have been among the film-makers' most valuable property, and sometimes grossly exploited by greedy adults. Films for children have been big box-office, as have those with equal appeal to adults.

1   Like Abracadabra, the words Walt Disney are magic, having cast a spell on generations of children (and adults) from the day Mickey Mouse made his debut in 1928. Undoubtedly Disney's greatest contribution to the cinema was the genius he brought to the art of animation. Test your knowledge of the Disney World:

a Who provided the falsetto voice for Mickey for almost twenty years? Who created Donald Duck's distinctive squawk and in what film did this irascible fowl make his debut?

b What was technically new for Disney about SILLY SYMPHONY: FLOWERS AND TREES (1932), LADY AND THE TRAMP (1955) and SLEEPING BEAUTY (1959)?

c Which short film of 1933 contained a hit tune that swept the nation? What was the song and who wrote it?

d The names of the seven dwarfs in SNOW WHITE AND THE SEVEN DWARFS were chosen by public poll. What were they?

e Name the eight composers represented in FANTASIA and say who conducted their works?

f In ROBIN HOOD, what animals portrayed Robin Hood, Prince John, and Little John. What was the name of Prince John's snake companion and who dubbed his voice?

g Which of Disney's cartoon features:
   i   opens with the camera pulling back from a large white star, panning across the roofs of a village and closing in on the lighted window of a cottage
   ii had Nelson Eddy dubbing the voice for a whale whose ambition is to sing at the Met
   iii had Roy Rogers singing the tale of 'Pecos Bill'
   iv was the last to be made during his lifetime
   v   is set in Paris

h Name the films from which the following songs come i) 'Look Out For Mr Stork' ii) 'When You Wish Upon A Star' iii) 'I'm Wishing' iv) 'The Bare Necessities' v) 'Bibbidi-Bobbidi-Boo'

i After Disneyland and Disney World comes EPCOT. What does it stand for?

j Name the films in which the following animated characters appear
   i) Jacques and Gus-Gus ii) Timothy Mouse
   iii) Brer Fox iv) Jock and Trusty v) Cruella de Vil

2   Unlike the Victorian era, children were seen *and* heard abundantly in Hollywood. Which child star precociously asked the director:

a 'When I cry, do you want the tears to run all the way, or shall I stop halfway down?'
   . . . and who, in each case, made the following remarks about her?

b 'If that child had been born in the Middle Ages, she'd have been burned as a witch'

c 'She's the only actress outside of Ethel who's made me take out my handkerchief in thirty years'

d 'She was at her most appealing, I might say, most appalling age . . . She was a quiet, almost too well behaved child, when her mother was on the set. When mother was absent, it was another story and she was a pain in the neck'

e 'It was very cold and she was waiting with a blanket around her shoulders and I said, '. . . I hate to tell you this, but somebody is going to kidnap your little dog and shoot it, you know.' And she said, 'Will there be lots of blood?' And I went on and elaborated – and finally said, 'Turn 'em' and jerked the blanket off her and she went out there and did this hysterical scene all in one take.'

3   Mickey Rooney's short stature cast him many times as a jockey. He played one in the first of ten films in which he appeared with Judy Garland. What was it? In which film did he train Elizabeth Taylor to ride? What future British politician auditioned for Elizabeth Taylor's role? Who played the same character in the 1978 sequel? What was it called? Rooney again appeared as a horse trainer in a 1979 movie. What was it called and name its sequel?

a **Who is the waifish actress in the picture?**
b **Name the film and the author of the story on which it was based**
c **Who played the man behind the puppets?**
d **What was the name of the song the puppet asks the girl to sing?**
e **The film inspired a Broadway musical. What was it called?**

4   Schooldays, happy or otherwise, have provided sentimental, nostalgic, comic or social scenarios for countless movies. Stay in after school if you don't get at least five out of ten questions right:

a Which teacher calls her class the 'crème de la crème' and who played her?

b What teacher on hearing that it was a pity he never had any children, replied, 'You're wrong. I have thousands of them – and all boys.' Who played him and how did Clark Gable lose out to him?

c Which film featured the following exchange: Girl student: I've missed two periods Teacher: That's all right, you can make them up after school

d Which film set in a school opened with 'Rock Around The Clock' behind the titles? What future film director had a bit role in it?

e What film, made in 1931, was set in an oppressive boarding school for the daughters of Prussian officers, and who directed it? In the 1958 colour remake which stars played the sympathetic teacher and the pupil infatuated with her?

f In which films is the headmistress played by a man? Who is the actor?

g In which film is the headmaster played by a midget? Who was its director?

h What British film of 1969 was influenced by the above, who directed it and who wrote the poem from which its short title derives?

i Name the film in which the 'plucky youngster' overcomes the bully Flashman? Who played the schoolboy hero in the 1940 and 1951 versions?

j In which film did a black teacher gain the respect of a class of tough white pupils at a London school? Who played the teacher and who made her feature film debut as a fresh schoolgirl?

5   Sometimes adult stars have been forced to play children. In which films, and why, did:

a Ginger Rogers pretend to be a 12-year-old girl?

b Jerry Lewis pretend to be a 12-year-old boy?

c Katharine Hepburn pretend to be a young boy?

d Cary Grant revert to childhood?

e Fred Astaire revert to babyhood?

6   Classic children's novels adapted to the screen have been perennial favourites. Who played the title roles in the stories below?

a THE ADVENTURES OF TOM SAWYER (1930, 1938, 1973)

b THE ADVENTURES OF HUCKLEBERRY FINN (1939, 1960, 1974)

c THE PRINCE AND THE PAUPER (1937, 1962, 1977 – US: CROSSED SWORDS)

d POLLYANNA (1919, 1960)

e LITTLE LORD FAUNTLEROY (1921, 1936, 1980)

7   Charles Dickens' stories have always been a popular source for the cinema. NICHOLAS NICKLEBY was first filmed as early as 1903. David Lean called Dickens 'the perfect screenwriter'. Answer the following Dickensian questions:

a Which of Dickens's novels did Lean direct and name two actors who each appeared in both of them?

b Who won the role of Oliver Twist in the musical OLIVER! after some 2000 boys had been auditioned? Who played the role straight in 1922, 1933, 1948 and 1983? What other Dickens tales have been made into screen musicals?

c In MICKEY'S CHRISTMAS CAROL, Mickey Mouse made a comeback after retiring many years before. What was his previous film and when was it released? In the Dickens-Disney cartoon what roles did Mickey, Donald Duck, Minnie Mouse and Goofy play?

d In 1934, MGM made a successful version of DAVID COPPERFIELD, directed by George Cukor. From the following list of 14 names, select the 10 correct names to complete the film's cast credits below: Donald Crisp, Freddie Bartholomew, Basil Rathbone, Roland Young, Lionel Barrymore, John Barrymore, W. C. Fields, Lewis Stone, Edmund Gwenn, Jackie Cooper, Hugh Williams, Lennox Pawle, Hugh Walpole, Frank Lawton
   Mr Micawber
   Dan Peggotty
   David Copperfield (as a boy)
   David Copperfield (as a man)
   Uriah Heep
   Mr Murdstone
   Mr Wickfield
   Steerforth
   Mr Dick
   The Vicar

e Who was originally cast as Micawber, but withdrew after a week's work? His wife, however, played Micawber's maid. Who was she?

8   Lassie became one of the most popular of all kids' animal heroines, inspiring a string of 'Lassie' films and a TV and radio series. In fact, Lassie was played by a male collie dog whose son, grandson and great-grandson succeeded him. Why was a male dog chosen and what was his real name? LASSIE COME HOME (1943) was the first of the series. In it, who played the boy who owned Lassie and who was the 10-year-old girl, making her second screen appearance? The boy's stunts were done by somebody who went on to star on Broadway in 'West Side Story'. Who was he? When and where is the Lassie story set? Name five other films with 'Lassie' in the title. In which film did Lassie share the honours with Jeanette MacDonald? In what musical is there a lyric which states, 'He may have hair upon his chest, sister, but so has Lassie'?

A scene from a film tailored to the talents of the 'Lilliputian in ringlets' illustrated. Name the little girl and the film. Who wrote the story on which it is based and how was it altered to suit her personality. Who directed it? Who is the actor she is confronting? One of the director's favourite actors is in the kilt. Who is he? Where is the film set?

9 Other animals besides Lassie had their moments of cinematic glory. Can you identify the various fauna represented by the names below and the films in which they appeared?
a Balthazar
b Flicka
c Bonzo
d Joe Carioca
e The Pi
f Cheeta
g Rhubarb
h Thumper
i Tarka
j Pushmi-Pullyu

10 European directors have coaxed brilliantly authentic performances from children who are not professional actors. Give the titles and directors of the films described below:
a A father and his small son spend a Sunday searching for something on which the man's job depends. What is that something? A previous film by the same director traced the misfortunes of two youngsters who get involved in the black market because they want to buy a horse. What was it?
b A 14-year-old boy is sent to reform school for stealing a typewriter. Name the actor and the character he plays. What is the last shot of the film? A later film by the same director detailed the 'civilising' of a child. What was it called?
c A boy throws himself off a ruined building in post-war Germany. What other film by the same director also concerns a child's suicide?
d Two children bury animals with full rites during the war. Who played the five-year-old Paulette?
e Urchins live from hand to mouth, at one stage beating up a blind man

11 Many child stars suffered from the many pressures imposed upon them. Some had their lives blighted by accidents, financial distress or emotional problems. Who:

a Appeared in over a dozen films in the early 50s, played the son of James Stewart, Robert Mitchum, Richard Widmark among others, featured in the 'Lassie' TV series, was arrested for growing marijuana in 1972, spent five years in prison for drug smuggling?

b Made his Broadway debut at the age of seven in a hit play – a role he repeated in his first film, was nominated for an Oscar in a classic western of the 50s, died at thirty as a result of a car accident?

c Was the first 'live' actor to sign a long-term contract with the Walt Disney studios, won a special Academy Award as 'the outstanding juvenile actor of 1949', became a drug addict, was buried in a pauper's grave, his body only identified a year later through fingerprints?

d Was given an MGM contract at the age of thirteen, was manipulated and controlled by the studio, was on pills from an early age to control her weight and nerves, married five times, died of an overdose of sleeping pills?

e Made his screen debut aged eighteen months in SKINNER'S BABY, was earning one of Hollywood's highest salaries at the age of seven, married starlet Betty Grable, sued his mother and stepfather in order to recover what little was left of the money they had spent of his fortune?

12 'During this depression, when the spirit of the people is lower than at any other time, it is a splendid thing that for just fifteen cents an American can go to a movie and look at the smiling face of a baby and forget his troubles'. Thus spoke President Franklin D. Roosevelt in 1935 of the most famous of all child stars – Shirley Temple:

a For what studio did she make most of her films?

b For what role did the studio refuse to loan her out to MGM when asked by Louis B. Mayer?

c Give the titles of three of her films that described something about her appearance

d In which two films did she appear with her first husband and who was he?

e In which films, when she had grown into a teenager did she co-star with i) Clifton Webb ii) Cary Grant iii) Ginger Rogers iv) David Niven v) Claudette Colbert

f In which films did she first sing 'On The Good Ship Lollypop', 'Animal Crackers In My Soup', and 'Baby Take A Bow'?

g In which films was she i) a little Swiss girl taken away from her grandfather ii) an orphan girl raised by a Canadian mountie iii) convinced she was Ronald Reagan's illegitimate daughter?

h Under what name, and in what capacity, did she have a political career in later life?

i One of Shirley's most frequent dancing partners was a great black hoofer. Who was he? In how many movies did they dance together? In which film was he her choreographer?

j Complete the following titles:
  i THE LITTLE––– (2 titles)
  ii THE LITTLEST –––
  iii LITTLE MISS ––– (2 titles)
  iv OUR LITTLE –––
  v POOR LITTLE –––

13 In Hollywood, show biz babies often follow in their parent's footsteps. Can you name the mothers of the following?
a Mary Crosby
b Lorenzo Lamas
c Jamie Lee Curtis
d Desi Arnaz Jr
e Carrie Fisher
f Tatum O'Neal
g Ricky and David Nelson
h Vanessa and Lynn Redgrave
i Larry Hagman
j Catherine Allégret

No, not Theda Bara or Marlene Dietrich, but an extremely mature child star of the 70s! Who is she? From what film does this vampish pose come? Name the character she played in it. What was her most notorious role? In which film did she play a murderess? Who stood in for her for the nude scenes in the latter? In what film did she play Barbara Harris's mother?

'He is alone . . . He is afraid . . . He is 3 million miles from home' – ran a publicity line for the movie illustrated. Who is 'he'? Where is '3 million miles from home'? 'He' is not really alone. Who is 'he' with? (Name the character and actor.) What are they trying to do? Who directed the film and who wrote the Oscar-winning score? What film does 'he' watch on TV while his friend is at school? What did Carlo Rambaldi have to do with the film?

---

14 Now for a mélange of moppetry:
a What roles did W. C. Fields, Cary Grant, Gary Cooper, and Edward Everett Horton play in the 1933 version of ALICE IN WONDERLAND? Who played the March Hare in the 1972 version?
b 'More laughs than LOVE FINDS ANDY HARDY . . . More thrills than TEST PILOT . . . More tears than CAPTAINS COURAGEOUS . . . with the stars that made them great . . .' What was the film and who were the stars that this publicity copy was shouting about?

c Who said of whom, 'The kid's no trouper', after spiking the infant's milk with gin?
d Who said, 'I stopped believing in Santa Claus when I was six. Mother took me to see him in a department store and he asked for my autograph.'
e In which film did Bob Hope, Mel Brooks, Richard Pryor, Telly Savalas, Carol Kane and Orson Welles all make guest appearances?
f Which two films by the same director caused a rumpus because of mother-son incest in one and child prostitution in the other? Who played the 12-year-old girl in the latter? Who was the director?
g Bald British character actor Lionel Jeffries has directed three classic children's stories. What are they?
h Who played the child who bumps off her classmates in THE BAD SEED, and who was the brat who ruins the lives of two teachers by her malicious gossip in THESE THREE?
i Where would you have found Spanky, Alfalfa and Pete? And Huntz Hall and Leo Gorcey?
j How are Harold Gray, F.D.R. and Charles Strouse connected?

The Generation Gap

In the mid-1950s, during the economic recovery from World War II, the gap between parents and children widened and films began to exploit their differences: it was only a matter of time before Youth had its own movies.

1 Which side of the gap are you on? Find out from this easy batch of opening questions:
a What does the title 9/30/55 refer to?
b In which film does Terence Stamp sleep with every member of a family plus the maid?
c Which star is common to WHERE THE BOYS ARE, FOLLOW THE BOYS and WHEN THE BOYS MEET THE GIRLS?
d In which film does William Holden fall for a young hippie?
e Which films with 'young' in the titles were directed by Alfred Hitchcock and Luis Buñuel?
f Which films with 'young' in the titles starred Cliff Richard, Burt Lancaster and Doris Day?
g Who played TAMMY AND THE BACHELOR and TAMMY AND THE DOCTOR?
h Which film was based on a Pink Floyd album and who did the animated sequences?
i In TOMMY, who played the title role, Pinball Wizard, Acid Queen and The Preacher?
j In what film are the kids of a small Mid-western town forbidden to disco-dance, and who played the big-city boy who fights the ban?

2 'Nostalgia isn't what it used to be' reads a famous graffito, but in movies about adolescence nostalgia is as present as ever it used to be:
a Which 1982 movie, set in Baltimore, about a reunion of kids for a football match, had the publicity line: 'Remember what life was like in 1959? Girls wore their hair long; guys wore theirs short'?
b Which 1981 movie, set in Florida in the early 1950s, featured college kids called Pee Wee and 'Meat' who visit the sleazy place of the title?
c Which 1971 movie, set in a small Texas town in 1951, told of teenage affairs and the closing down of a place of entertainment?
d Which 1961 movie, set in Kansas in 1926, about a young couple prevented from marrying by their parents, had a title taken from a line by Wordsworth?
e Which 1971 movie, set in a New England holiday resort, told of the growing pains of three boys on vacation many moons ago?

3 Teen movies often have high school settings:
a At which school would you find Sean Penn as a permanently stoned surfer?
b Where would you find Donald Sutherland as a pot-smoking English professor?
c At which school would you find Professor Kingsfield and who played him?
d In which 'class' would you find i) Gary Grimes ii) Timothy Van Patten iii) Rob Lowe?
e Which countries produced the following films about school kids? i) PEPPERMINT SODA (DIABLE MENTHE) ii) LEMON POP-SICLE iii) MEATBALLS?

4 Drug taking has been associated with youth culture since the 60s. In which movies did
a Al Pacino become a junkie in a New York ghetto?
b Peter Fonda as a director of TV commercials take LSD?
c Peter Sellers try out hash cookies made by his hippie girlfriend?
d A fifteen-year-old German girl become a heroin addict?
e Joe Dallesandro have constant fixes?

5 A CLOCKWORK ORANGE gained notoriety for its depiction of violence and its bleak vision of the future. Anthony Burgess wrote the novel, but who wrote the screenplay? Who directed the film? Where was it set? What was the name given to the teenage gang of four? Who played Alex Delarge? Who was the character's favourite composer? What was the last line that Alex spoke?

A scene from an Elvis Presley vehicle in which he is singing the title number:
a **What is the name of the film?**
b **It was only his i) first ii) second iii) third film?**
c **His co-star was i) Judy Tyler ii) Dolores Hart iii) Juliet Prowse?**
d **Among the songs were i) 'I Don't Wanna Be Tied' ii) 'Treat Me Nice' iii) 'Blue Suede Shoes'?**
e **Name three films he made with 'Girl' in the title**

9 In the early 70s, the word 'rockumentary' was coined to describe film records of rock festivals. Which rockumentary:
a Featuring the Rolling Stones was shot in Canada?
b Featuring the Rolling Stones included the fatal stabbing of a youth by a Hell's Angel?
c Was a three-hour split-screen affair which ended with Jimi Hendrix singing 'The Star-Spangled Banner'?
d Celebrated The Band's final concert?
e Was the final appearance in a feature film of the Beatles together?

10 Pop stars have often taken straight roles in films. Name the male pop idols you would find in:
a PAT GARRETT AND BILLY THE KID
b BRIMSTONE AND TREACLE
c THE HUNGER
d LISZTOMANIA
e THE JAZZ SINGER (1980)
f PERFORMANCE

11 Love and/or sex has often bridged the generation gap. Can you name the older people that the following fell for?
a Bud Cort in HAROLD AND MAUDE
b Debbie Reynolds in SUSAN SLEPT HERE
c Warren Beatty in THE ROMAN SPRING OF MRS STONE
d Debbie Reynolds in THIS HAPPY FEELING
e Murray Head in SUNDAY BLOODY SUNDAY
f Deanna Durbin in THAT CERTAIN AGE
g Richard Beymer in THE STRIPPER
h Jane Powell in NANCY GOES TO RIO
i Peter McEnery in VICTIM
j Warren Beatty in ALL FALL DOWN

12 'This boy, this girl were never properly introduced to the world we live in' was a pre-credit title of a 1948 film about young lovers on the run from the law in the 30s. What was the film called, who played 'this boy, this girl', and whose debut film was it? It was remade in the 70s with the title of the original novel by Edward Anderson. Name it, the director and the young lovers.

13 Freud's figurative expression 'Strike the father dead' underlies many father-son relationships in the movies. In which films were the following fathers and sons at odds?
a Donald Sutherland and Timothy Hutton
b Paul Dooley and Dennis Christopher
c Jack Lemmon and Robby Benson
d Robert Duvall and Michael O'Keefe
e Gary Cooper and Anthony Perkins

Marlon Brando, one of the icons of modern cinema, in one of his most famous poses:
a Name the film and the role he played
b Of what was the film a forerunner?
c Who played Brando's girl, and who was the leader of a rival gang?
d Name the films in which Gene Kelly (1957) and Peter Boyle (1973) take off Brando in this role?
e In which films did Brando play the other rebels Stanley Kowalski, Terry Malloy and Val Xavier?

14 What two things do TEX, RUMBLEFISH and THE OUTSIDERS have in common and which is the odd one out?

15 A 1948 British film, starring Jean Simmons and Donald Houston, told of the shipwreck of a boy and girl on a tropical isle and their subsequent growing up there. Name the film and the stars of the remake. The director, Randal Kleiser, said 'It's very attractive to work with young people because they look for guidance and they don't argue about interpretation.' He should know, as he directed a hot John Travolta movie and a 1983 film whose publicity slogan was 'They Spent a Summer of Love to the Sounds of Chicago'. Name the two films.

16 Which young female stars played:
a POOKIE
b GIDGET
c GEORGY GIRL
d MARJORIE MORNINGSTAR
e WANDA NEVADA

Lynn Carlin and Audra Lindley in a scene from a generation gap comedy of the 70s. Name the film. In what way is the game they are playing related to the title? What other meaning is given to the film's title? Which two pop stars appeared in it as themselves? Who directed the film and in what way was it a debut for him? Name two other generation gap pictures he directed previously.

---

17 · The Vietnam war created protests among college students all over America, many of them burning their draft cards. Several movies reflected this atmosphere:

a What notable Italian director tackled the subject and name the film? What set-piece takes place on the sands of Death Valley and how does the film end? Who was its young male star and what happened to him subsequently?

b In what picture did Elliott Gould play a postgraduate at Everywhere University, surrounded by radical students? Who was the female lead? What did Ingmar Bergman's liking of the film lead to?

c THE STRAWBERRY STATEMENT was about student protests. Explain the title, and name the two young leads

d What movie was expanded from a talking blues number by Arlo Guthrie? Who wrote the song 'Pasture of Plenty' used in the film? Who directed it?

e What movie celebrated 'the age of Aquarius', and who choreographed it?

18 Street gangs are all here in the questions below:
a In which movies would you find i) the Sharks and Jets ii) the Greasers and the Socs?

b Which street gang movie took its inspiration from a novel based on Xenophon's 'Anabasis' which told of how Greek soldiers had to make their way home after their leader had been killed?

c Which movie of the 70s told of clashes between Mods and Rockers in the 60s?

d In what film and for whose benefit did James Cagney go screaming and struggling to the electric chair?

e What 1979 movie told of street gang clashes in the Bronx at the time of Kennedy's assassination?

Identify the two actors in this scene from one of the cult movies of the 70s. What was its title? Where are they headed for? Who made his mark as the dropout lawyer? Name the producer, and the director. Both of them wrote the screenplay with a third writer. Who was he? How does the film end?

19 Elvis Presley, the rock singing idol, gyrated in many different locales throughout his film career. Can you name the films in which he was to be found in the places below?
a West Germany
b Seattle
c Mexico
d England
e The Middle East
f Hawaii (twice)
g Nevada
h Tennessee
i New Orleans
j Miami

20 In road movies no-one stays anywhere for very long. It's 'keep on trucking' through the vastness of American space. In which movie did
a Goldie Hawn and William Atherton get chased by every cop in Texas while trying to reclaim their baby?
b Characters called The Driver, The Mechanic, The Girl and GTO race from California to Santa Fe?
c Lovers Martin Sheen and Sissy Spacek go on a killing spree while moving across America?
d Peter Fonda and Susan George rob a bank and try to evade the cops in a long chase?
e A German journalist travel down the East Coast of America with a nine-year-old girl?

21 Motor cycles emerged in the 60s as erotic-narcotic symbols, becoming the ultimate freedom machines:
a Who owned the SILVER DREAM RACER?
b Who was THE GIRL ON THE MOTOR-CYCLE?
c Which two offspring of more famous stars were members of THE WILD ANGELS?
d In which film did a young motorcycle messenger become involved with an opera star? Who was she, and whose directorial debut was the film?
e In which French classic is a poet run over by a pair of motorcyclists?

22 THE GRADUATE was one of the first American films to appeal to middle class students because of its rejection of middle class values. Although Benjamin Braddock, the graduate of the title, makes no protest against the war in Vietnam, the roots of the anti-draft counter culture are to be found in the movie. What business did one of Benjamin's father's friends want to interest him in? Who played Benjamin, his girlfriend Elaine and her mother? What was Elaine's mother's first name? Who sang the two hit songs in the movie and what were their titles? One of the scriptwriters also played a hotel clerk. Who was he?

Guessing Games

This chapter has no boundary in time or space, ranging as it does over seven decades of movies, from New York to New Delhi. Obviously, we don't expect you to know all the answers – some you will, some you won't. . . .

1 'What's in a name?' The movie industry evidently thought there was plenty. The stars of the films below are billed under their real names. By what names are they better known?
a Bernie Schwartz and Rosetta Jacobs in THE PRINCE WHO WAS A THIEF
b Julius Garfinkle and Julia Jean Turner in THE POSTMAN ALWAYS RINGS TWICE
c Lucille Le Seuer and Ira Grossel in FEMALE ON THE BEACH
d Anna Italiano and Melvin Kaminsky in TO BE OR NOT TO BE
e Marion Morrison and Betty Perske in THE SHOOTIST
f Constance Ockleman and Ernest Bickel in I MARRIED A WITCH
g William Beedle Jr and William Mitchell in NETWORK
h Frederick Austerlitz and Joan de Beauvoir de Havilland in A DAMSEL IN DISTRESS
i Issur Danielovitch and Tula Finklea in TWO WEEKS IN ANOTHER TOWN
j Allen Konigsberg and Diane Hall in LOVE AND DEATH

2 Beautiful friendships are often begun in the strangest manner in the movies. Who met whom in what films in the following ways?
a He jumps into her open jalopy in order to escape from his fans
b They both buy the same pair of pyjamas
c She drops a tomato plant from her balcony almost on top of him
d He takes a cinder out of her eye on a railway station platform
e She complains about his tap-dancing in the room above
f She emerges from the sea towards him with virtually only a knife at her waist
g She drops her purse, he helps her to retrieve the contents, and then takes her to a bomb shelter
h They fight over a book he has come to borrow from the library where she works
i They are attending a school concert in which one of their children is taking off Maurice Chevalier
j He saves her as she falls from a building

3 A number of Hollywood's top male stars chose to marry virtually unknown starlets. Can you match the stars with their wives in the following list?
a Bing Crosby
b William Powell
c Cornel Wilde
d Ronald Reagan
e Cary Grant

A Nancy Davis
B Betsy Drake
C Diana Lewis
D Jean Wallace
E Kathryn Grant

4 Now for an odd mixture of motion picture posers:
a Who played Rupert Pupkin, Trudy Kockenlocker, J. D. Hackensacker III, Sugar Kane and Badass Buddusky, and in what films?
b Who played Pa and Ma Kettle, and in what film did the characters make their first appearance?
c Maude, Claire and Pauline are heroines of which film director? Complete the titles in which their names appear
d Name the films in which Mickey Rooney, Marlon Brando play Japanese; Katharine Hepburn plays a Chinese; Jean Simmons an Indian; and Shirley MacLaine, Jennifer Jones play Eurasians
e What American writer was the focus of a 1982 film by a German director? Name the director and the actor who took the title role
f Who, in 1981, played a film actor playing a 19th-century scientist?
g Who said 'The difference between me and Lubitsch is that he shows you the king on the throne, and then shows you the king in his bedroom. I show you the king in his bedroom first. That way when you see him on the throne you have no illusions about him'?
h Who said, 'If I made Cinderella, the audience would be looking out for a body in the coach'?
i Who says and in what film, 'Quick, the Renaissance will soon be here and we'll all be painting'?
j What film of 1978 begins with a title that is usually the final one, and who was its director and star?

**Who are the celebrated couple pictured here?
What is the film called, who directed it and who
played the title role? Who wrote the screenplay based on his own play? Name another film
in which the couple appeared together. What
was her last movie?**

---

5 As in the literature of the past, alternative titles
have sometimes been offered in the movies, and in
these days of multiple sequels are often used. Add the
first half of the following titles:
a ... THE HERETIC
b ... FLYING KILLERS
c ... SEASON OF THE WITCH
d ... or HOW I LEARNED TO STOP
WORRYING AND LOVE THE BOMB
e ... or PARDON ME, BUT YOUR TEETH ARE
IN MY NECK
f ... 3D
g ... or THE 120 DAYS OF SODOM
h ... THE SHAME OF THE NATION
i ... THE POSSESSION
j ... THE STORY OF A WOMAN

6 When Jack Warner was told in the 60s that
former Warner Bros. contract actor Ronald Reagan
had been nominated to run for Governor of California, he said, 'No, no. Jimmy Stewart for governor –
Reagan for his best friend.' In which films were the
following contenders for high political office?
a Robert Redford
b Alan Alda
c Henry Fonda
d Don Murray
e Spencer Tracy

7 In 1959, a group of French directors was given
a generic name by a journalist. What was it? Which
of the group made what is considered to be the first
film of the movement and what was it called? At the
Cannes Film Festival in 1959, two other directors
were given awards for their debut features. Who
were they and what were the films? A fourth director
made a sensational debut in 1960. Who was he? His
film was remade by an American in 1983. What was
it? What film magazine was especially linked with the
group?

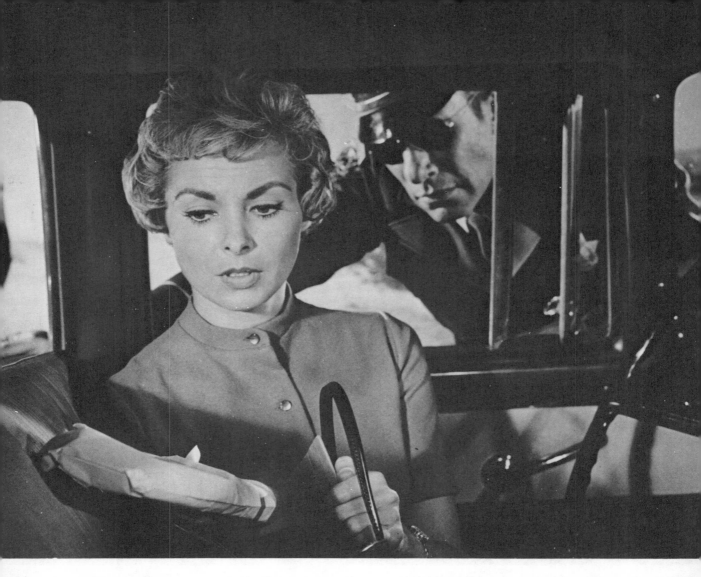

8   The car chase, comic or dramatic, has been camera fodder since the beginnings of the silent cinema. Other forms of pursuit have also been popular in pictures. Answer the following questions:

a Which film, set in San Francisco, is remembered for one of the most spectacular car chases ever committed to the screen? Who directed it? Name two other films by the same director featuring chases, one with Robert Redford and George Segal, and the other involving ambulance drivers

b In what film does Noel Coward mastermind 'history's biggest traffic jam'?

c Bubber Reeves escapes from prison only to face the threat of lynching from the inhabitants of his home town, who pursue him. Name the film, and the stars who played Reeves, and the Sheriff who tries to get him a fair trial

d Who is pursued by whom through the sewers of Vienna, and in what film?

e Victor Hugo's classic novel 'Les Miserables' has been filmed a number of times. Who played the ex-convict and who the detective that trails him all his life in the 1935 and 1952 versions, and the 1957 French version?

Janet Leigh in a scene from Alfred Hitchcock's PSYCHO.
a What has she in her bag and why should she be nervous of the man at the car window?
b Who played the detective hired to find her and what happens to him?
c One of the key scenes was allegedly directed by someone other than Hitchcock. Do you know who?
d PSYCHO was one of the first films to have a special contract with exhibitors. What did it entail?
e Who reprised their roles in PSYCHO II?

9   Name the Polish director who made his reputation with a war trilogy. Who was the brilliant young actor, known as the Polish James Dean, who appeared in many of his early films? How did the actor die? What film by the director paid tribute to him? What was the title of the film about a worker-hero in the 50s, and its sequel about Solidarity? What film did he direct in France about the French revolution?

10 Eating in films often takes on a significance beyond the satisfaction of hunger. The questions below might give you some food for thought:

a With whom does Albert Finney share a chicken as a prelude to other activity? What was the film?

b Who, and in what film, has a hard time at a roadside diner getting chicken without having to take a toasted sandwich?

c In what film is a group of people's attempts to eat a meal constantly interrupted? Who wrote the screenplay?

d Who played the four friends who decide to eat themselves to death, and in what film?

e In the famous boot-eating scene from THE GOLD RUSH, what part of the boot does Chaplin carve for himself, and what provides a wishbone and spaghetti? In the same film, what does Chaplin do with two bread rolls?

f In what film did a middle-aged couple called Paul and Mary Bland pose as a kinky sex duo, and bump off their clientele? Who played the couple, and who the title role?

g Who serves whom a large rat with vegetables? Name the film

h In what film is an injured rabbit served up as a ragout in a restaurant?

i Who did Wallace Shawn have dinner with, and who directed the film?

11 It took until the 70s for Australia to produce a number of movies that made an impact on the international market. It now has a film industry to be reckoned with. Give the titles and directors of the films mentioned down under:

a Based on a novel by Thomas Keneally, it was about a half-breed aborigine who goes on a rampage

b Based on an autobiographical novel by Miles Franklin (a *nom de plume*), it was about a young girl growing up in rural Australia at the turn of the century. Who played the girl?

c Based on a novel by Joan Lindsay, it was about some schoolgirls who disappeared on a St. Valentine's Day outing

d It told of a lawyer's attempt to defend an aborigine charged with ritual murder. Who played the lawyer?

e It proved that an Aussie film could out-bike, out-stunt, out-cult any Yankee exploitation movie, as did its sequel, made with American money

12 A number of highly dramatic movies, which brought marvellous performance from stars, concerned themselves with the horrors of addiction. Identify the addiction and the victim(s) in each case:

a LONG DAY'S JOURNEY INTO NIGHT

b THE LOST WEEKEND

c THE MAN WITH THE GOLDEN ARM

d LA BAIE DES ANGES/BAY OF ANGELS

e DAYS OF WINE AND ROSES

13 Try your hand at the following movie mélange:

a In what film did the hero play chess with Death, and who was the brave man?

b A pet monkey is given a solemn funeral. Who did it belong to and in what film?

c Who, and in what film, plays the piano while travelling in the back of an open truck?

d The hero, in this film, reads of his own death in a newspaper. Give the actor and the title

e Who was the protagonist pursued by a truck with an unseen driver, and in what film?

f Which heroine has her hands viciously caned while she is playing the piano? Name the film, and the actor who wielded the stick

g Who was THE FATHER OF THE BRIDE, and who the bride? Name the mother, too

h Who won the Sarah Siddons award for acting? Name the film

i Who played the same English king in two historical romances and was Oscar nominated for both? What were the films and who was the king?

j Who played THE GREAT WALDO PEPPER? What was its subject, and what films starring Rock Hudson and Burt Lancaster had a similar subject?

14 Since early this century, the Italians have been in the forefront of the world's film makers, contributing greatly to the 'seventh art'. Test your knowledge of Italian cinema:

a Which director regained some of his past esteem by winning the 1971 Foreign Language Oscar with a film set in Italy during the rise of fascism? Name the film and its two non-Italian leads. Who wrote the music for it?

b Who is the composer most associated with the films of Fellini, and for which American films did he win an Oscar?

c For which film was the term 'neo-realism' first used, who directed it, and from what novel was it adapted?

d Name the three films that Pasolini made based on three great collections of stories. What artist did he play in one of them?

e Name the films by Fellini, Bertolucci, Rosi, Antonioni, and Visconti in which Donald Sutherland, Burt Lancaster, Robert De Niro, Rod Steiger and Richard Harris appeared

15 Who played the *title* roles in:

a GENEVIEVE?

b EDWARD MY SON?

c THE BLUE ANGEL?

d WHO'S AFRAID OF VIRGINIA WOOLF?

e THE TROUBLE WITH HARRY?

f FRANKENSTEIN (1931)?

g COME BACK LITTLE SHEBA?

h HARVEY?

i REBECCA?

j LOOKING FOR MR GOODBAR?

16 During the golden age of cinema the studios reigned supreme. Can you name the studios from which the following films emanated, and state the decade in which they were produced?

a GILDA
b HE WHO GETS SLAPPED
c BUS STOP
d THE EMPEROR WALTZ
e HUE AND CRY
f THE CIRCUS
g WAKE OF THE RED WITCH
h MORNING GLORY
i THE PAJAMA GAME
j THE MUMMY

17 There are certain classic moments from the movies that stand out and are forever associated with that film. With which films would you immediately associate:

a The 'butter' scene?
b The 'coathanger' scene?
c The 'stateroom' scene?
d The 'shower' scene?
e The 'beach' scene?

Name the film, the characters, and the performers in this still. Which veteran Yiddish actress played Yente the Matchmaker? Where and when is the film set? Where was it filmed? Who played the music for the title role? On whose original stories was the show based?

18 Here are some quotes from stars about their acting careers. Do you know who said:

a 'I was a 14-year-old boy for 30 years'
b 'So I never worked with Cooper, Gable, Grant – any of the real kings of the screen. They had their films and I had mine'
c 'After THE WIZARD OF OZ I was typecast as a lion, and there aren't all that many parts for lions'
d 'When I was training for POPEYE, I had that dream of getting up to thank the Academy . . . After the first day on POPEYE, I thought: Well, maybe this isn't it; and finally I wound up going, Oh, God, when is it gonna be over'
e 'I may not be a great actress but I've become the greatest at screen orgasms. Ten seconds of heavy breathing, roll your head from side to side, simulate a slight asthma attack, and die a little'

Reach for the Stars

A Born illegitimate and brought up in the slums of Naples, she won a beauty contest at the age of 14 and became a film extra and model. Under the auspices of an Italian film producer whom she later married, she went to Hollywood, became an international star and won the Best Actress Oscar (for a foreign film):

a Who is she?

b For what film did she win the Oscar?

c She appeared in a screen version of a Eugene O'Neill play. What was it, and who were her two male co-stars?

d What was her real family name?

e In what films were her co-stars Alan Ladd, Frank Sinatra, Cary Grant, Charlton Heston, Marlon Brando?

B Born in 1925, he remains a star in 1984. Nominated five times for the Oscar, he has never won it. Among the vast range of characters he has played are a boxer, an ice-hockey player, a racing driver, a pool player, a seal hunter and a broken down lawyer:

a Who is he?

b For what movies were his Oscar nominations?

c Name five real-life people he has played.

d In which movies did he appear opposite foreign actresses Elke Sommer, Sylva Koscina and Dominique Sanda?

e He directed his actress wife in two films. What were they, and who is she?

C The son of unsuccessful music hall entertainers (British), he first appeared on the stage at the age of five. On his second visit to America in 1913, he accepted a film contract with Mack Sennett's Keystone company to make one- and two-reel silents and, by 1921, was accepted as one of the world's greatest comic geniuses. He survived the coming of sound and went on directing films into the 1960s:

a Who is he?

b He was a founder of a famous film company in partnership with two other major stars and a renowned director. What was the company and who were his partners?

c The first film he made for this company, in the capacity of director only, starred Edna Purviance and remained unreleased for virtually half a century. What was it called?

d His last wife was the daughter of a famous playwright. Name him, name her, and name their well-known film actress daughter.

e What is the title of the famous film, anti-Nazi in subject, in which he played a dual role? Name the female co-star.

D English-born Archie Leach first went to America with a troupe of acrobats. He has had one of the longest star careers in the history of motion pictures and with his looks, casual elegance and wit undimmed by time, he has co-starred with almost everybody you can think of from Mae West to Leslie Caron. Married five times, one of his wives was heiress Barbara Hutton.

a Who is he?

b Name the four Alfred Hitchcock films in which he starred, and his leading lady in each

c He played the lead in a wildly inaccurate biopic about a famous composer of musicals. What was it called, and who was the composer?

d In two of his most famous comedy hits, he donned female garb. Name the films and the distinguished director of both of them (again, let's have the leading ladies)

e He retired from the screen to devote himself to big business. His last film was made in 1966, and was also its director's last. Name film and director

E As Phyllis Isley (her real name), this actress first appeared as John Wayne's leading lady in a B western, but four years later was hailed as a new discovery when she won an Oscar for playing a young peasant girl who claimed to have seen the Virgin. One of Hollywood's most celebrated producers promoted her career and became her second husband, but her film career was nevertheless uneven:

a Who is she?

b A hit title song helped one of her films to great success. It was the tragic love story of a Eurasian woman and a soldier. What was the film and who was the leading man?

c In the screen version of a Theodore Dreiser novel she reduced Laurence Olivier to poverty and degradation. Give the title and the director

d At the climax of one of her best remembered films she and the hero shot each other in the desert then crawled into each other's arms to die. Again, title and leading man

This Sporting Life

Sport embraces action, suspense, violence, stories of struggle and triumph. Most sports films encourage the ethic of football coach Vince Lombardi that 'Winning isn't the most important thing – it's the only thing'.

1   VISIONS OF EIGHT, the official film of the 1972 Olympics, was prefaced by the following:
'There is no chronological record, no summary of winners and losers. Rather, it is the separate visions of eight singular film artists.' Can you match the eight 'singular film artists' with the sequences they directed?
a Milos Forman
b Kon Ichikawa
c Claude Lelouch
d Yuri Ozerov
e Arthur Penn
f Michael Pfleghar
g John Schlesinger
h Mai Zetterling

A The Losers
B The Marathon
C The Starting Line
D The Pole Vault
E The Women
F The Weight Lifters
G The 100 Metres
H The High Jump and The Decathlon

2   Match the following athletic stars with the long-running films in which they appeared:
A Dustin Hoffman
B Michael Douglas
C Peter Strauss
D Jim Hutton
E Tom Courtenay

a THE JERICHO MILE
b THE LONELINESS OF THE LONG DISTANCE RUNNER
c WALK DON'T RUN
d RUNNING
e MARATHON MAN

3   Boxing, as a subject, has attracted many directors of stature, among them Alfred Hitchcock, King Vidor, Rouben Mamoulian, John Huston, Luchino Visconti, Jerzy Skolimowski and Franco Zeffirelli. Name the films they directed in which boxing plays a central role.

4   In sports movies, women are invariably seen in reaction shots to men's actions. But some films have given them a chance to play a more active role. Give the titles of the films indicated below and the names of the performers underlined:
a *A girl* replaces a boy in the position of striker in the school soccer team
b *Two girl athletes,* more than good friends, find themselves competing against each other in the trials for the 1980 Olympics
c *Two female wrestlers* travel around the halls with *their manager* until they hit the big time by beating the Toledo Tigers in a no-holds-barred match
d *An attractive TV executive* recites the names of all the heavyweight champions to the amazement of a gym full of boxers who promptly compliment her by singing, 'Baby, You Knock Me Out'
e *An up-and-coming woman skier* has a tragic accident during a competition which leaves her paralysed from the neck down. She later falls in love with *another skier* who is killed in an air crash
f *The new owner-manager* of a turn-of-the-century baseball team turns out to be a woman much to the disgust of *one of the leading players*
g *An American champion swimmer* makes preparations to swim the English Channel with the help of her family
h *A Norwegian refugee ice skater* finds herself entertaining at an American ski resort
i *A female professional golfer and tennis player* alienates her macho fiancé and marries *her promoter*
j *A woman* dying of leukemia meets *a Formula One racing driver* at a Swiss clinic

Sylvester Stallone in a pose from one of the ROCKY movies – which? What is Rocky's surname? Name the veteran character actor who played Rocky's trainer. Which of the three ROCKY films to date did Stallone direct himself? Which one featured a fighter known as Clubber Lang, and which had Rocky working in a butcher's shop?

5 Kung Fu or 'chop-socky' movies consist mainly of a series of brilliantly choreographed fights accompanied by shrieks and groans. What does Kung Fu mean? Who was its most famous exponent on screen? His reputation is based mainly on four films. Two of them have a mythical beast in the title. What are these two called? Another karate-chopping cult hero of the 70s was the subject of three films; he was played by Tom Laughlin, but what were the titles of the films that contained the character's name?

6 More films have been made about boxing than any other sport. Its attraction lies in its clear-cut one-to-one dramatic situation, its ritualised violence and its crooked connections. In which films did the following pugilists face each other in the ring? Only one of the first named lost the fight. Which was he?
a Errol Flynn vs Ward Bond
b Danny Kaye vs Steve Cochran
c Jeff Chandler vs Rock Hudson
d Charles Bronson vs Robert Tessier
e Max Baer vs Mike Lane

7 In which film would you find
a 'The Fonz' in a wrestling ring
b 'Conan' winning the Mr Olympia contest in South Africa
c 'Zorba' taking punishment in a boxing ring
d 'Darth Vader' winning the heavyweight boxing title
e 'Rocky' keeping goal in a soccer match

Paul Newman as the player-coach of an ice-hockey team at the centre of abuse being hurled at them by the spectators. Why is the crowd angry? The team comes from Charlestown, but can you work out its name? What is the title of the film? Who directed it and what two other movies did he make with Newman? This is one of the only major features on the sport. In which films, however, did Ryan O'Neal and Robbie Benson play ice-hockey? Who were the stars of two minor ice-hockey movies, IDOL OF THE CROWDS (1937) and PAPERBACK HERO (1973)?

8   'Anyone for tennis?' Film makers have generally ignored this request, but can you respond to the questions below?

a   Which two Alfred Hitchcock movies contained murderous tennis players, and who portrayed them?

b   Which world class tennis player appeared in which James Bond film?

c   Whom did Guillermo Vilas beat in five sets at the Wimbledon final in 1979, and in what film?

d   In what film is a game of tennis played with an imaginary ball, and which actor watched it?

e   Where did Ian Carmichael go in order to learn to beat caddish Terry-Thomas at tennis, and who gave him the advice, 'If you're outclassed, you must try to take your opponent's eye off the ball.'

f   Who did Richard Pryor and Sheila Frazier play in a disastrous mixed doubles match and where?

g   Who – and in what film – imagines during a tennis match that her opponent, 'Gorgeous' Gussie Moran, has a gigantic racket, that the net is way above her head, and that many balls are coming to her at once?

h   What comedian, wearing a hat made of newspaper, a jacket and long trousers, served unreturnable balls after making an eccentric shuffling movement with his racket?

i   In which film is Celeste Holm a tennis-playing nun?

j   Which tennis champion was HARD, FAST AND BEAUTIFUL, and who directed her?

9   Film titles don't always immediately reveal the sport with which the picture deals, or in which it features. Can you name the sport featured, in each case, in the following films (the answers are never the same):

a   CHAMPIONS
b   STAY HUNGRY
c   THE DOVE
d   DRIVE, HE SAID
e   THE FINAL TEST
f   THE BINGO LONG TRAVELING ALL-STARS AND MOTOR KINGS
g   NORTH DALLAS 40
h   GEORDIE (US: WEE GEORDIE)
i   THE WORLD ACCORDING TO GARP
j   C.C. AND COMPANY

10   Some films have condemned pro boxing as a vicious racket that exploits the boxer. Which film ends with a sports columnist typing the words, 'Professional boxing should be banned even if it takes an Act of Congress to do it.' Who wrote these words and what was particularly poignant about his appearance in the picture? Who played the gangster Nick Benko? Which former world heavyweight boxers had roles in it?

Who is behind the helmet in this film about a futuristic game? The game is the name of the movie. What is it? Of what three sports is the game a combination? Which distinguished English actor made a surprising appearance in the film? In which films did the actor illustrated portray a stock-car racer and a compulsive gambler?

11   THE BAD NEWS BEARS were a team of Little League baseball players. Who played Amanda Whurlizer, their twelve-year-old pitcher, and Morris Buttermaker, their broken-down beer-swilling coach? The screenplay was written by the son of a very athletic actor. Who is he? The director's favourite theme is competition as seen in his SMILE and THE CANDIDATE. Who is he and what football movie did he make with Burt Reynolds? Name the two sequels to THE BAD NEWS BEARS.

12   A film of 1981 told how Harold Abrahams and Eric Liddell managed to overcome a series of figurative hurdles to win the 100 and 400 metres respectively for Britain at the 1924 Olympics. What was the name of the film? Who played Abrahams and Liddell, and what was a precondition of their getting the roles? What particular problem did each of the two characters encounter? Who said, and on what occasion, in connection with this film, 'The British are coming'?

13 Some stars fancy themselves as sportsmen. Identify the films in which you would find

A Robert De Niro as a) baseball player b) cyclist c) boxer
B Robert Redford as a) ski champion b) motor cycle racer
C Jan-Michael Vincent as a) athlete b) surfer
D Ronald Reagan as a) baseball player b) footballer
E Anthony Perkins as a) baseball player b) basketball player
F Joe E. Brown as a) speed boat racer b) swimmer c) wrestler
G Harpo Marx as a) jockey b) football player
H Paul Newman as a) pool player b) racing driver c) poker player
I James Cagney as a) racing driver b) boxer (three films)
J Jerry Lewis as a) football player b) jockey

14 In what film did

a Michael Crawford, Ryan O'Neal, Athol Compton and Charles Aznavour compete in a race, what was the race and who won?
b Yves Montand, Brian Bedford, James Garner and Antonio Sabato compete in a race, what was the race and who won?
c Gregory Peck have a flashback while skiing and what was the flashback?
d Chevy Chase play golf blindfolded, backwards and between his legs, and yet never complete a hole?
e Jack Lemmon end up in hospital after being injured at a football game and how did the accident occur?

15 Who said to whom and in what movie – 'I coulda had class. I coulda been a contender. I coulda been somebody instead of a bum, which is what I am.' In which more recent film is this quoted?

16 'Ladies and Gentlemen – five rounds of boxing questions . . .':

a In which film would you find Apollo Creed and who played him?
b Who had his first major role as GOLDEN BOY, and who was the female lead?
c John Garfield starred as a boxer in THEY MADE ME A CRIMINAL. Who was the extremely unlikely director of the film? In what other film did Garfield put on boxing gloves?
d How did the bullfighter Escamillo become the prizefighter Husky Miller?
e Joey Popchik, a poor law student, abandons his studies for the boxing ring in order to pay for his sister's eye operation. His faithful trainer 'Gloves' Malloy dies saving him from gangsters. What was the movie called, who directed it and which actors played the two characters mentioned above?

17 The 1936 Olympic Games in Berlin took place a few months after Hitler's armies reoccupied the Rhineland. Hitler and Goebbels perceived the immense propaganda potential of the Games, and its propagation through the medium of cinema:

a Who directed the film of the 1936 Olympics?
b The film lasts i) three hours ii) four hours iii) five hours?
c It is in two parts. The first part is called 'The Festival of Nations', and the second 'The Festival of Beauty'. How do the two parts differ in content?
d What documentary was made by the same director the year before, and what was its subject?
e What was the director's first film and who played the female lead in it?

This is a scene from the musical DAMN YANKEES (GB: WHAT LOLA WANTS). In what way does the word 'damn' in the title relate to the plot, and what sport is involved? Who are the two stars pictured? What is she attempting to do and who played her immediate boss? In what way was she related to the film's choreographer and who was he?

18 The idea that democracy in America provides equal opportunities for all and that sport is the best demonstration of this, is embedded in the American consciousness. What sports are represented by the films below and who took the leads in them?

a THE ALL-AMERICAN BOY

b THE ALL-AMERICAN

c THE LAST AMERICAN HERO (aka HARD DRIVER)

d THE GREAT AMERICAN PASTIME

e CRAZYLEGS – ALL AMERICAN

19 'The square ring' is not always as 'square' as it seems. Name the film in which the following unusual events take place, and the actor who plays the character underlined in each case:

a A puny pugilist is made into a champ by the hypnotic powers of *his manager*

b *A multi-millionaire* pays boxers to mince around in an effeminate manner in a heavyweight championship

c *A would-be boxer* walks out into the streets with his fiancée wearing a top hat, frock coat and . . . boxing trunks

d *A prizefighter* is killed in an airplane crash and returns to earth in another man's body to win the world championship

e *An unsuccessful boxer* owns the Knockout Driving Academy, a driving school in the shape of a boxing glove. ('The thumb leaks a little')

a **What is the title of the film illustrated?**

b **What game is being played?**

c **Who are the three actors around the table?**

d **In what period is the film set and in what city?**

e **What famous black bandleader of the 30s and 40s appeared in it?**

---

20 What sports do these films involve and who played the title roles in all of them?

a KID GALAHAD (1937)

b KID GALAHAD (1962)

c THE KID FROM SPAIN

d THE LEMON-DROP KID (1951)

e THE KID FROM LEFT FIELD

21 Now try to complete the last lap with this multi-sports question:

a What was MAN'S FAVORITE SPORT?

b What was PARADISE ALLEY?

c What film features a game between prison guards and cons, what was the game, who was the leading con and who won?

d 'The Barber Of Seville' overture was used as background music to a young man's sporting efforts. Why? What was the sport and the name of the film?

e What game was the subject of THIS SPORTING LIFE?

95

For King and Country

War movies are wonderful vehicles for propaganda and morale building, or for expressions of anti-war sentiment. They have also serviced stories of heroism, or merely displays of blood-and-guts violence.

1 Who were the actors who played Hitler in THE HITLER GANG, HITLER, THE MAGIC FACE, THE GREAT DICTATOR, and HITLER, THE LAST TEN DAYS?

2 Complete the film titles which contain the following names and say who played the title roles:
a McHale
b Sergeant O'Farrell
c Major Benson
d Private Hargrove
e Angelo

Happy landings in a scene from an army comedy. What is it called and who is the girl playing the title role? Who is the principal man in the cast? Where does most of the movie take place? Name three earlier films about women in uniform that featured a) Esther Williams and Vivian Blaine b) Lana Turner and Laraine Day c) Betty Hutton and Betty Hutton.

3 Inspirational endings were common during World War II to convince Americans at home of the rightness of the cause. If you don't know the titles of the films that end in the following way, try an inspired guess!
a 'We want to live by each other's happiness-not by each other's misery. Greed has poisoned men's souls – has barricaded the world with hate – has goose-stepped us into misery and bloodshed . . . You, the people, have the power to make this life free and beautiful'
b 'This is the people's war! It is our war! We are the fighters! Fight it then! Fight it with all that is in us! And may God defend the right!'
c 'It's as if the lights were all out everywhere, except in America. Keep those lights burning there. Cover them with steel, ring them with guns, build a canopy of battleships and bombing planes around them. Hello, America! Hang on to your lights! They're the only lights left in the world!'
d 'Be of good courage and He shall strengthen your heart, all ye that hope in the Lord'
e 'Now for Australia and a crack at those Japs'

4 In 1959 a French actress filming in Japan has an affair with a Japanese she meets there. Their different memories of the war flash into their minds. What is the film called and who directed it? Who wrote the screenplay? Name the two leads. What was the male character's profession? Which films by the same director dealt with:
a Auschwitz?
b the war in Algeria?
c the Spanish Civil War?

This film won Oscars for Best Picture, Best Director, Best Supporting Actor and Actress, Best Screenplay and Best Black and White Cinematography. Can you supply the names of the winners? Who is the actor pictured and who is the lady in the portrait? What is their relationship in the movie? How was the film a breakthrough for the actress? When and where is the film set?

A scene from a milestone in anti-war movies:
a Name the film and its director
b Who is the actor on the left?
c What nationality is the character on the left?
And the other one?
d From which side is the story told and of
which war?
e Describe the famous last scene of the film. In
what way was a substitution made in it?

---

5   Films have not ignored the physical disabilities
accrued from the war. Morbid as it may be, can you
name the injuries suffered by the people below and
the wars in which they occurred?
a John Heard in CUTTER'S WAY
b John Savage in THE DEER HUNTER
c John Garfield in PRIDE OF THE MARINES
d John Wayne in THE WINGS OF EAGLES
e Jon Voight in COMING HOME
f Timothy Bottoms in JOHNNY GOT HIS GUN
g Marlon Brando in THE MEN
h Harold Russell in THE BEST YEARS OF
   OUR LIVES
i William Devane in ROLLING THUNDER
j John Gilbert in THE BIG PARADE

6   'The war to end all wars' was the optimistic
label attached to World War I. Answer the following
questions on films to end all World War I films:
a What film took its ironic title from a World
   War I song? It was the director's first film
   behind the camera. Who is he? He made his
   screen debut as an actor in a World War II
   movie. What was it called and who directed it?
b 'Journey's End', the celebrated play about
   tensions in the trenches, was the first film made
   by its stage director soon to become renowned
   for his horror movies. Who was he? What was
   the name of the 1976 remake, transferred to the
   air war?
c Which anti-militarist film was banned in
   France, Switzerland, and in US military
   cinemas in Europe on its first release. Who
   played Colonel Dax and who directed it? What
   was the Joseph Losey film which dealt with a
   similar subject?
d A wounded American ambulance driver falls in
   love with his nurse during World War I in Italy.
   Name the film and the two leads in both the
   1932 and 1957 versions
e Who directed the silent war classic THE BIG
   PARADE and who played the female lead?

7   Aerial dog fights during World War I provided exciting action for a number of movies:

a Can you supply the last line of the drinking song from the DAWN PATROL (1930)?
'So stand by your glasses steady,
The world is a world of lies.
Here's to the dead already.....
Who directed it and in what way was it a first for him? It starred Richard Barthelmess and Douglas Fairbanks Jr. Which of the two dies? Who played their roles in the 1939 remake?

b What was the first film ever to win an Academy Award for Best Picture and which future star had the small role of a young pilot who gets killed in the first reel?

c Some of the spectacular flying was forgotten when an actress, in her second featured role, uttered the immortal line, 'Would you be shocked if I put on something more comfortable?' to which the reply was 'I'll try to survive'. Who was she, to whom was she speaking, what was the film and who both produced and directed it?

d Who played the title roles in Roger Corman's VON RICHTHOFEN AND BROWN (GB: THE RED BARON)? What did Corman give up after this film?

e George Peppard was the German war ace who falls for a beautiful countess. Who was she and what was the film?

8   The publicity people at the studios, just like recruiting officers, try to coax the public to join a queue and watch a war. Can you attribute the five slogans below to the correct films? (10 titles are given from which to choose):

A 'The guts, gags and glory of a lot of wonderful guys'
B 'The truth about the Nazis from the cradle to the battlefront'
C 'The epic of the American doughboy'
D 'Love-starved women in uniform... Men whose days are numbered... thrown together in the mad whirl of life and death, love and laughter that is war'
E 'He felt the Lash of Nazi Terror! When they torture you for hours and then sneer that your mother is held hostage... you think you'll go mad!'

a BEACHHEAD
b THE BIG PARADE
c WOMEN IN WAR
d THE MORTAL STORM
e HITLER'S CHILDREN
f BATTLEGROUND
g MEN OF THE FIGHTING LADY
h I ESCAPED FROM THE GESTAPO
i AT THE FRONT
j CONFESSIONS OF A NAZI SPY

9   'Yesterday, December 7th 1941, a date which will live in infamy, the United States of America was suddenly and deliberately attacked by naval and air forces of the Empire of Japan... With confidence in our armed forces, with the unfloundering determination of our people we will gain the inevitable triumph, so help us God!' announced President Roosevelt. And Hollywood went to war on the Japanese. Test your cinematic knowledge of the soldiers of Nippon with the following questions:

a What movie contained the uplifting line, 'Fried Jap going down', and who directed it?

b 'The oriental way of life holds a great appeal for me.... You probably don't share my enthusiasm for the Japanese.... Wonderful little people, wonderful. Greatly misunderstood, believe me', says someone on board ship to the hero. Who is the speaker, who is he speaking to, what is the film's title and who directed it? The same three leads and the director made a film together the year before. Name it and the third lead

c The bombing of Pearl Harbor was the subject, seen from both sides, of a 1970 movie. Name the film and its American director. A. D. Flowers and L. B. Abbott won an Academy Award for their work on the movie. What did they contribute?

d Charlton Heston is a U.S. naval officer whose son falls in love with a Japanese girl on the eve of a crucial battle against the Japanese. The title of the film derives from the battle. Name it. Who plays Admiral Chester W. Nimitz in it?

e Who Played AN AMERICAN GUERRILLA IN THE PHILIPPINES (GB: I SHALL RETURN) and who was the film's unlikely director? What famous American soldier was impersonated at the end?

f Which American film of 1945, about a renowned campaign against the Japanese, was withdrawn from British cinemas after an official protest? What was the reason? What was added to it when it was reshown in Britain in 1952?

g What war film took 138 minutes to tell the story of a half-minute? Who directed it and what future comedy director had a small role in it?

h What actor playing a dying General in MERRILL'S MARAUDERS died himself soon after completion of the film? Who directed the film and where was it set?

i Eight American airmen shot down over Japan are put on trial for their lives. Name the film, and its veteran war-film director. In the final scene i) all eight Americans are executed ii) seven out of the eight escape alive iii) six of them are rescued by a commando?

j In which journal, in 1941, might you have read 'War between the United States and Japan broke just as it began to look as though the sheet music business would have its biggest year end since 1938'?

10 Answer the questions on the following provocative quotes:

a 'They tell me everything isn't black and white. Well, I say why the hell not?' What star said this in defence of the second of two films he directed. What was the film?

b 'Viewed as drama the war is somewhat disappointing.' What famous early director said this of World War I?

c What film by the director quoted in 'b' above, caused 'hundreds and thousands of men and women in more or less pro-German audiences in the United States to have a complete change of heart' – or so claimed one of his contemporaries, also a director? Who was he?

d 'I've got your happy ending. We'll let the Germans win the war.' What director said this when disgruntled with the Universal front office? What was the film?

e 'It's a great picture without political significance. We are not for or against anybody,' said Paramount studio chief Adolph Zukor, not wishing to offend anyone about the Spanish Civil War. What was the film?

11 THE DEER HUNTER won five Academy Awards and exactly caught the mood of the time – the need for America to find some justification for the war in Vietnam. What song ends the movie? Who directed it? How many films had the same director made previously? Which of the cast won an Oscar? Which actor died soon after completing the movie? Who shoots a deer with one bullet and how does this action relate to a central scene in the movie?

12 In which two films did James Mason portray German Field Marshal Rommel? Name two later pictures in which he played a German officer in World War I.

Identify the actors in this scene from THE BRIDGE ON THE RIVER KWAI. What are their ranks? What is their relationship? Why does the bridge of the title only appear briefly in the film? What are the final words spoken, and who speaks them?

A portrait of the character, von Rauffenstein, in one of the classics of world cinema. Name the film and its director. Who is the actor and what is his job in the picture? Why is he wearing a neck brace? In which films did he appear as Rommel and Beethoven? Name the three French actors who played Marechal, the proletarian, Rosenthal, the Jew, and Boieldieu the aristocrat.

---

13 Nasty Nazis abound in World War II movies. Name the actors who portrayed the overt (or covert) Nazis in the following:
a THE NIGHT PORTER
b DEAD MEN DON'T WEAR PLAID
c CONSPIRACY OF HEARTS
d THE BOYS FROM BRAZIL
e SABOTEUR
f STALAG 17
g INVISIBLE AGENT
h THE MORTAL STORM
i THE NORTH STAR (ARMORED ATTACK)
j MARATHON MAN

14 Match the following 'Operation' movies with the female stars below:
a THE GREAT SPY MISSION (GB: OPERATION CROSSBOW)
b OPERATION PETTICOAT
c OPERATION DAYBREAK (aka PRICE OF FREEDOM)
d OPERATION AMSTERDAM
e OPERATION SECRET

A Nicola Paget
B Dina Merrill
C Phyllis Thaxter
D Eva Bartok
E Sophia Loren

15 Name the captains courageous in the following movies:
a THE CRUEL SEA
b THE SEA CHASE
c SINK THE BISMARCK
d THE EXTRAORDINARY SEAMAN
e YANGTSE INCIDENT (US: BATTLE HELL)

16 There are not too many laughs during a war, but what laughter there is has been mined by many a film comedian:

a The first starring vehicles for Bud Abbott and Lou Costello, Dean Martin and Jerry Lewis, and Danny Kaye were army comedies. What were they?

b Martin and Lewis were together again in uniform in two other comedies. Name them. Jerry Lewis solo was a soldier in two pictures and a sailor in another. What were their titles?

c Two vacuum cleaner salesmen join the army accidentally in a 1941 comedy. What was the film and who were they?

d Who starred in PACK UP YOUR TROUBLES, GREAT GUNS and BLOCK-HEADS?

e The American soldier in the trenches and on the battlefield was Charlie Chaplin. What was the film and who played the French girl and the dual role of a sergeant and the Kaiser?

f An American G.I. impersonates a British intelligence officer and does a Marlene Dietrich impersonation. Who was he and what was the title – a play on words – of the film?

g Brian Keith, Tony Curtis and Ernest Borgnine were in this army farce. Name it, and the veteran star of 40s Fox musicals who appeared in it?

h Who played the title roles in the British army comedies, CARRY ON SERGEANT and PRIVATE'S PROGRESS?

i The title of a 1966 comedy set in 1943 Italy is the question put to James Coburn by his child. What was the question and who directed the film?

j Jack Lemmon starred in both of the following: i) a decrepit destroyer disguised as a sailing ship, confuses the Japanese ii) set in Normandy, where a smooth operator gets around the rule that soldiers cannot fraternise with nurses. Titles, please. An actor-comedian, killed in a car crash in 1962, made his debut in the latter. Who was he?

A moment from the final sequence of THE DIRTY DOZEN. Name the actor with the gun in the foreground and the one in the front seat behind him. Why are the soldiers shooting? Why were they referred to as the 'dirty' dozen? Which of the following were members of the 'dozen': Ernest Borgnine, John Cassavetes, Clint Walker, Telly Savalas, Ralph Meeker, Robert Ryan, Jim Brown?

---

17 Each of the following films takes place during a particular war. Put them in the correct chronological order related to the events depicted (*not* to the films' release dates). Name the leading male actors in each case:

a FOR WHOM THE BELL TOLLS
b BATTLE CIRCUS
c OPERATION PACIFIC
d BREAKER MORANT
e WHAT PRICE GLORY (both versions)

18 Prisoner-of-war camp movies have given British actors a chance to keep a stiff upper lip and Americans to display bravado. 'The first duty of a prisoner of war is to escape,' was the motto. Try not to get out of answering the following questions:

a How did P.O.W's escape in i) THE WOODEN HORSE ii) ESCAPE TO VICTORY iii) ALBERT R.N. (US: BREAK TO FREEDOM) iv) VERY IMPORTANT PERSON (US: A COMING-OUT PARTY)

b How did THE MACKENZIE BREAK and THE ONE THAT GOT AWAY differ from most other P.O.W. stories? Who played the title role in the latter?

c 'This picture is dedicated to the fifty.' What picture, and who were the fifty?

d What is the password in a film that recounts the exploits of the inappropriately named Sergeant-Major Charles Coward played by Dirk Bogarde?

e Who played the title role in MERRY CHRISTMAS, MR LAWRENCE? Name the book on which it was based, and its author. Who directed the film? Who played Major Celliers and how does he prevent the camp commandant from killing a fellow prisoner?

f What film set in Auschwitz, and then on board ship years later, was left unfinished when the director was killed in a car crash during the shooting in 1961? Who was the director, and what is the running time of his incomplete work?

g Richard Burton and Clint Eastwood are agents assigned to rescue an important American from an impregnable fortress. Name the film and the setting

h An English woman is among prisoners being held by the Japanese in Malaya. She meets and falls in love with an Australian soldier. Who were they, what was the film and who wrote the book on which it was based?

i Name the prisons in which you would find a) John Mills and Eric Portman b) William Holden and Don Taylor c) Andre Morell and Edward Underdown

j Name the films in which the following were war captives i) Meryl Streep ii) George Segal iii) Ronald Reagan iv) Susan Strasberg v) Michael Redgrave

19 War heroes are often depicted as having mutual respect for their opposite numbers. Identify the films in which the following Allied officers begin to admire their enemies:

a American Burt Lancaster and German Paul Scofield
b British John Gregson and German Peter Finch
c American Robert Mitchum and German Curt Jurgens
d British David Niven and Italian Alberto Sordi
e American Lee Marvin and Japanese Toshiro Mifune

20 On the other hand, sometimes officers of the same army are at loggerheads and have no respect for each other. In which films did the characters played by the following actors conflict?
a Humphrey Bogart and Van Johnson
b James Cagney and Henry Fonda
c Clark Gable and Burt Lancaster
d John Mills and Alec Guinness
e Frank Sinatra and Trevor Howard

The title of this war film was taken from the name of an epic battle. Give its title, the country that produced it, and its director. Who is the running actor? Why is he running and in what way did part of his civilian life affect his job in war? Name the movie with the same director and actor that was set in Indonesia.

---

21 'War knows no frontiers.' Can you supply the English titles of the films below? Identify the country of origin in each case, and name the director:
a LETYAT ZHURAVLI was a story of a love affair destroyed by war. The actress who played Veronica won first prize at Cannes in 1958. Who was she?
b BIRUMA NO TATEGOTO starred Shoji Yasui as a musician who tries to bury as many bodies as he can after a terrible battle
c OSTRE SLEDAVONE VLAKY described an adolescent's days at a country railway station while under German occupation
d POKOLENIE was the first of a war-time resistance trilogy. Name the other two films
e OBCHOD NA KORZE told of the relationship between an old Jewish woman and a carpenter in a small town under the Nazis. Who played the woman?

22 Military academies have prompted a number of movies, many of them relishing the sadism that is sometimes to be found in such establishments:
a The publicity of which film carried the disclaimer that the events depicted 'do not, nor are they intended to, reflect the educational philosophy or teaching of the Valley Forge Military Academy and Junior College'? The lead was played by the son of an actor who died of cancer aged forty-five. Name father and son
b John Ford made a film about West Point. What was it? Who were the male and female leads?
c Which musicals starring Doris Day and Lucille Ball took place in military schools?
d Ben Gazzara made his screen debut in a movie set in a Southern military academy. Name the film and the play from which it was adapted. Volker Schlöndorff made his feature film debut as director with the same subject. Name the film
e LORDS OF DISCIPLINE was directed by the director of QUADROPHENIA. Who is he? It starred David Keith who played a similar role in a similar setting in an earlier movie. What was it called and who played the roles of Zack Mayo, Paula Pokrifki and Sergeant Emil Foley? The latter won an Oscar as Best Supporting Actor. What was exceptional about the award?

23 Army ranks feature in many a title. Name the films below from the clues given. Amongst the titles there are two generals, two sergeants, two colonels, one major, one lieutenant, one corporal and one private. In which film did:
a Danny Kaye play Jacobowsky?
b The Bee Gees and Paul Nicholas sing the title song written by others?
c John Cleese play a major?
d Rod Steiger nurse a forbidden passion?
e Is Tom Ewell married to a soldier?
f Is Jack Buchanan married to a Frenchwoman?
g Mercenary Gary Cooper clash with warlord Akim Tamiroff?
h Con-man Vittorio de Sica become a martyr?
i Roger Livesey take part in three wars?
j Jean-Pierre Cassel refuse to stay put in his P.O.W. camp?

24 TO BE OR NOT TO BE is one of the great satirical war comedies of the 40s. Who directed it? Who says of whom, 'I saw him on the stage when I was in Warsaw once, before the war. Believe me, what he did to Shakespeare we are doing now to Poland.' Why does the title soliloquy cause a young man in the audience to get up and leave the theatre every time he hears it? Who played him? What Shakespearean speech causes a diversion near the end? Who played Maria Tura? In the 1984 remake, who were the leads, what did the name Tura become, and what song was sung in Polish?

Name the film in which these strange warriors appear. What is the name of the character under whose command they are, and who is the actor that plays him? Why have they come out in such numbers? In which country does this scene take place? By what book, by which author, was the film inspired, and who directed?

25 To end hostilities, take a shot at this last battle of wits:

a In Fritz Lang's MAN HUNT, who played the hunter and who was his prey?

b What have FIRST BLOOD, TAXI DRIVER and THE VISITORS in common?

c Who played the title role in A GUY NAMED JOE?

d Where was A BRIDGE TOO FAR? Who directed THE BRIDGE (DIE BRUCKE)? Which film about a battle for a bridge starred George Segal and Robert Vaughan? And what two films about bridges starred William Holden?

e What was the main theme of HOME OF THE BRAVE?

f In which contemporary trouble spots were UNDER FIRE and CIRCLE OF DECEIT set?

g What three German exiles were responsible for the direction, screenplay and music of HANG-MEN ALSO DIE?

h Gregory Peck, David Niven, Stanley Baker and Anthony Quinn were members of a team whose task was to blow up two giant German guns. What was the film and who were the two women among them?

i Name the directors of THE AMERICAN SOLDIER and BALLAD OF A SOLDIER

j Who was the teenage star who plays a computer whizz, thus almost causing World War III? Name the movie

Spine Tinglers

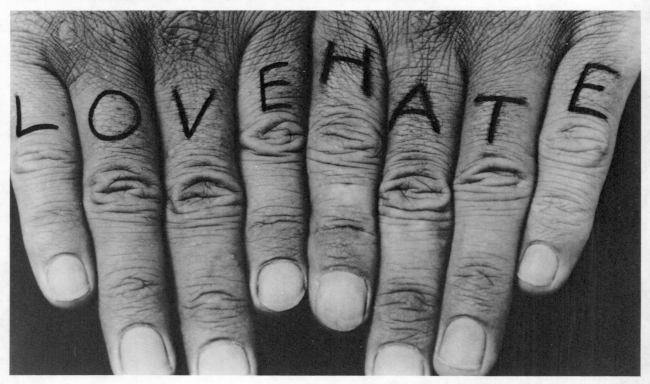

ABOVE
A distinguished black-and-white thriller about a murderous preacher whose hands are shown here. Can you name the picture, the actor who played the preacher, and the two female stars? This was the only picture directed by a distinguished British-born actor. Who was he?

RIGHT
The actor illustrated here also directed the film in which this scene took place. Identify him, his co-star, and the film. What was his profession in the film and how does it relate to the title?

FAR RIGHT
Can you identify the actresses playing mother and daughter in this dramatic, effective and eerie film of the 70s? What is the film's title and who directed it? Three young actors who played schoolmates of the girl illustrated later graduated to starring roles. Can you name them?

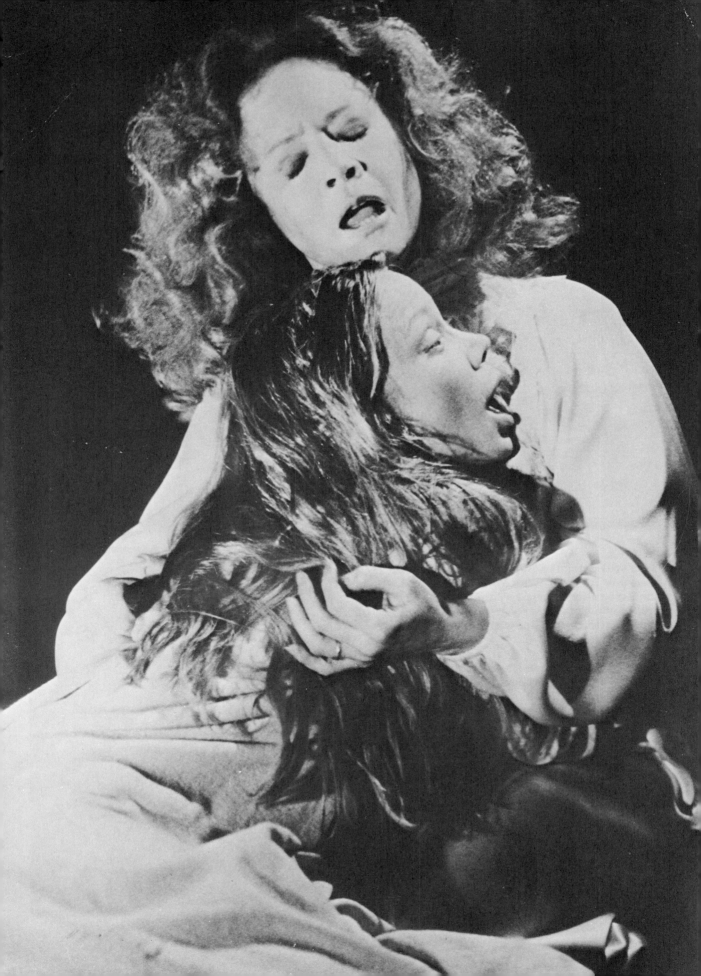

ABOVE
This still is from a popular and successful 1967
suspense thriller. What was it called and who is
the actor shown here? Whom is he terrorizing
and to what purpose? Who played the victim of
the situation and what was unusual about her?

RIGHT
The actor seen here appeared, early in his
career, in two Hitchcock thrillers. Who is he,
what were the Hitchcock films, and who were
his female co-stars in each? This scene is from
a well-known 70s horror film. Can you identify
it and name the boy actor seen with the star?
What is his connection with the boy, and why is
he trying to kill him?

FAR RIGHT
A few of Hollywood's ageing female stars found
themselves frightened and menaced in the 60s.
The star seen here appeared in two notable
spinetinglers filmed in 1964, one of which is
illustrated. Can you name her and the two
movies? Identify the pair of young hoodlums at
whose hands she is suffering – one of them developed into a major star in the 70s.

ABOVE
The English community in Hollywood made some bizarre contributions to 30s cinema. Can you identify these two British stars and name the picture in which they are appearing? What British actor played Baron Frankenstein and who played his bride? The picture's English director was a master of the genre. Who was he and can you name any of the other well-known horror films he made during the early 30s?

ABOVE
This still is from a famous horror classic filmed in 1931 by Paramount. Can you name it and the two stars shown here, one of whom won an Oscar? Who wrote the novel on which the film was based, and who were the stars of the 1941 MGM remake?

LEFT
This still shows Christine Gordon, Frances Dee and Darby Jones in one of the best of a classic series of 40s chillers. What is the film, who was its innovative producer, and which studio made the series? Can you name the director, and the two other pictures he made in this series? And do you know who the director's father was?

ABOVE
Isabelle Adjani is the tasty morsel here, but who is the actor enjoying her? What is the movie and who directed it? This 1979 picture was a remake of a classic German horror silent. Can you give the date of the original version, the name of its distinguished director and its star?

RIGHT
Here is Humphrey Bogart in a somewhat uncharacteristic role. The title of the movie sounds like a sequel to a 1932 Lionel Atwill classic, but in fact it was nothing of the kind. Nonetheless, give the titles of both movies. To what use did Bogart put the instrument he is holding?

ABOVE
This picture was the first of Universal Studio's horror cycle of the 30s. Can you name the picture and the two stars shown here? The small British studio, Hammer Films, remade this, and other Universal pictures, in colour, beginning in the late 50s. Can you give the titles of the first four Hammer remakes and name the two new stars who emerged from this cycle?

RIGHT
This still comes from the 1943 remake of one of the most famous of all silent horror movies. The story was filmed four times in all, most recently in a rock music version with a slightly different title. Can you give the titles of all four versions and name the stars of each? The 1943 version was a stylish Technicolor production which won a pair of Oscars – what were they for?

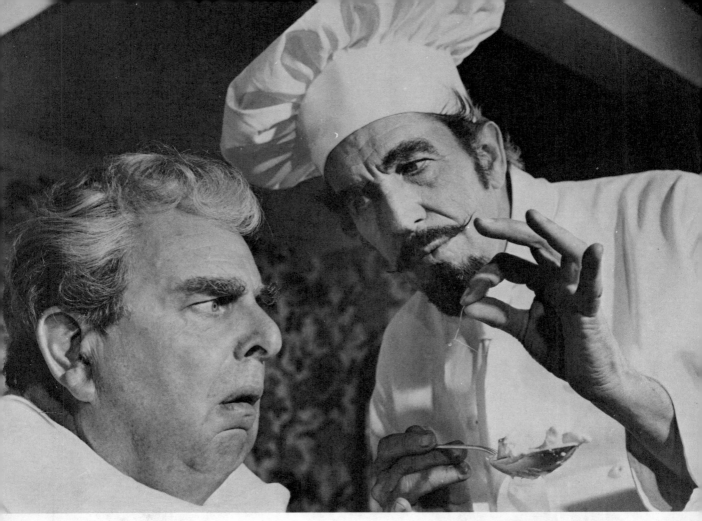

ABOVE

Vincent Price has long been a staple figure of the horror film. Identify the following Price movies from the brief descriptions:

a In this still Price is seen playing a ham actor who wreaks a terrible vengeance on London's theatre critics, represented here by Robert Morley

b Price plays a French judge who leads a double life as a knife murderer

c Price is the proprietor of a wax museum

d Price and Boris Karloff are sorcerers and deadly rivals, in this black comedy

RIGHT

This sequence comes at the opening of a thriller directed by Sam Fuller whose pictures often featured tough and resourceful heroines. From the following, identify the stars and the Fuller movies in which they appeared:

a A prostitute attacks the pimp who has been exploiting her (illustrated). She then exposes the hypocrisy and corruption in a small town

b A gangster's moll joins forces with a pick-pocket to help the FBI catch a gang of Red spies

c A Eurasian girl leads a dangerous mission behind Communist lines in 1954 Vietnam

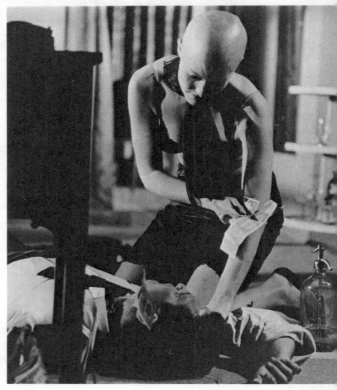

114

Reach for the Stars

A Christened Maurice Micklewhite, this virile, blonde Londoner from the East End made an impact on audiences as the bespectacled hero of a 1965 thriller directed by Sidney Furie. International stardom followed when he accepted a role in the movie version of a successful Bill Naughton play. Though initially underrated as a serious actor, his career, in the last few years, has shown the doubting Thomases that he is one of the most talented male actors on the screen today:

a Who is he?
b He first attracted attention as an effete young army officer. What was the film?
c In what films was he directed by Otto Preminger, Ken Russell, and Joseph L. Mankiewicz?
d In what recent thriller did he play Sidney Bruhl, and who were his co-stars?
e He received rave reviews and an Oscar nomination for his performance as a disillusioned University tutor. What was the film and who was his co-star?

B German-born, he became a star in his first film although he had only 12 lines of dialogue. In his first Hollywood film he was a bald-headed transplant specialist. He marked time as a judo-loving Oriental sleuth, and then found an outsize partner while hunting for a crusader's bauble:

a Who is he?
b In THE BEAST WITH FIVE FINGERS (1947) he was strangled by a disembodied hand. The sequence was reputedly devised by a Spanish film maker of discretion and charm. Who was he?
c His last film with his most famous co-star was also the first film by a famous director. Name the film, the co-star, and the director
d In 1957 he played a comic Russian in a musical remake of which Greta Garbo film? Name the musical.
e He played a taxi driver in the 1960 SCENT OF MYSTERY. What was special about the film? Which leading lady made a surprise appearance at the end?

C He became an All-Star Southern Conference Halfback and, at the beginning of his movie career (following such TV series as *Riverboat, Gunsmoke* and *Hawk*), many of his critics thought he should have remained one. But experience and the full-

ness of time, coupled with his virile good looks and an endearing ability to send up his own macho image, has resulted in his becoming one of Hollywood's most bankable superstars. He achieved a certain notoriety by posing nude for the centrefold of *Cosmopolitan* magazine. Despite his ladykiller status, he has only been married once: to *Laugh-In*'s Judy Carne. They divorced in 1966:

a Who is he?
b In 1976 he directed his first film. What was it?
c In which film did he play a stunt man?
d His one foray into musicals was a disaster. Name the movie, the director, and the female co-star
e In what film did he appear with Liza Minnelli?

D Born in Hollywood, her father was a successful writer-director, her mother an MGM star of the 30s. Brought up in Britain, she returned to the USA, became an actress and gained some notice in the TV serial of PEYTON PLACE. She first got into the international limelight, however, because of her marriage to one of the world's most famous crooners:

a Who is she?
b Name her two famous husbands.
c Ira Levin wrote it, Roman Polanski directed it, she starred. Name the film, and the eminent elderly actress who took a major supporting role.
d In what film did she co-star with Elizabeth Taylor? Who was the male star and the director?
e In what films did she play opposite Laurence Harvey, Topol, Dustin Hoffman, Jean-Paul Belmondo?

E Born Sarah Jane Fulks, this durable actress spent ten years playing mainly 'best friend' roles and perky 'B' picture heroines before winning an Oscar as a deaf mute. Subsequently, she starred in drama, comedies and musicals, then after a period of semi-retirement emerged to star in a popular TV series:

a Who is she?
b For which film did she win the Oscar, and who was its director?
c Partnered by a famous crooner, she introduced 1951's Oscar-winning song. Name the song, the crooner, and the film in which they sang it.
d Her second husband, then a fellow actor, went on to hold a notable position in public life. Who is he, and what position does he hold?

Lust for Lives

Although a genre in its own right, the biopic encompasses all other genres. Most biopics could justifiably state that 'any resemblance of the characters to any persons living or dead is purely coincidental'!

1 Who were the famous subjects of the following films and who played them?
a BOUND FOR GLORY
b P.T.109
c THE SPIRIT OF ST LOUIS
d MOMMIE DEAREST
e TONIGHT WE SING
f MAN OF A THOUSAND FACES
g MONTPARNASSE 19
h SUEZ
i TOO MUCH TOO SOON
j MILLION DOLLAR MERMAID

2 Identify the biopics by the publicity blurbs or critical comments below:
a 'They're young . . . they're in love . . . and they kill people'
b 'Heston hits the Ceiling' – *Time Magazine*
c 'The story of a homosexual who married a nymphomaniac'
d 'When poets love . . . heaven and earth fall back to watch'
e 'How fitting that America's Beloved First Star returns to millions of picturegoers in the role of the warm, vital young beauty who became queen of France in an era that shook the world'
f 'It achieves one feat which is not inconsiderable. It manages to libel even the despised Rasputin' – *New York Herald-Tribune*
g 'Because the Hollywood story builds relentlessly to (the) ear-slicing for its climax, (it) falls midway between being a first-rate art film and high-pitched melodrama' – *Time Magazine*
h 'It took one remarkable man to defeat an Empire and free a nation of 350 million people. His goal was freedom. His strategy was peace. His weapon was his humanity'
i 'What Senator Joseph McCarthy did to people's reputations is nothing compared with what Ken Russell does, and if his victims aren't around to lose their livelihoods, neither are they around to defend themselves . . . (He) has the incomparable gall to attack Hollywood and the American public for their callous exploitation of this orange-lover' – Pauline Kael
j 'See Don Ameche invent the telephone'

3 Disease and affliction have always been the bread and butter of biopics. Identify the films and their subjects from the clues below, and name the stars who portrayed the unfortunate people concerned:
a A great jazz singer becomes a heroin addict
b A popular songstress is crippled in an airplane crash
c A singer of stage and screen ruins her career with eight marriages and a descent into alcoholism
d A nightclub singer has his vocal chords cut by gangsters, becomes a comedian, and takes to the bottle
e A jockey fights back after harrowing treatment for cancer
f An opera singer returns to the stage after being crippled by polio
g A girl who was born deaf, dumb and blind, learns to communicate by touch
h A baseball player makes a comeback after having a leg amputated
i A baseball player suffers a nervous breakdown because of his father's high expectations for him
j A man who is so disfigured that he is exhibited as a freak, then kept locked away from the public, before finally being seen in society

4 For what film does the publicity read, 'On November 13, 1974, an employee of a nuclear facility left to meet with a reporter from the *New York Times* . . . She never got there'? Who played this employee? What was the gist of the message she was to give the reporter? Why did she never get there? Who played the two people she lived with? What 1979 movie had a similar message?

Newsweek **called it 'Hollywood's most profound exploration of the artistic life.' The actor pictured won the New York Critic's Circle Award and an Oscar nomination. What is the film called? Who is the actor? Who directed the film? The title comes from whose biography of which artist? Who won the Best Supporting Actor Oscar and for which role?**

A well-known country singer was the subject of this biopic:
a Name the movie
b Who is the actress illustrated and who is the singer she is portraying?
c Did the actress do her own singing or was she dubbed?
d Who played her supportive husband?
e The scene takes place in a town celebrated by a Robert Altman film. What is its name?

5   In each of the following questions one star portrayed the various real-life characters described. Can you name the star, the characters and the titles of the films in each case?
a A nurse who helped wounded soldiers on the battlefields during World War I, a flying pioneer in the 30s, a woman who reformed the nursing service in the late 19th century
b A great escapologist at the turn of the century, a Red Indian World War II hero, the Jewish head of Murder Inc. in the 30s
c A British colonial general under siege by the Arabs in 1883, one of a pair of explorers through the Louisiana Purchase territory in 1803, a U.S. President forced to get support from a pirate during the war of 1812
d A famed model and mistress of an 18th century Spanish painter, a 19th century Austrian Empress, a beautiful actress of the late 19th century
e A medieval Italian explorer, a hillbilly who became a World War I hero, an American general who accused the top military brass of negligence
f A Mexican revolutionary hero, a French-Canadian trapper who opened up the northern wilderness, a composer and teacher of Chopin
g A prostitute executed in the gas chamber, a 19th century First Lady with a past, a seductress of the King of the Jews
h A 15th century Italian explorer, a 19th century English poet, a great American humorist and novelist
i A 17th century French poet, philosopher, wit and duellist, a 19th century French officer tried for treason, a turn-of-the-century French painter
j A German dictator, a Roman Emperor, a 17th century English king

Ken Russell directed this biopic of a composer. Whose life did this one depict, who played him and what was the title of the film? Russell made two other biopics of composers. Who were they, and who played them? Which actress is seen in the still and what role did she play? Name another Ken Russell film in which she had a leading role.

6   Modern world leaders or their surrogates crop up from time to time in the movies:
a What recent film featured Eisenhower, Lyndon Johnson and John Glenn lookalikes?
b Who are Richard M. Dixon and Jeanette Charles?
c In what film did Glenda Jackson become Richard Nixon?
d Four presidents were impersonated in THE PRIVATE FILES OF J. EDGAR HOOVER, but who played the title role?
e Which world leaders were disguised under the names of Hynkel and Napoloni, and who played them?
f What fictitious character was offered $500,000 to assassinate General De Gaulle and who played him?
g Which political figures are addressing each other in the following dialogue and who played them?
'When we lost the missiles, Cuba lost its promise. My departure is long overdue'
'Yes, I know! You've told me. Things are moving too slowly for you here. You've told me a dozen times ... I don't understand you!'
h Which famous statesman's parents were played by Anne Bancroft and Robert Shaw?
i What role did Wallace Beery and Yul Brynner have in common?
j What did Burt Lancaster, Robert Ryan and Will Geer conspire to do in order to change the course of history, and in what film?

7   Certain risible moments occur in biopics to disturb one's concentration on 'high art'. In which films
a Was a composer inspired to write the opening bars of a symphony by the sound of the rent-collector knocking on the door?
b Did a composer gain inspiration for a complete waltz in an open carriage after taking his melody from the birds?
c Did a composer write a suite in a Moroccan nightclub for the dancer there?
d Did a pianist step up the tempo of one of her husband's works during a recital to get to her baby being held in the wings?
e Was a performance at the Met disturbed by the news going around the auditorium that the leading tenor had just become a father?

8   What one thing do the following biopics have in common and who were the subjects of the first three?
a THE GREATEST
b BROADWAY
c TO HELL AND BACK
d THE FABULOUS DORSEYS
e THE TOMMY STEELE STORY

9 Historical figures are often impersonated on the screen. Name the characters that the following stars have in common and, if possible, the titles of the films in which they appeared:
a Bette Davis, Glenda Jackson, Flora Robson
b Marlon Brando, Rod Steiger, Eli Wallach
c Claudette Colbert, Vivian Leigh, Rhonda Fleming
d Henry Fonda, Raymond Massey, Walter Huston
e Anna Neagle, Irene Dunne, Peter Sellers
f Charles Laughton, Robert Shaw, Richard Burton
g Boris Shchukin, Maxim Straukh, V. Nikandrov
h Marlene Dietrich, Jeanne Moreau, Elisabeth Bergner
i George Arliss, John Gielgud, Alec Guinness
j Claude Rains, Rex Harrison, Louis Calhern

10 What profession did characters played by each of the following groups of actors have in common, in what films did they practise it, and who did they play in each case?
a Paul Newman, Errol Flynn, Robert De Niro
b George C. Scott, Gregory Peck, James Mason
c Carroll Baker, Jessica Lange, Kim Novak
d Robert Walker, Robert Alda, Tom Drake
e Charles Laughton, Mel Ferrer, Anthony Franciosa
f Dirk Bogarde, Trevor Howard, Jean-Pierre Aumont
g Patrice Munsel, Mario Lanza, Kathryn Grayson
h Ralph Bellamy, Charlton Heston, Brian Keith
i Paul Muni, Spencer Tracy, Walter Pidgeon
j Dustin Hoffman, Rod Steiger, Keefe Brasselle

11 Match the stars with the celebrities they played and name the films in which they played them:
a Richard Chamberlain
b Alan Bates
c Stewart Granger
d Ronald Colman
e Jason Robards Jr
f Claude Rains
g Beau Bridges
h Robert Donat
i David Niven
j Richard Todd

A Ben Hecht
B David Belasco
C William Pitt
D Lord Byron
E Beau Brummell
F Bonnie Prince Charlie
G Robert Clive
H Rob Roy
I Howard Hughes
J Sergei Diaghilev

12 Pick out the biopics from each of the following groups, naming the subject and the star. Who were the stars of the remaining purely fictional movies?
a i) THE STAR ii) THE ACTRESS iii) STAR!
b i) BLONDE BOMBSHELL ii) INCENDIARY BLONDE iii) BLONDE VENUS
c i) PRINCE OF PLAYERS iii) ACT ONE iii) STAGE STRUCK
d i) THE MAGIC BOX ii) MAGIC iii) MAGIC FIRE
e i) THE GIRL IN THE RED VELVET SWING ii) THE GIRL MOST LIKELY iii) THE 'I DON'T CARE' GIRL

13 Sometimes biopics offer two famous characters for the price of one. In which films would you find the following pairs?
a Jill Clayburgh and James Brolin
b Betty Grable and June Haver
c Jane Fonda and Jason Robards Jr
d Janet Suzman and Ian McKellen
e Robert Morley and Maurice Evans
f Julie Andrews and Daniel Massey
g Deborah Kerr and Gregory Peck
h Spencer Tracy and Cedric Hardwicke
i Paul Newman and Robert Redford
j William Katt and Tom Berenger

14 Whether to circumvent the law of libel or to allow for more poetic licence, the names of real people are often changed in the movies. Who inspired the following thinly disguised biopics? Who took the roles in each case?
a CITIZEN KANE
b DANIEL
c YOUNG CASSIDY
d THE MOON AND SIXPENCE
e THE GREEK TYCOON
f ALL THE KING'S MEN
g THE GREAT WHITE HOPE
h CABARET
i YOUNG MAN WITH A HORN
j THE ROSE

15 'Stories' are generally fictions, and film stories of real people are not much different. Who portrayed the famous people in the following 'stories':
a THE JOLSON STORY
b THE BUSTER KEATON STORY
c THE BUDDY HOLLY STORY
d THE GLENN MILLER STORY
e THE GEORGE RAFT STORY
f THE HELEN MORGAN STORY
g THE JAMES DEAN STORY
h THE STORY OF VERNON AND IRENE CASTLE
i THE STORY OF DR WASSELL
j THE STORY OF WILL ROGERS

Rose, June and Louise Hovick are the subjects of this musical biography. Name the film. Under what names did two of the Hovicks become better known? Which of the three, did the girl in the cap (foreground) play, and who is the actress? Why is she dressed as a boy? What was the nature of the solo act which later made her famous? How was the song 'Let Me Entertain You' used in the film? Who played the girl's ambitious mother?

---

16 With which biopics would you associate the stars below:
a Ben Kingsley?
b William Powell?
c Doris Day?
d William Bendix?
e John Mills?

17 It might be possible that the real personages actually said the things that scriptwriters put into their mouths. However, some lines create serious doubts as to their verbal authenticity. In which films would you hear the following unlikely dialogue?
a 'Discontinue that so-called Polonaise jumble you've been playing for days'
b 'Oh, Nicolo Paganini, you could make a tin whistle sound like a Stradivarius'
c 'It's hard living with an old revolutionary. You should have been with us when we stormed the Winter Palace! With Lenin in Moscow in the early days. What happiness to be alive and to be fighting then!'
d 'You cannot die an old maid'. 'I have no intention to, Chancellor. I shall die a bachelor'
e 'What's your name, son?'
'Jesus, sir'
'That's a good name'

18 Coincidentally, two films on Wilde, the Irish playwright, poet and wit, were made in 1960 in Britain. One was called THE TRIALS OF OSCAR WILDE (US: THE MAN WITH THE GREEN CARNATION) and the other OSCAR WILDE:
a Who took the title role in each?
b Which was in colour?
c Which was directed by Gregory Ratoff?
d Who played Lord Alfred Douglas and Oscar's long-suffering wife in each?
e What role did Ralph Richardson play in one and James Mason in the other?

What actress is portraying which famous dancer? What is the film? Where and when is this scene taking place? In what way did the Dancer marry a Singer? Who played the Singer? In which three other films did this actress play the title role?

19 Actors playing Gustave Flaubert, Rudyard Kipling and Somerset Maugham have made appearances in films based on the writers' novels. Name the actors and the films.

20 The casting of stars with totally different accents and nationalities from the people they were playing never bothered the makers of Hollywood biopics. In which films did
a An English-born actress play a great French actress?
b A Russian-born dancer play an Italian-born film star?
c A Welsh-born actor play a Macedonian warrior?
d A Mexican-born actor play the scourge of the Roman Empire?
e An Irish-born actress play a Polish-born scientist?
f A New York-born actor play a Persian poet?
g An Ohio-born actor play an Irish patriot?
h A Nebraska-born actor play an Austrian psychoanalyst?
i A Roumanian-born American actor play a a German scientist?
j An Iowa-born actress play a French saint?

21 Overt homosexuality on the screen was, in many countries, taboo for some decades. The following actors played people who were known or thought to have been homosexuals, but the idea was never mentioned in the films. Who were the characters they played and in which discreet biopics?
a Cary Grant
b Charlton Heston
c Mickey Rooney
d Peter O'Toole
e Innokenti Smoktunovsky

22 Fanny Brice was one of the great comediennes of the Broadway musical stage and her life was the subject of three musicals. The earliest one, based on her first marriage, claimed to be 'entirely fictional', but Miss Brice sued the studio. What was it called and who was the female star? Who made her screen debut as Fanny Brice, and what was the film called? Name the sequel. Who played her two husbands in the movies? What was Fanny Brice's theme song, used in these musical biopics? In which biographical film did Fanny Brice appear as herself?

23 Each of the following real people has been portrayed in a film. Who are they and who portrayed them in which films?
a Pearl White
b Douglas Bader
c John Reed
d Gaudier-Brzeska
e Dorothy Stratten
f James Walker
g Lou Gehrig
h Ernie Pyle
i Jack Kerouac
j Coco Chanel

24 History, we are told, has been male-dominated, thus, by extension, so has the biopic. We try to redress the balance by giving renowned women the last word in this chapter:
a Which three authors were played by Ida Lupino, Olivia de Havilland and Nancy Coleman, and in which film?
b Who was THE STORY OF ADELE H about? Who played the title role and who directed the movie?
c Both Judy Garland and June Haver have portrayed a famous Broadway musical-comedy star. Who was she and what were the films?
d In which films did Ginger Rogers play a president's wife and a film star's mother?
e Can you name the female lead in a musical-bio whose cast included Eleanor Parker, Peggy Wood and Anna Lee?
f In which film does the author of 'Frankenstein' make an appearance and who played her?
g Sarah Miles appeared in a film about a scandalous 19th century aristocrat written by her husband. Name the film and her author husband
h Diane Keaton and Maureen Stapleton played two radical women in a 1981 movie. Who were the women and what was the film?

A biopic about a night club entertainer:
a Name the film, the entertainer and the actor
b Who played his wife Honey?
c Who directed the film?
d What semi-autobiographical film did the director make?
e In which other film did the actor play a contemporary real-life person?

Behind the Scenes

You may know what film won last year's Oscar, but do you know who wrote it? Or who composed the score? Or who was behind the daredevil stunts? Did the stars get on? What were the problems of getting it made?

1 Jean-Paul Sartre might have been referring to the movie industry when he wrote that 'Hell is other people.' Who said of – or to – whom?

a 'I have more talent in my smallest fart than you do in your entire body'

b 'If you were more of a woman, I would be more of a man. Kissing you is like kissing the side of a beer bottle'

c 'It's like kissing Hitler'

d 'Directing her was like directing Lassie. You needed fourteen takes to get each one right'

e 'She has breasts like granite and a brain like Swiss cheese, full of holes. Extracting a performance from her is like pulling teeth'

f 'Just how garish her commonplace accent, squeakily shrill voice, and the childish petulance with which she delivers her lines are, my pen is neither scratchy nor leaky enough to convey'

g 'My experience with him was an unhappy one. There seemed to be a malevolence in him, a determination to make other human beings unhappy'

h 'What's extraordinary is that I've never worked with this man . . . And yet he goes around saying these terrible things about me'

i 'She thinks she doesn't get old. She told me once it was her cameraman that was getting old. She wanted me to fire him!'

2 A 1983 film was advertised as 'The Biggest Gross in History'. What was the film? How much did it earn in its first 14 days? In January 1983, it overtook the highest grossing movie to date. What was it? Place the following movies in order of box office receipts as published in *Variety* in 1980:

  i THE GODFATHER
 ii SUPERMAN
 iii GONE WITH THE WIND
 iv CLOSE ENCOUNTERS OF THE THIRD KIND
  v THE STING
 vi THE SOUND OF MUSIC
 vii JAWS
viii THE EXORCIST
 ix SATURDAY NIGHT FEVER
  x GREASE

3 Film stars are often revealing when they analyse themselves. Who said?

a 'I have a face like the behind of an elephant'

b 'I have eyes like those of a dead pig'

c 'I'm a very physical person. People don't credit me with much of a brain, so why should I disillusion them?'

d 'Roger comes in the humour door, and I go out it'

e 'I choose my roles carefully so that, when my career is finished, I will have covered all our recent oppression'

f 'I've carried stillness and non-reaction as far as I can go. I've got to pedal on furiously to something else'

g 'Sobriety's a real turn on for me. You can see what you're doing'

h 'My real name is Ramon Estevez. I've never changed it legally. I never will. It's my favourite name in the world. On paper, you know, in America, I'm a Chicano. I'm a minority.'

i 'Accents? I can do Irish, Welsh, Manchester, Liverpool, Birmingham, Cockney and New York Jewish lesbian' . .

j 'I only thought about what my father would think. He sat behind me at the opening night of THE STUD. Every time a nude scene came on, I turned round to see his reaction. He seemed to be enjoying it'

4 Here are a few more questions about the legendary antagonisms between stars:

a Which member of a comedy team sued the other for $222,000 in unpaid royalties?

b What star was completely ignored by Clark Gable when they were not filming because he hated 'high-toned ladies'?

c What star refused to continue to play love scenes with Clark Gable unless he did something about the bad breath caused by his dentures?

d To whom did Bette Davis deliver a slap on camera that did not require added sound effects?

e During the making of which 1983 Don Siegel movie, whose title says it all, did the director have violent 'creative differences' with its volatile star? Who was she?

This is the most memorable moment from a documentary demonstrating a new screen process which one newspaper described as 'the most astounding development in cinema history since sound'. What was the film called, who first developed the process, and how did it differ from other screen techniques? What was the first story feature released in the process?

5   1981 and 1982 produced two of the most expensive flops of all time made by two of the biggest money-making directors of all time. The first was a $36 million western and the second a $27 million musical. Name the films and their directors. What was Steven Spielberg's gargantuan $28 million dollar flop? What was the title of the disastrous $40 million movie about the Korean war and whose money enabled it to be produced?

6   William Holden remarked in SUNSET BOULEVARD that 'Audiences don't know anybody writes a picture. They think the actors just make it up as they go along.' Answer the following questions on screen writing:

a Which was the only film for which Scott Fitzgerald received a writing credit?

b Which American novelists wrote the screenplays for i) STRANGERS ON A TRAIN ii) THE BIG SLEEP iii) VIVA ZAPATA iv) SUDDENLY LAST SUMMER v) CITY STREETS

c Name the films that Paul Schrader wrote for Sydney Pollack, Martin Scorsese and Brian de Palma before becoming a director himself?

d Who wrote 'Adventures in the Screen Trade'?

e With which directors are the screenwriters I.A.L. Diamond, Cesare Zavattini, Suso Cecchi d'Amico, and Marshall Brickman associated?

This is a scene from a film which deals with an historic event. What was the event, and on what date did it take place? Who are the characters represented in the picture? Name the film and the author of the book on which it was based? What real events were featured in a) ALL THE PRESIDENT'S MEN b) OPERATION THUNDERBOLT c) THE YEAR OF LIVING DANGEROUSLY d) UNDER FIRE.

---

7   Not all big Hollywood stars are American. In which countries were the following born?
a Jose Ferrer
b Audrey Hepburn
c George Sanders
d Ray Milland
e Ann-Margret
f Vivien Leigh
g Olivia de Havilland
h Peter Lorre
i Stan Laurel
j Errol Flynn

8   Film stars often have an influence far beyond the screen. What fashions were created by the following?
a Valentino
b Diane Keaton in ANNIE HALL
c Barbra Streisand in A STAR IS BORN
d Clark Gable in IT HAPPENED ONE NIGHT
e Ingrid Bergman
f James Dean
g Joan Crawford
h Audrey Hepburn
i Jean Harlow
j Veronica Lake

9   'A designer was as important as a star. The magic of a dress . . . was part of selling a picture. Sets, costumes and make-up just aren't considered the art form they used to be,' commented top Paramount designer Edith Head. Behind many a glamorous film star there stood an exceptional costume designer to help shape their image. Match the star with the designer with whom they are most associated:
a Greta Garbo
b Audrey Hepburn
c Rita Hayworth
d Bette Davis
e Marlene Dietrich

A Orry-Kelly
B Adrian
C Jean Louis
D Travis Banton
E Givenchy

10   To continue in a glamorous fashion:
a In which film did one star wear 65 different costumes designed by Irene Sharaff at a cost of $130,000, and who was she?
b Who wore, and who designed, a cape of peacock feathers plucked from Cecil B. DeMille's own peacocks?
c Who said 'Who could ever believe my whole career would rest on Joan Crawford's shoulders'?
d Which films did Cecil Beaton design for Leslie Caron, Barbra Streisand, and Audrey Hepburn?
e Which late 60s movie, designed by Theadora Van Runkle, started a fashion for campy early 30s clothes design?
f Which 1974 movie won an Oscar for Best Costume Design for its evocation of the Jazz Age?
g Whose swimming costumes for Esther Williams influenced bathing suit manufacturers such as Catalina and Jantzen?
h In which black-and-white movie did Bette Davis wear a dress that had to suggest the colour red in order to show her lack of convention during an all-white ball?
i Who designed a $4,000 period costume for Vivien Leigh in GONE WITH THE WIND?
j In which film did Ginger Rogers wear a dress with $35,000 worth of ranch mink skins sewn onto her skirt?

11   Who was paid over $2½ million for 12 days' work and a 10-minute appearance, and what was the film? How much were John Travolta and Olivia Newton-John reputed to have earned each as a percentage of the profits of GREASE? Who was the first star to demand a share in the profits of a film before agreeing to take part, and what was the film? Who was the first performer whose life was insured during the making of a film, and what was the film?

12 Answer these Oscar-winning questions:
a Who was the first black to win an Oscar?
b Who was the first actor to receive the Best Actor award posthumously?
c Who was the first President of the Academy of Motion Picture Arts and Sciences?
d Who won an Oscar while on his death bed?
e Who were the first winners of the Best Supporting Actor and Actress awards?
f Who were the first co-stars to win Best Actor and Actress awards and for what film?
g Which was the first Foreign Language Film winner?
h Who was the first to win the Best Actor Oscar in a musical?
i Which actresses have won an Oscar two years in succession?
j Which of the following never won an Oscar for Best Actor or Actress: Greta Garbo, Cary Grant, Marlene Dietrich, Charles Chaplin, Judy Garland, Bob Hope, Ava Gardner, James Dean, Barbara Stanwyck, Tyrone Power?

13 Stars are often not all they appear to be on screen. Who
a lost a thumb and index finger when a prop exploded and thereafter always appeared either with gloves or dummy latex fingers?
b lost a leg in World War I and acted with an artificial one?
c has a glass eye?
d had a metal plate inserted in his forehead after a motor accident?
e had plastic surgery on his face after a motor accident?
f was completely bald under her wigs, although the comedians she worked with never took advantage of it?
g had her breasts painfully bound to suggest a girl of twelve when she was seventeen?
h had all his profuse body hair shaved off, including under his arms, for the role of Christ?
i had his protruding ears pinned back by surgery when he first arrived in Hollywood?
j had chronic asthma for most of his life and was only able to complete his last role with the aid of oxygen tanks?

14 Can you name the first
a film made in Hollywood?
b film shown publicly?
c CinemaScope feature?
d feature in 3D with Stereophonic sound?
e musical with an original score?
f film in Sensurround?
g feature-length western?
h country to nationalise its cinema industry?
i all-talking feature film?
j talkie made in Britain?

15 The director of photography or cameraman often makes as important a creative contribution to a film as its director. Match the following films with their photographers:
a CITIZEN KANE
b BARRY LYNDON
c CABARET
d AMERICAN GRAFFITI
e RAIDERS OF THE LOST ARK
f LAWRENCE OF ARABIA
g THE BIRTH OF A NATION
h SHANGHAI EXPRESS
i APOCALYPSE NOW
j FANNY AND ALEXANDER

A Geoffrey Unsworth
B Gregg Toland
C Sven Nykvist
D Billy Bitzer
E Freddie Young
F Haskell Wexler
G Vittorio Storaro
H John Alcott
I Lee Garmes
J Douglas Slocombe

A dramatic moment from one of the legion of films adapted from Shakespeare, the most filmed of all writers. Which is it, and who directed this version? Who is the actor playing the king? Which Shakespeare play has been filmed more than any other, and who played the title role in the very earliest version? Which Shakespeare film had the immortal credit line, 'additional dialogue by Sam Taylor'?

16 Make-up artists have always played a vital role in the presentation of a character on screen. Answer the following questions on memorable cosmetic creations:

a For what film did Gordon Bau and eight assistants take almost two days to apply special make-up to an actor's whole body, making it the longest make-up job ever? Who was the actor who submitted to this lengthy process?

b During the shooting of which film did Elsa Lanchester have to be fed through a tube because of the stiffness of her facial make-up?

c For which film did the make-up budget take up nearly 17% of the total production cost, because most of the cast had to appear convincing in their new faces?

d In which film did acrobats, dancers and stunt-men in monkey-suits, mix with real apes so that it was impossible to tell them apart?

e Which two Dustin Hoffman movies required the most elaborate make-up and why?

f In which film was Alec Guinness made up to look like Alastair Sim?

g In which films did Lon Chaney, Claude Rains, Herbert Lom and Paul Williams reveal a horribly scarred face?

h Which great make-up man at Universal created the Monster in FRANKENSTEIN, and how was Boris Karloff made to walk in the manner he did?

i Of whom and in what film did one critic write 'They have put pudding in (his) cheeks and dirtied his teeth, he speaks hoarsely and moves stiffly, and these combined mechanics are hailed as great acting.'?

A scene from one of the last silent spectaculars:
a Name the three actors pictured
b Name the film and its director
c What special qualification did the director have for making the film?
d How did the film make cinema history?
e During the shooting of which 1930 war drama were three aerial stuntmen killed?

---

17 Winning an Oscar is worth an extra $10 million at the box office and allows the winners to dictate their terms for any future projects. Which famous art director designed the Oscar statuette? After whom, reputedly, did Margaret Herrick, the librarian at the Academy, name it? What is the actual value of the statuette and how high does it stand? In what year was it first awarded and which film, director, actor and actress were its first participants? Who won the same awards in 1984?

18 So many people with different skills contribute to the making of a motion picture. Can you name the particular job of each of the following creative people?
a Vilmos Zsigmond
b Douglas Shearer
c Van Nest Polglase
d John Briley
e Leo Forbstein
f Sydney Guilaroff
g Natalie Kalmus
h Dave Gould
i Claudia Weill
j Willis O'Brien

Reach for the Stars

A This beautiful British actress made her screen debut at fourteen and had become a top star by the time she followed her actor husband to Hollywood. Having already had an Oscar nomination for portraying a Shakespearean heroine, she was to gain another for her roles as a disillusioned wife in a film directed by her second husband:

a Who is she?

b Who was her actor husband, and who was the director who became her second husband?

c What was the film in which she made her screen debut?

d She co-starred with Marlon Brando in two films – can you name them?

B He was discovered playing in a drama school production of 'Journey's End'. He was signed to a seven year contract starting at $35 a week and got his first chance in a 1934 'Crime Does Not Pay' short. He accidentally blinded Irene Dunne in a classic tearjerker and was already romancing his wife-to-be when he co-starred with her in THIS IS MY AFFAIR (1937). He grew a moustache to play opposite Vivien Leigh, and dropped the A-bomb on Hiroshima. He equalled Clark Gable's record of service at the studio to which they both belonged:

a Who is he?

b He had perhaps the most memorable real name among the great stars. What was it?

c In what film was he jilted by Garbo?

d In 1938 he returned to college. In what film?

e Which legendary western outlaw did he play in 1941?

C For this actress, a show business cliché came true when, as understudy, she took over in a Broadway show the night a Hollywood producer was out front and was thus signed to a movie contract. Her offbeat, kooky personality was particularly well showcased when playing warm-hearted floozies, the sort of role for which she won her first Oscar nomination. Other Oscar nominations were for roles as an elevator attendant in love with a married man, a bubbly Parisian tart, and an off-beat mother, for which she finally won the award:

a Who is she?

b Her first film was directed by Hitchcock. Name it

c One of her most finely etched portrayals was that of a schoolteacher accused of having an affair with her best girlfriend. What was the film, who directed it, and who was her female co-star?

d She has a famous actor brother – who is he?

D As a result of an unsettled childhood, and long before he was bitten by the acting bug, he undertook a variety of decidedly odd jobs, and in quick succession found himself employed as a nightclub bouncer, a maintenance man on a freighter and a public relations officer to an astrologer. Then, after a short stint as a drop hammer operator for Lockheed Aircraft, he joined the Long Beach Theatre Guild, entering movies in 1943 in a succession of Hopalong Cassidy westerns. His big break came in 1945 with a movie about a soldier, which won him an Oscar nomination:

a Who is he?

b He appeared in two films with Shirley MacLaine. What were they?

c He appeared in the only film directed by Charles Laughton. What was its title?

d In what films did he play Philip Marlowe?

e David Lean directed him only once. Name the film

E The son of tomato growers from an island in the Bahamas, he made his Broadway debut in 1946 in *Lysistrata* before going to Hollywood where, in the mid-50s, he became one of the first black superstars. For a while, his presence was usually more impressive than the films he was asked to make. The situation changed in 1963 when he was cast as a black itinerant workman in New Mexico, and won an Oscar for his efforts:

a Who is he?

b In which films did he play a concerned store clerk, and a Samaritans' telephone volunteer, and who were the actresses who benefitted from his help?

c In which film did he break new ground by becoming engaged to a white girl? Who was she?

d In which film did he create the role of detective Virgil Tibbs?

e He made a 1966 western because he wanted to play a black cowboy. What was it called?

Adventure Playground

Spies and pirates, jungles and deserts, submarine or outer space. This chapter covers a vast field of storytelling, ancient and modern, all connected with the thrill of adventure and romance.

1 Audiences in recent times have had their need for adventure satisfied by living out their worst fears. The films that provide this have become known as 'disaster' movies. Here is a selection of questions with which to grapple:

a What disaster overtook the characters in THE POSEIDON ADVENTURE?

b What calamity happened on A NIGHT TO REMEMBER (1958)?

c What catastrophe threatened to overwhelm Rock Hudson and Mia Farrow in a 1978 disaster movie?

d It unnerved Dorothy Lamour and Jon Hall in 1937, and Mia Farrow and Dayton Ka'ne in 1979. What minor difference was there in the titles of the two films?

e A mad bomber has threatened to blow up a transatlantic liner. Only Richard Harris can save the situation. How and in what film?

f Who played the architect of the burning building in TOWERING INFERNO, and what famous dancer was among those trapped in the conflagration?

g In what disaster film did someone billed as Walter Matuschanskayasky play the cameo role of a drunk?

h What menacing creature of the deep did Richard Harris and Charlotte Rampling have to conquer?

i Who wrote the screenplay for JAWS and THE DEEP, and the novels on which they were based?

j What leading actor survived the terrors of JAWS to reappear in JAWS 2?

2 'Far away places with strange sounding names' goes the song:

a Which men did Marlene Dietrich meet in Morocco, Shanghai and Monte Carlo?

b Who would you find at both THE BRIDGES AT TOKO-RI and THE BRIDGE ON THE RIVER KWAI?

c Where would you find Humphrey Bogart with i) Walter Huston ii) Ingrid Bergman iii) Michele Morgan iv) Florence Marly v) Lloyd Bridges?

d Which women did Clark Gable meet in Bombay, Naples and on the China seas?

e Which romantic actor would you find in Castile, the Khyber Pass and Suez?

3 Too much sand and too little water have been the cause of much discomfort in desert dramas. Answer the following questions from the oases of information supplied, and name the film in each case:

a A group of ten plane crash survivors try to rebuild their plane in the middle of the desert. Of the actors four are American, four British, one German and one French. Who are they?

b John Wayne and Rossano Brazzi on a treasure hunt in the Sahara fight over a woman. Who is she?

c Plane crash survivors, including Susannah York and Stanley Baker, battle through the desert of the title and against wild baboons. Who was the American star of this British movie?

d John Ford directed this tale of a British military group lost in the Mesopotamian desert fighting hostile tribes. What favourite Ford stalwart leads the patrol and what horror-movie star plays a religious fanatic?

e Erich von Stroheim as Rommel stays at a Sahara oasis hotel. Franchot Tone tries to obtain secrets from him. Who played the owner of the hotel and the chambermaid and who directed the movie?

f Foreign Legionnaire Alan Ladd is the sole survivor of an ambush. He's nursed back to health by a beautiful redhead. Who was she?

g John Mills, Harry Andrews, Anthony Quayle and a woman try to make their way through the desert in a truck. Who played the girl? What nationality did Quayle play? Explain the title

h A CinemaScope French film about gold-smuggling in North Africa with Michele Morgan. The title comprises one refreshing word. Who directed it?

i A British army captain leads a group of ex-cons into the North African campaign in World War II. Similar to THE DIRTY DOZEN even in its title. Who played the captain?

j Two friends join the Foreign Legion to forget. They perform 'Shine On, Harvest Moon' and one of them is reincarnated as a horse. Who are they?

This is a scene from TARZAN THE APE MAN. Who played Tarzan and what was his claim to fame before the film? Who played Jane and name her famous daughter? This was the first Tarzan movie – true or false?

4 P. C. Wren's romantic Foreign Legion adventure BEAU GESTE has been filmed three times – in 1926, 1939 and 1966. How does the story begin? Who played the title role and the sadistic sergeant in each case? In which version did Donald O'Connor appear and what part did he play? Who played the two other Geste brothers in the 1939 version? Who directed and starred in THE LAST REMAKE OF BEAU GESTE? Do you know which star appeared in it posthumously?

5 Africa, the Dark Continent, has been a favourite hunting ground for many Hollywood scenarists. Who or what did the following find – or search for – in Africa?
a Stewart Granger and Deborah Kerr
b Spencer Tracy
c Bill Travers and Virginia McKenna
d John Wayne and Red Buttons
e William Holden and Capucine

Queen Elizabeth I looking down on two of her subjects.
a **Name the film.**
b **Who played the queen and in which film did she repeat the role?**
c **Name the couple seated.**
d **What was their relationship at the time?**
e **What other films did they make together?**

6 Two of Herman Melville's great sea stories have been made into films – MOBY DICK (1956) and BILLY BUDD. Name their directors. Who played the title roles? Who played the captains in each? Who played the narrator Ishmael in the former, and the evil Claggart in the latter? What great actor-director had a cameo role in MOBY DICK? What were the names of the ships in each film? Who wrote the screenplay of MOBY DICK and where was it filmed? Who played his first major role in BILLY BUDD?

7 Where there's a hero at sea, there is generally bound to be a villain. Name the salty hero and the heavy in each of the following:
a THE SEA HAWK
b AGAINST ALL FLAGS
c TWO YEARS BEFORE THE MAST
d BOTANY BAY
e HMS DEFIANT (US: DAMN THE DEFIANT!)

8 A group of people survive a plane crash in the Tibetan mountains and come across an 'ideal society'. Give the film's title. What was the only law of the valley community? Who wrote the novel from which the film was adapted? Who directed the film? Who played Conway, Chang and the High Lama? Who played them in the 1973 remake and how did it markedly differ from the original?

9 Agent 007, otherwise James Bond, the modern equivalent of the swashbuckling heroes of yesteryear, has been at the centre of many a spy adventure. Answer the following questions on Bondage:
a Place the films listed in the order in which they were made:
   i) DIAMONDS ARE FOREVER
   ii) THE SPY WHO LOVED ME
   iii) MOONRAKER
   iv) FROM RUSSIA WITH LOVE
   v) THUNDERBALL
   vi) NEVER SAY NEVER AGAIN
   vii) LIVE AND LET DIE
   viii) DR NO
   ix) GOLDFINGER
   x) THE MAN WITH THE GOLDEN GUN
b In which of the above films was Bond played by Roger Moore?
c Which Bond film was set in the West Indies, and which one in Japan?
d James Bond's arch-enemies differ from film to film. In which films did he confront i) Christopher Lee ii) Curt Jurgens iii) Louis Jourdan iv) Gert Frobe v) Joseph Wiseman?
e Who played Sir James Bond and in what film?

10 Spies have variously been treated in the movies as mysterious, sinister, shabby or romantic figures. Give the names of the spies played by the stars below:
a Monica Vitti
b Dean Martin (in a series)
c Greta Garbo
d James Mason
e Michael Caine (in a series)
f James Coburn (in a series)
g George Lazenby
h Robert Vaughan (in a series)
i Virginia McKenna
j Anna Neagle

11 Alfred Hitchcock was the master of the spy-chase film. It gave him the chance to create picaresque pursuits and menace in the most unexpected places. Name the films where there were murderous goings-on in
a A chocolate factory
b A small cinema
c A music hall
d The Albert Hall
e The United Nations building

12 In which of Hitchcock's movies would you find the following pairs:
a Bruce Dern and Karen Black?
b Paul Newman and Julie Andrews?
c John Forsythe and Dany Robin?
d John Forsythe and Shirley MacLaine?
e Leslie Banks and Edna Best?
f Robert Montgomery and Carole Lombard?
g John Gielgud and Madeleine Carroll?
h Joel McCrea and Laraine Day?
i Henry Kendall and Joan Barry?
j Gregory Peck and Alida Valli?

13 The monster gorilla, unrequited lover and martyred pet, KING KONG (1933), has become absorbed into American myth and the film is still considered, fifty years on, to be the best of Hollywood's adventure-fantasies. How much of a Kong buff are you? To find out, test yourself on the following questions:
a What is the fade-out line of the movie and who speaks it?
b 'Scream, Ann, scream for your life!' In what circumstances is this said and who played Ann?
c Where was the great ape discovered and where did it meet its death?
d How high was the actual model for the ape and who led the special effects team? How high was it in the 1976 remake?
e Oscar Levant said that the 1933 film 'should have been advertised as a concert of ———'s music with accompanying pictures on the screen'. Whose music was he referring to? Who wrote the score of the remake?
f Jessica Lange played the role of Dwan in her screen debut in the 1976 version. True or false?
g What duo directed the original movie and in which scene do they appear?
h In the 60s, there was a popular badge that read 'King Kong ———'. Complete the phrase
i What prolific British crime story writer contributed the script but died during the shooting of KING Kong (1933)?
j Complete the titles of three follow-up movies: SON OF———, KING KONG VS———, MIGHTY ———. Which British film of the mid-60s used scenes from KING KONG to comment on the hero's psyche?

Name the film from which this still comes. What is the name of the actress and of the sinister character she plays? What particular weapon did she use in the film? Who was the actress married to in real life?

---

14 The desert is not only about the thirst for water, it is also a setting that satisfies the thirst for romance. Shapely, exotic queens of the sand dunes, Maria Montez and Yvonne de Carlo (née Peggy Middleton) made a series of 'tits and sand' adventures for Universal Pictures in the 40s and 50s. Sort out the Montez titles from the de Carlo ones, giving the ladies four each. Who were the female stars of the remaining two?
a ARABIAN NIGHTS
b ALI BABA AND THE FORTY THIEVES
c THE DESERT HAWK
d VEILS OF BAGDAD
e SLAVE GIRL
f SUDAN
g FLAME OF ARABY
h SONG OF SCHEHERAZADE
i WHITE SAVAGE
j CASBAH

15 Who were
a S·P·Y·S?
b THE SPY WHO CAME IN FROM THE COLD?
c THE SPY WITH A COLD NOSE?
d THE SPY WHO LOVED ME?
e THE SPY IN BLACK?

16 Robin Hood, the legendary outlaw, has been the subject of many colourful adventure pictures. Match the following Robin Hoods of the screen to the titles of the films they appeared in, and say which was actually shot in Sherwood Forest:
A Richard Todd
B Douglas Fairbanks
C Sean Connery
D Errol Flynn
E Don Taylor

a THE ADVENTURES OF ROBIN HOOD
b MEN OF SHERWOOD FOREST
c ROBIN HOOD
d ROBIN AND MARIAN
e THE STORY OF ROBIN HOOD AND HIS MERRIE MEN

17 Still in Sherwood Forest, answer the following:
a Which character actor played Little John in three films? Name the films
b Who played the son of Robin Hood in BANDIT OF SHERWOOD FOREST and ROGUES OF SHERWOOD FOREST?
c What was curious about the role that June Laverick played in SON OF ROBIN HOOD?
d Name the Robin Hood spoof featuring Frank Sinatra's 'rat pack'? Where was it set?
e In which film did John Cleese appear as Robin Hood?

18 There is a *world* of adventure in the following films. Can you unearth the titles from the information given and identify the performers of roles in italics?
a Pat Boone sang 'My Love Is Like A Red Red Rose' before going on an expedition with Gertrude the goose and *a Scottish professor*
b It was originally shown in Sensurround
c Only *three people* are left alive after a nuclear war
d Kirk Douglas and Yul Brynner fight over the possession of an island and *a beautiful shipwreck* victim
e It was the third of a great Bengali trilogy – directed by whom?
f The long journey took approximately two-and-three-quarter months
g A pastoral visual tone poem dedicated to the foundation of a collective farm in the Ukraine
h *He* was a captain of a seal schooner and *she* was a Russian countess. Anthony Quinn was a seal poacher
i David McCallum and other scientists go underwater to test tidal waves. *One woman* comes along on the trip
j *Time* magazine commented, 'Literally, the picture is a mad chow mein of Chinese laundry English. Dramatically, it is just one long touristic stagger through the better bars and restaurants of Hong Kong. *He* looks more like an ageing bellboy than an artist, *she* seems more Piccadilly than Wanchai'

19 In each question below, one star did all the things described, in various films. Identify the performer in each case, and name the films:

a Who searched for El Dorado in the Andes; tried to bring opera to primitive tribes of the Amazon; stabbed his mistress to death?

b Who met Audrey Hepburn in the Congo; brought Elizabeth Taylor to his Ceylon tea plantation; played Lord Nelson?

c Who played Lady Hamilton, Queen Elizabeth and Charlotte Corday?

d Who drove bootleg beer from Georgia to Texas; dived for sunken treasure while being disturbed by sharks; spent a horrific weekend canoeing in the Appalachians?

e Who spent a horrific weekend canoeing in the Appalachians; tracked down a Nazi war criminal; taught black children on an island off South Carolina?

Name the director and the title of this popular adventure movie. Who is the actor on the right? What is the character's name and profession? When and where was the film set?

20 The sun never set on the British Empire during the golden days of Hollywood. Answer the following questions:

a Who played the title role in a 1939 adventure set in India and based on a famous narrative poem? Who wrote the poem and which stars were the three British army sergeants?

b Christopher Plummer played Rudyard Kipling in a film based on a Kipling novel. What was it and who were the other two male stars?

c A British Imperialistic epic from a novel about heroism and cowardice has been filmed a number of times. What was it called? What was the title of the 1955 version? Who directed the 1939 and 1955 versions? Who was the star of the 1977 interpretation?

d Douglas Fairbanks Jr and Basil Rathbone were stiff-upper-lip soldiers fighting for king and country in Africa in a film whose title referred to the British Empire. What was it called and who was the woman in it?

e Gary Cooper and Franchot Tone were two soldiers in India in a film based on a novel by Major Francis Yeats-Brown. What was it and who played the callow third soldier?

21 Adventure films have profited from the era when knights were bold, and ladies fair:

a What role do the following actors have in common and name the films in which they played it.
   i) Robert Taylor ii) Cornel Wilde iii) Franco Nero iv) Luc Simon?

b Robert Taylor played the title role in two costume dramas based on novels by Sir Walter Scott. What were their titles, and name the damsels in distress in both films?

c What role did Nicol Williamson play in EXCALIBUR, and who directed it?

d Which cartoon features were based on the writings of i) T. H. White ii) J. R. Tolkien?

e Which satire set in the Middle Ages had a title derived from a Lewis Carroll poem?

One of the most dashing of Hollywood's swashbuckling heroes in his first success. Who is he? What was the film? What studio produced it? Was it in black and white or Technicolor? Who is the fat man on the far left?

---

22 In which films did

a Kirk Douglas play a bearded, peg-legged pirate?

b Jean Peters play a swaggering lady pirate?

c Tommy Lee Jones as Captain 'Bully' Hayes set out to find a kidnapped girl?

d Donald O'Connor as a shop assistant find himself arrested for piracy?

e Peter Ustinov return to earth to stop his descendants' home being taken over by racketeers?

23 Who played the colourful pirates below?
a THE CRIMSON PIRATE
b THE SCARLET BUCCANEER
c YELLOWBEARD
d BLACKBEARD THE PIRATE
e THE BLACK PIRATE

24 'I never saw the original picture. I liked the script and the story. I liked the set-up and I'd never been to that part of Africa – so I just did it.' What veteran director said this and of what film was he speaking? What was 'the original picture'? To what part of Africa was he referring? Who was the director of the earlier version and who played the male lead, the floozie and the married lady? Who was the male star of the remake? Both his female co-stars were nominated for different Oscars. Who were they, and who was nominated for which?

This still comes from the climax of a classic spy thriller. Name the film and its director. Where does most of the action take place? Name the actor in the hat. Who were the romantic leads and who played them in the 1979 remake? Who played the title role in each version?

25 Pick your way through the jungle of questions that follow:
a What cliché phrase would you expect Denny Miller, Mike Henry, Elmo Lincoln and Miles O'Keefe to utter on introducing themselves to their female companion? Who would the last-named say it to?
b In which 'Tarzan' film is the name Tarzan never mentioned?
c Who played the title roles in each case in THE AFRICAN QUEEN, SHE (1965), WHITE WITCHDOCTOR, THE JUNGLE PRINCESS?
d What role did Johnny Weissmuller play from 1948–1955, and who did Johnny Sheffield play from 1949–1955?
e Gregory Peck starred in two movies based on Ernest Hemingway's African stories. What were they?

26 In which swashbuckling costume dramas did
a Keith Carradine duel with Harvey Keitel?
b Stewart Granger duel with Mel Ferrer?
c Robert Wagner fight James Mason?
d Tony Curtis confront David Farrar?
e Danny Kaye cross swords with Basil Rathbone?

Reach for the Stars

A His real name was Roy Fitzgerald, and he was born in Winnetka, Illinois in 1925. Discovered by the same man who discovered Tab Hunter, Robert Wagner and John Saxon (among others), he ditched his job as a postman for a career in Hollywood. After a one-line part in a Raoul Walsh film at Warner Bros. he moved to Universal where, after a string of B features established him as the best-looking man on the lot, he entered the kingdom of stars in a glossy remake of a Lloyd C. Douglas weepie:

a Who is he?
b He was nominated for an Oscar in James Dean's last film. What was it?
c Who was the buttercup blonde crooner with whom he made three comedies?
d In the 1970s he starred in a popular TV series. What was it called?
e In 1978 he appeared in a disaster movie. What was it called?

B Scenic designer, distinguished actor and, more recently, a successful writer, he signed a movie contract after returning from World War II service and fast became the male equivalent of a Rank starlet. But he soon proved his versatility and in 1960 was given his most complex role to date, that of a homosexual. He has since worked for such eminent directors as Joseph Losey, Luchino Visconti and John Schlesinger:

a Who is he?
b Give the titles of his two beautifully written volumes of autobiography
c In what film did he play a decadent valet, and who starred as his master?
d One of his best roles was in a film version of a Thomas Mann novel. What film?
e Who was his female co-star in DARLING, and who directed it?

C After being expelled from several Catholic schools in France, he became a butcher's apprentice, a parachutist in Indo-China and a porter at Les Halles in Paris. His extraordinary good looks, however, led to a 1957 move debut (the picture was called QUAND LA FEMME S'EN MELE), after which he became France's newest heart-throb. Directors such as Clement, Visconti and Antonioni sought his services, but his matinée-idol image made it difficult for him to be accepted as anything other than a pin-up boy. In 1968 he and his former wife became the key figures in a murder scandal:

a Who is he?
b Which of his films was based on a book by Patricia Highsmith?
c Terence Rattigan wrote the script of a 1964 film he was in. What was it called?
d What were the films he made for Visconti?
e In which film based on the work of a celebrated 19th-century French writer did he play a middle aged roué. Who were his male and female co-stars?

D One of the most versatile of British character actors, he made both his film and stage debuts in 1934. But it wasn't until 1946, in the classic David Lean screen version of **GREAT EXPECTATIONS**, that his film career could honestly be described as being launched. His very best work was done during the 40s and 50s, particularly in the field of comedy. His many screen portrayals include Charles I, Marley's Ghost, Hitler and Pope Innocent III.

a Who is he?
b In what film did he invent a wonder cloth renowned for its durability?
c In what Arnold Bennett novel did he play the titular hero?
d What was the 1959 Ealing film he co-produced and in which he played a dual role?
e In what film did he appear opposite Rosalind Russell? And what did he play in it?

E Few Hollywood stars of the 30s had her glamour, her sophistication and her wit (as well as her reputation for foul language). Specialising in whacky screwball comedies directed by such experts in the genre as Gregory La Cava, William Wellman and Ernst Lubitsch, it was her work in a Howard Hawks comedy in 1934, in which she starred opposite John Barrymore, that really established her as a comedienne to watch. Her life, and second marriage to one of Hollywood's superstars, ended tragically when, in 1942, she was killed in a plane crash:

a Who is she?
b Who was her second husband?
c Which 1976 flop brought her life story to the screen, and who had the two leading roles?

d In what film did she star with her first husband and who was he?
e What was her real name?

F She was Theodosia Goodman from Cincinnati, but William Fox decided that she had been born 'in the shadow of the Sphinx'. The film which made her famous was inspired by a Kipling poem, and helped to coin a new word in the English language. By 1926 she was burlesquing herself, with Oliver Hardy, in a short directed by Stan Laurel and Richard Wallace. She married the director Charles Brabin:

a Who is she?
b Why was there such a fuss when she made KATHLEEN MAVOURNEEN (1919)?
c In 1932 she came third in a poll to find the greatest all-time female star. Who were first and second?
d On which Victor Hugo novel was her DARLING OF PARIS (1917) based?
e Her most famous film is also the only one that survives intact. What is it called and what, in it, did she order the dying Ed José to do?

G Born in 1949 in Syracuse, New York, his well-developed torso, which his most recent spate of films has exhibited without inhibition, is almost as well-known as his face. One of his latest forays was into Graham Greene territory, as well as a remake of a Jean-Luc Godard success, neither film being as good as its inspirational source. Very much an actor in the contemporary 'macho' mould, he also scored a personal success on Broadway recently, playing a gay concentration camp victim in Martin Sherman's play 'Bent'.

a Who is he?
b In what film did he make his debut?
c He appeared in a film whose leading character was a teacher of deaf children. What was it called? Who was the teacher?
d Lauren Hutton co-starred with him in which film? What did he play in it?
e Who directed his first British film, and what was it called?

H Born Ruby Stevens in 1907, she was to become one of Hollywood's greatest and most durable stars. Though nominated four times for an Oscar, she never won, but was given every other professional accolade and won ever major TV award in later years. Emotional dramas, comedies and westerns comprised her main film fare, while for one of her greatest *femme fatale* portrayals she wore a blonde wig.

a Who is she?
b The bewigged role is probably her most famous

– what was the film, who directed it and who were the two male stars?
c HIS BROTHER'S WIFE was the first of three films she made with the man she was to marry in 1939. Who was he, and what were the other two films?
d She appeared in a murder mystery based on a book by stripper Gypsy Rose Lee. What was the film, who directed it, and what was the name of the song she sang?
e When finally given an honorary Oscar, she paid tribute to an actor who had his first break opposite her in a 1939 boxing film and who had sent her roses every year in appreciation for her help. Name the film, and the actor?

I She was born in Paris in 1943, and made her screen debut at the early age of thirteen, changing her surname to her mother's maiden name. A ravishing beauty, described by Time Magazine as 'eerily evocative of a warmer Grace Kelly', she enjoyed a liberated private life, having borne children to a well-known French director and a famous Italian screen actor, although she was married to neither of them. She married British photographer David Bailey, a liaison which ended in divorce. The film which first brought her general recognition contained no spoken dialogue:

a Who is she?
b She made two films for Buñuel. Name them
c Name the fathers of her children referred to above
d In what film was she directed by Polanski?
e What was the name of her actress sister, and what became of the latter?

J His parents were both mutes and he ended his own life speechless. After years as a stock player, he became a star playing a bogus contortionist. Two of his later roles gave him magnificent views of Paris and an interesting tour of its sewers. Intensely private, he claimed that he 'ceased to exist' between films. His entry in The Encyclopedia Britannica was for many years the standard work on make-up:

a Who is he?
b To which MGM star did he offer the advice, 'Mystery has served me well – it could do the same for you'?
c Jackie Coogan thought he was 'a miserable old bastard'. In which film did they co-star and what roles did they play?
d What was so novel about the knifethrower he played in THE UNKNOWN (1927) and who was his human target?
e Which actor impersonated him in a 1957 biopic and what was it called?

Out of This World

Ever since George Méliès's A TRIP TO THE MOON in 1982, the cinema has been invading space. Science has almost caught up with fiction and, in some cases, surpassed it, but the flow of Sci-Fi pictures has not stopped.

1   Destruction on a mass scale, or at the very least the threat of it, lies at the heart of the science fiction tradition. In the following films which cities were terrorized or laid waste by
a A nuclear strike in PANIC IN YEAR ZERO?
b An oversize ape in KONGA?
c A wandering warhead in THE LOST MISSILE?
d An Ymir in 20 MILLION MILES TO EARTH?
e THE BEAST FROM 20,000 FATHOMS?

This is a scene from a popular sci-fi series of five movies. Name all five films. From which does this still come? Who played the two humans pictured and who is the actress behind the make-up in the centre? What was the job of the character in the loin cloth before finding himself in this predicament? What revelation ends the film?

2   H. G. Wells is one of the fathers of science fiction, and his works have frequently been adapted for the screen:
a Who directed THINGS TO COME (aka THE SHAPE OF THINGS TO COME) and who played The Boss in that film? THINGS TO COME established a notable first – what was it?
b Who appeared as the God of Indifference in THE MAN WHO COULD WORK MIRACLES?
c Who played Dr Moreau in the 1977 version of THE ISLAND OF DR MOREAU? What was the title of the 1933 screen adaptation of the story, and who played Moreau then?
d Who was the enterprising exploitation producer who turned Wells' 'Food of The Gods' into a low-budget feature? What effect did the food have?
e In which film did Wells appear as a character and who played him? Which famous criminal was he hunting down in the film?

3   Space travel can take a number of unconventional forms:
a How did the inhabitants of the Duchy of Grand Fenwick power their rocket in MOUSE ON THE MOON?
b How was the rocket launched in WHEN WORLDS COLLIDE?
c What was the means of propulsion in LE VOYAGE DANS LA LUNE (1902)?
d What got Lionel Jeffries and his companions to the Moon in FIRST MEN IN THE MOON?
e How did the aliens arrive on Earth in THEY CAME FROM BEYOND SPACE?

Name the characters from left to right, the actors who played them and the three films in which they appeared together. Who was the villain of the piece in all three films? Which outsize actor filled his forbidding costume, and which other actor provided his equally menacing voice? The character on the extreme left has a mentor in the Merlin mould – what was his name and who played him?

ESS·6
PROD 50

4 Flash Gordon, space hero and king of the serials, was played by Buster Crabbe three times – in 1936, 1938 and 1940 – but do you know:

a On whose comic strip the Flash Gordon adventures were based?

b Who was Flash's power-crazed enemy in all three serials? Who played him, and his voluptuous daughter Princess Aura?

c Who were Flash's three companions in FLASH GORDON'S TRIP TO MARS and who played them?

d What other futuristic hero of the comic strips did Buster Crabbe play in 1939?

e FLASH GORDON was remade in 1980. Who was Crabbe's successor in the role and who, this time, portrayed his arch enemy?

5 Robots, androids and often machine 'people' are the most durable of science fiction stand-bys. In which films do the following non-humans appear?

a C3P0

b The Gunslinger

c Colonel Saunders

d Hal 9000

e Megalon

This still comes from the 1956 film version of a futuristic novel. Give its title, the novel's author and the year it was written. Who directed the film and who were the American stars of this British production? In what way does the film's ending differ from that of the book? (The still offers a clue.)

6 What unthinkable terror menaced everything we hold dear in

a FLASH GORDON CONQUERS THE UNIVERSE?

b NO BLADE OF GRASS?

c FIEND WITHOUT A FACE?

d THE GIANT CLAW?

e THE FORBIN PROJECT?

7 What do the following films all have in common?

a FIVE

b ON THE BEACH

c THE OMEGA MAN

d THE WORLD, THE FLESH AND THE DEVIL

e DAMNATION ALLEY

142

8 Close encounters with our alien friends have provided a mixture of laughs and terror. Who played the following unearthly ones and in what films:
a The Stranger?
b Mr Johnson?
c Nyah?
d Barbarella?
e Mr Spock?

9 An alien's mission can take many forms:
a In which film does a famous disc jockey become the target of a robot army? Who was he and in what other feature film did he play a prominent part?
b What were the alien visitors after in LIQUID SKY?
c In which film did a space creature hitch a ride on the wing of a jet airliner?
d What startling fact did Peter Graves discover when he made contact with the Martians in RED PLANET MARS?
e What vital resource was David Bowie seeking in THE MAN WHO FELL TO EARTH?

10 Complete the following titles:
a DR GOLDFOOT AND ...
b SANTA CLAUS ...
c CAT-WOMEN ...
d GAS-S-S-S OR ...
e ROBINSON CRUSOE ...

11 Scientists, inevitably of the mad variety, have striven for the secrets of invisibility, usually with distressing results for all concerned:
a Who made his first film appearance (or disappearance!) as THE INVISIBLE MAN (1933)?
b In the same film, which actor, playing what character, uttered the immortal lines, 'E's invisible, that's what's the matter with him'?
c How did the Invisible Man finally betray himself to the pursuing police?
d THE INVISIBLE MAN returned in 1940. Who played him on this occasion, and why did he seek the cloak of invisibility?
e Who was THE INVISIBLE AGENT in 1942 and into whose arms did he finally materialise?
f Who kept a transparent Alsatian as a pet in THE INVISIBLE MAN'S REVENGE?
g Who manufactured THE INVISIBLE WOMAN?
h Who was Richard Eyer's non-human co-star in THE INVISIBLE BOY?
i In which film does an irradiated Boris Karloff melt a statue of one of the Deadly Sins after each of his murders?
j How did the INVISIBLE INVADERS plan to take over the earth?

12 The watchword of all science fiction films is 'Destroy All Monsters' – and as spectacularly as the budget will allow. What methods were used to dispose of the menace in the following films? One of these efforts was completely unsuccessful; do you know which one?
a THE BLOB
b THE MAGNETIC MONSTER
c IT (US: RETURN OF THE GOLEM)
d X THE UNKNOWN
e THE DAY OF THE TRIFFIDS

13 Possession by an alien intelligence is one of the enduring themes of science fiction:
a What tell-tale detail betrayed the human zombies to little Jimmy Hunt in INVADERS FROM MARS? Among those taken over by the aliens were his Mom and Dad – who played them? What form did the Martian leader take?
b INVASION OF THE BODY SNATCHERS, filmed in 1955, has become a minor classic. Who directed it and who were its stars? How did the alien intelligence take over its human victims? How does the original cut of the film end? Who were the male and female leads in the 1978 remake? How did the settings of the two films differ? Who, with a connection to the first version, played cameo roles in the remake?
c Who woke up to find that she had MARRIED A MONSTER FROM OUTER SPACE?
d IT CAME FROM OUTER SPACE, in Jack Arnold's 1953 chiller, but where did it land?
e Who played the surviving member of the spaceship crew in ALIEN?

14 Many a budding star, early in their careers, made an appearance in a low-budget science fiction quickie. So have well-known performers who have known better days. Who played
a A young hot rodder in THE BLOB?
b Machine gun Joe Viterbo in DEATH RACE 2000?
c A fighter pilot in TARANTULA?
d An anthropologist who discovers a missing link in TROG?
e A vampire from beyond the stars in PLAN 9 FROM OUTER SPACE?
f THE ATOMIC KID in the film of the same name?
g A woman searching for her child who has made contact with an alien in THE WATCHER IN THE WOODS?
h A singing cowboy who finds a lost civilization in THE PHANTOM EMPIRE?
i A sinister scientist with a white streak in his hair in THE RETURN OF DR X?
j A masochistic dental patient in THE LITTLE SHOP OF HORRORS?

22 Which films do the following plot-lines describe?

a UFOs appear to various people around the globe. They become obsessed with a pyramid shape that they don't understand, until they are drawn to a mountain in Wyoming

b A woman is attacked and raped by an invisible manifestation. Scientists manage to freeze it with liquid helium, thus defining its shape. But it takes control of the equipment and escapes to do more damage

c In five different locations on Earth an alien presents an ordinary human being with a box of capsules. Each box, which can only be opened by the telepathic command of the recipient, is capable of completely wiping out human life on a continent. The exercise turns out to be a test of our maturity, which we just manage to pass

d As a result of simultaneous test explosions of Russian and American nuclear devices, the Earth is thrown out of its orbit towards the Sun. The great powers unite to explode four more devices to push us back into our correct orbit. The closing shot is of two alternative news headlines – 'Earth Saved' and 'Earth Doomed'

e In the year 2274 a life of unending pleasure is somewhat mitigated by extinction at the age of 30. One of the 'sandmen', who are responsible for carrying out this unpleasant task, decides to investigate the world outside the pleasure dome

23 In the 50s, giant insect invasions were all the rage. The theme was taken up again in the 70s. What monstrous mutations went on the rampage in

a THEM!?

b THE MONSTER FROM GREEN HELL?

c THE BEGINNING OF THE END?

d THE MONSTER THAT CHALLENGED THE WORLD?

e THE SWARM?

24 The Saturday-morning serials boasted a small army of power-crazed scientists, each one bent on world domination:

a In which serial did Dr Vulcan invent the deadly Decimator?

b In keeping with the tiny budgets of the serials, the Decimator looked suspiciously like The Cyclotrode from an earlier epic, THE CRIMSON GHOST. Which stalwarts of the serials were the stars of THE CRIMSON GHOST?

c Who played Superman in the 1948 serial of the same name, and in the 1950 sequel, ATOM MAN VERSUS SUPERMAN?

d From which planet did the menacing Roy Barcroft travel in THE PURPLE MONSTER STRIKES?

e How did Eduardo Ciannelli plan to take over the world in THE MYSTERIOUS DR SATAN?

25 Distant planets have played a part in many a space opera. In what films do the following appear?

a Altair 4

b Terra Eleven

c Davanna

d Metaluna

e Mongo

26 Now, a final journey through space:

a Which film about a kinky TV cable outfit had characters called Bianca O'Blivian and Brian O'Blivian and what female pop singer had a role in it?

b What was the mission of the spaceship in DARK STAR and how did it come to an abrupt end?

c What was the mission of the DEVIL GIRL FROM MARS?

d What was unique about the tentacled monster created by Ray Harryhausen for IT CAME FROM BENEATH THE SEA?

e Charlton Heston starred in a film which showed New York beset by pollution, overcrowding, and synthetic food. No – not today, but in the year 2022. What was the film's title?

f Who played the title role in THX-1138, and who made his directorial debut with this film?

g How many astronauts were done away with by the spaceship's computer in 2001: A SPACE ODYSSEY?

h In what Russian film did astronauts discover a planet covered by a living, intelligent sea?

i Which classic of the genre ends with the words 'Keep watching the skies!'?

Name the film in which this scene is taking place and its location. Who is the worried character on the phone, to whom is he speaking and why? Who is the actor and what other two roles did he play in the film? Who is the stout actor in the Homburg and what character is he playing? Name the actors who played Colonel 'Bat' Guano and General Jack D. Ripper. What was the song that closed the film and who sang it?

Silence is Golden

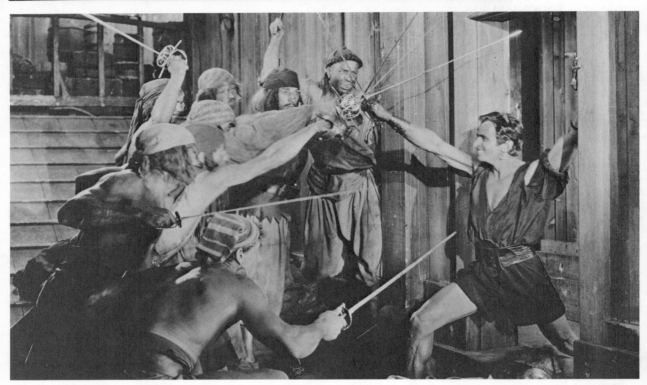

ABOVE LEFT
The most famous swashbuckler of them all was Douglas Fairbanks Sr, seen here in a 1926 film which he also produced and scripted, along with others of his movies, for a particular Hollywood film company. What was the company and his relationship to it? And can you identify this film and say why its technique makes it of special historical interest?

LEFT
American football is a brutally tough sport, yet it has often been used as a source of comedy on the screen. Can you name the comedy picture from each of these stars which featured a football sequence:
a Harold Lloyd (illustrated here)?
b The Marx Brothers?
c Warren Beatty?
d Elliott Gould and Donald Sutherland?
e Burt Reynolds and Kris Kristofferson?

ABOVE
The Christmas spirit in sunny California!This delightful silent short, entitled BIG BUSINESS, could just as easily be called 'Tit For Tat'. What is the business and who are the actors pictured? Who is doing what to whom – are they
a chopping down the tree?
b building the house?
c chopping firewood?
d destroying the house?
e having a free-for-all?
This scene illustrates the theme of the picture, but one important inanimate object is missing. What is it? The scriptwriter and cameraman both went on to become famous, Oscar-winning directors. Who were they?

149

ABOVE

A dramatic still from QUEEN KELLY, but how did she become a 'queen' and what was she before? Can you name the two ladies pictured here? The one on the left became a Hollywood screen-writer during her later years. Here she is attacking the star with a whip – what did the latter do to deserve such treatment? Who was the wealthy, politically connected executive producer from a well-known Boston family who financed the picture? In which of the star's films many years later did she view herself in QUEEN KELLY on a home movie screen?

RIGHT

MGM was formed in 1924 and had three smash hits during 1925 and early 1926. The first was the silent version of THE MERRY WIDOW, a scene from which is pictured here. Name the two stars illustrated. One of Hollywood's most famous stars made one of his first screen appearances as an extra in this film – do you know who he was? MGM produced remakes of THE MERRY WIDOW in 1934 and 1952. Who were the stars, and who the director in each case? Which Hitchcock villain is haunted by the music of 'The Merry Widow Waltz'?

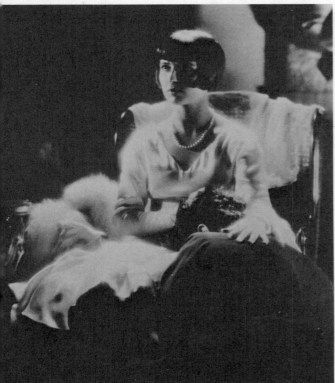

ABOVE

Answer the following statements, True or False:

a This picture shows Rudolph Valentino with Vilma Banky in THE SHEIK

b Valentino was born in Naples, Italy

c Valentino's real name was Rodolfo Alfonso Raffaelo Pierre Philibert Guglielmi di Valentina d'Antonguolla

d Valentino made his living as a nightclub taxi dancer for a time before he broke into pictures

e Valentino's first big hit movie was THE FOUR HORSEMEN OF THE APOCALYPSE

f Valentino was 25 years old when he died

LEFT

It's well-known that many European performers became famous Hollywood stars, but certain Americans first achieved stardom in Europe. Here is a uniquely individual actress who was chosen as the 'eternal woman' by the German director G. W. Pabst. Can you identify her, and name the two classic silent pictures they made together? In what artistic field did she start her professional career and for which notable impresarios? In which American film, directed by William Wellman, did she dress as a boy and ride the freight trains?

BELOW
Here is Erich von Stroheim being throttled by the jealous husband of a lady he has tried to seduce, in a film he also directed. What was the film? Who is Von Stroheim's co-star pictured here? Can you name the other silent films Von Stroheim directed in which he also starred?

ABOVE
There are three well-known Hollywood versions of Somerset Maugham's play 'Rain', only one of which is actually called by its original title. Here, the star (and, indeed, the producer) of the silent version flirts with her director and co-star. Can you name both of them and give the title of this version? Name the two later versions, and the famous female star in each case.

LEFT
Can you name this film in which Charlie Chaplin essays his familiar tramp? Although best known for this portrayal, Chaplin in later years played a variety of other roles. Do you know in which films he was
a a wife murderer?
b a Jewish barber?
c The King of Estrovia?
What was the first picture he made for United Artists, the then new company of which he was a founder?

RIGHT
This film was a famous landmark in German Expressionism. What is the title, and who directed it? The young actor is best remembered for his performances in THE THIEF OF BAGDAD (1940) and CASABLANCA. Can you name him, and the character he plays here, and say what he is doing in this scene? The title was used again for a 1962 American picture starring Glynis Johns and Dan O'Herlihy. What, other than the title, did it have in common with the silent?

BELOW
Here is young Vladimir Roudenko in the famous silent NAPOLEON. The director also appeared in the film. Who was he and what role did he play? Which influential French theatrical figure played Marat? What wide-screen technique, referred to as Polyvision at the time, did the film anticipate by thirty years or so?

ABOVE RIGHT
If you can fill in the missing words in these well-known fantasy and science-fiction film titles, the first letters will spell out the title of the classic silent film illustrated here. Who directed it?
a ... JOE YOUNG
b ... vs THE FLYING SAUCERS
c ... TO COME
d ... OF THE CREATURE
e ... THE BEACH
f ... IN YEAR ZERO
g ... MILLION YEARS BC
h ... HORIZON
i ... CAME FROM OUTER SPACE
j ... WARS

RIGHT (opposite)
They don't make them like this anymore! This is a famous image from a 1916 epic employing thousands of extras and some of the most impressive sets ever seen in bringing ancient Babylon to life on the screen. Name the film and its director. What was unusual about the film's plot structure? Which country was the first to make lavish historical epics set in ancient times, and what was the first notable example to emerge?

Crime & Punishment

The heyday of the crime film was the 1930s. Since then each decade has produced its classics, but in recent years it has become increasingly difficult to tell the good guys from the baddies!

1 Test your general knowledge of crime movies with the following questions:

a In which film did Miss Marple, Hercule Poirot, Nick and Nora Charles, Sam Spade and Charlie Chan appear together and who played them?

b Who was the original creator of Miss Marple and which British actress made her famous?

c How were Alan Ladd, Humphrey Bogart and Veronica Lake all able to appear in a movie together in 1982, some years after their deaths?

d Who played the title role in THE THIN MAN in 1934? Who later became famous as The Thin Man, what was that character's real name, and who played his wife in the series?

e Who played the title roles in GODFATHER I and GODFATHER 2, and how many times was the word 'mafia' uttered in these movies?

f Name the three versions (1931, 1936 and 1941) of the movie, based on a famous crime novel, for which the headline 'Spade Digs Up Bird' would be appropriate.

g She had hot coffee thrown in her face by Lee Marvin because she befriended detective Glenn Ford. Who was she?

h Joan Fontaine, Ingrid Bergman, Kim Novak, Janet Leigh, Grace Kelly and Tippi Hedren have something in common. What is it?

i Who was THE WOMAN IN THE WINDOW and who directed it?

j And who was THE PHANTOM LADY and her director?

2 From the following statements about CHINA-TOWN, select the true fact in each case:

A The leading male star was a) Burt Reynolds b) Elliott Gould c) Jack Nicholson

B He played a) a private eye b) a cop c) a gangster

C The setting of the movie was a) Los Angeles b) Philadelphia c) San Francisco

D The period was a) the 20s b) the 50s c) the 30s

E It was directed by a) Roman Polanski b) John Huston c) John Boorman

F The title of the movie is a) the first word spoken in it b) the last word c) it is never mentioned

G The female co-star was a) Ellen Burstyn b) Faye Dunaway c) Catherine Deneuve

3 The following short synopses are attached to wrong film titles and wrong stars. Make the corrections:

a THE BATTLE OF THE CENTURY tells of attorney Frank Galvin (John Belushi) who takes on a case of medical malpractice. Ed Concannon (Dan Aykroyd) is his opposite number in court. Both actors were nominated for Oscars in 1982.

b SILVER STREAK is set in a small Mississippi town where Virgil Tibbs (Richard Pryor), a black detective from Philadelphia, has to face the bigotry of local red-neck chief of police (Gene Wilder)

c FANNY follows the events that befall a New York cop, Popeye Doyle (Clint Eastwood) who goes to Marseilles determined to catch the narcotics king (Charles Boyer) who eluded him in America

d SCARED STIFF is about a mystery story writer (Dustin Hoffman) who invites his wife's lover (Jon Voight) down to his country estate where they play a series of deadly games

e POCKETFUL OF MIRACLES tells of a pickpocket (Ron Moody) who robs a girl (Barbra Streisand) who is being followed by the FBI as a communist agent. With the aid of an elderly informant (Lila Kedrova) they eventually help round up the gang

4 Name the crime movies which begin or end with the following words:

a 'I steal . . .'

b 'Geronimo, Mike!'

c 'You'll see it, just as I saw it. You'll meet the people, you'll find the clues. And maybe you'll solve it quick, and maybe you won't'

d 'Mother of Mercy, is this the end of Rico?'

e 'This picture is dedicated to all the beautiful women in the world who have shot their men full of holes out of pique . . .'

A pose from one of the outstanding films of the 1960s. What was its name, who are the stars pictured here, and who played the brother and sister-in-law? Can you also name the director, the pair of writers, and the man responsible for the notable photography?

5 Gene Hackman and John Travolta starred respectively in two notable thrillers that made particular use of the technological advances in recent years of sound recording, both heroes becoming obsessed with tape recordings that may be vital clues to crime. Can you name the films and their directors?

6 The following motley assortment have all either robbed or attempted to rob a bank in a movie. Name the appropriate movie:
a Dustin Hoffman
b Walter Matthau
c Woody Allen
d Bette Davis
e Al Pacino

7 The tragic story of a pimp and prostitute in modern Paris whose love for each other enables them to be manipulated by the police into informers formed the basis for a successful thriller that won the 1981 Césars (the French Oscars) for best film, best actor and best actress. What was the film, and who were the award-winning stars?

This famous film from Germany was the first sound film for its director, the first film for its star, later a noted Hollywood character actor, and a film which created a sensation with its daring subject matter. Name the film, the director, the star and the film's subject. Who directed the ill-advised Hollywood remake in 1950, and who played the lead in that version?

8 Con-men (and women) have cheated their way merrily through a string of films:
a Who played an elegantly crooked duo in TROUBLE IN PARADISE?
b Who took on Michael Sarrazin as an apprentice in fraud in THE FLIM FLAM MAN?
c In which classic Preston Sturges comedy did a couple of card sharps take Henry Fonda for a ride? Who were they and what was the title of the 1956 remake?
d What did ventriloquist W.C. Fields sell to a gullible barman in POPPY?
e What was the crafty con which was perpetrated by James Garner and Lou Gossett in THE SKIN GAME?

9 Amnesia has played an important part in crime films, adding a disquieting element of uncertainty to the atmosphere of mystery and suspense. From the synopses below, name the films, and identify the performers of the characters in italics:

a The new *doctor* at a lunatic asylum is actually an amnesiac who has assumed the identity of the real doctor. A *female doctor* at the asylum helps him regain his memory through psychoanalysis and reveals the murderer of the real doctor as the asylum's *director*

b During a blackout in a New York building, a *man* meets a *girl* who knows him, but he discovers he knows nothing of the past two years. With the aid of a *private detective* who is murdered, he discovers a sinister plot

c A *composer* in Victorian London fails to remember that when in a rage he hears discordant noises and commits murder. He strangles a *female victim* and places her body on a bonfire, but a friendly *psychologist* helps him understand his illness and he dies in a fire while playing his concerto on the piano

d An alcoholic *pianist-composer* learns that his estranged *wife* has been murdered. He forms an act with a *singer* whose husband has been accused of murder and helps her investigate the activities of a *nightclub owner* who is a chief suspect. It transpires, however, that the composer murdered his own wife and has blotted it from his mind

e An *ex-Marine* suffering from amnesia returns from the war with two letters the only clues to his identity. A *Police Lieutenant* tells him that the signatory of one of the letters was a murderer who disappeared on the same day that the amnesiac joined the marines. With the aid of a *nightclub singer* he uncovers his identity and reveals the true murderer as the singer's *boss*

10 Each of the following groups of films was made by the same director. Name the director of each group:

a CHRISTMAS HOLIDAY
THE SPIRAL STAIRCASE
THE DARK MIRROR
CRISS CROSS

b PICKUP ON SOUTH STREET
UNDERWORLD USA
THE NAKED KISS

c QUE LA BETE MEURE
LA FEMME INFIDELE
LE BOUCHER
VIOLETTE NOZIERE

d THE ANDERSON TAPES
THE OFFENCE
DOG DAY AFTERNOON
PRINCE OF THE CITY

e MY NAME IS JULIA ROSS
THE UNDERCOVER MAN
GUN CRAZY

11 Many of Hollywood's top stars have resorted to murder on the cinema screen – match the murders below to their victims and name the films in which the crimes took place:

A Ronald Colman
B Charles Laughton
C Faye Dunaway
D Robert Walker
E Alain Delon
F George Brent
G Humphrey Bogart
H Joan Crawford
I Rod Steiger
J Merle Oberon

a Rhonda Fleming
b Rose Hobart
c Rita Johnson
d Ruth White
e Shelley Winters
f Charles Korvin
g Richard Burton
h John Gielgud
i Laura Elliott
j Van Heflin

12 One of the most bizarre thrillers of all time was THREE STRANGERS, which centred on a legend surrounding a Chinese statuette, said to grant a mutual wish to three strangers at midnight on New Year's Eve. The attempt by three people to fulfil this prophecy leads to death and disaster . . . Who played the three strangers, who directed the film, and who conceived the original story?

13 Real-life criminals have frequently been depicted by the cinema. Match the criminals below to the stars who played them and name the films in which the portrayals occurred:

A The Boston Strangler
B Baby Face Nelson
C Jack the Ripper
D John Christie
E Gary Gilmore
F Dr Crippen
G Landru
H Robert Stroud
I Pretty Boy Floyd
J Caryl Chessman

a Burt Lancaster
b Richard Attenborough
c Tommy Lee Jones
d Tony Curtis
e John Carradine
f Fabian
g William Campbell
h Mickey Rooney
i Donald Pleasence
j Laird Cregar

14 'Johnny' has been a favourite gangster name-tag. Who played the following 'Johnnies'?
a Johnny Eager
b Johnny O'Clock
c Johnny Cool
d Johnny Stool-Pigeon
e JohnnyApollo

15 Crime of the more ambitious, expansive kind always needs a criminal mastermind to dream it all up:
a Who directed dastardly operations underneath a silver wig in MODESTY BLAISE?
b Which crime czar hid his face behind a layer of contoured rubber in THE FACE BEHIND THE MASK?
c Who played Wilkie Collins's Count Fosco in the 1948 Hollywood version of his classic novel 'The Woman In White'?
d Who organised THE ITALIAN JOB from inside one of Her Majesty's prisons?
e Where do we find Fritz Lang's evil genius Dr Mabuse at the beginning of THE TESTAMENT OF DR MABUSE?

The still shows a scene from a feature film from which a famous TV series originated. The leading character was drawn from the true-life memoirs of a US government agent. Name the film and the TV series, name the true-life character and identify the star, shown here, who played him.

16 Screen villains have frequently met their end by means of a spectacular fall. From the scenes described below, name the player who died and the film title:
a Exposed as a former Nazi hiding in a small town, he is impaled on part of a mechanical clock and falls from the clock tower
b Confessing to the man she loves that she had murdered his wife then had him framed, she boasts that he will never have proof, then plunges from a top floor window
c Although the man he has tried to kill tries to save him falling by clinging to his coat arm, the seams slowly come apart and he plummets from the top of the Statue of Liberty
d Finding an innocent girl in the boat he is using to escape the police, he manages to set her on a piece of land before the boat is swept over a waterfall, carrying him with it
e A beautiful murderess in Edwardian England, suddenly remembering an incriminating poison phial, rushes to retrieve it, fails to realise the lift is no longer waiting, and plunges down the shaft

17 Hoods and gunsels come in all shapes and sizes, from the silkily menacing to the deranged and incompetent:
a Who raised a thin-lipped giggle as he pushed an old lady downstairs in KISS OF DEATH?
b Who gave Elisha Cook Jr a poisoned drink in THE BIG SLEEP?
c Who played a pair of gay hitmen in THE BIG COMBO?
d Who begged to hit 'Baby' just one more time in THE GLASS KEY? Who was 'Baby'?
e Who gave Edmond O'Brien a brisk pistol whipping in D.O.A. and on whose orders?

18 Guardians of the law – official, licensed and self-appointed – have come in many combinations, but most often in pairs. Which films featured the following partnerships?
a Godfrey Cambridge and Raymond St Jacques
b Orson Welles and Joseph Calleia
c Alan Arkin and James Caan
d Don Taylor and Barry Fitzgerald
e Francis L. Sullivan, Griffith Jones, Hugh Sinclair and Frank Lawton

19 The following stars all featured in films with 'MURDER' in the title. Name the films:
a Margaret Rutherford, Robert Morley, Flora Robson
b Peter Sellers, Maggie Smith, David Niven
c Stuart Whitman, May Britt, Peter Falk
d Jack Oakie, Kitty Carlisle, Carl Brisson
e Vera Hruba Ralston, William Marshall, Ann Rutherford

A meek clerk confronts the notorious gangster who is his double in a comedy-thriller of the 30s directed by a man more usually associated with the western. Who is the dual personality pictured, who played the clerk's girlfriend who pretended to be his moll, what was the film and who directed it?

---

20 Stuck for a storyline? Get your characters to organise a heist:

a How did Clint Eastwood open a bank vault in THUNDERBOLT AND LIGHTFOOT?

b FIVE AGAINST THE HOUSE was one of the best caper movies of the 50s. What was the House?

c In which polished comedy-thriller of the 60s does a group of crooks set out to steal a jewel-encrusted dagger from a museum in Istanbul? They look like getting away with it until an unforeseen twist of fate gives them away. What was it? In prison they are already planning their next job. What was it?

d Heists have a habit of going wrong, but in which film do Robert Redford's plans to secure the 'Sahara Stone' fall apart on three separate occasions before he makes off with the prize?

21 With due deference to his predecessors and successors, Sherlock Holmes remains the *nonpareil* of detectives, a fascinating combination of high definition and elusiveness:

a Who played Holmes in THE SPECKLED BAND, THE SCARLET CLAW and THE PRIVATE LIFE OF SHERLOCK HOLMES? Who was disastrously miscast as Holmes's remarkable brother Mycroft in the last film?

b In which film does Holmes say, 'Elementary, my dear Freud'? Who played Holmes and Freud and what had brought the detective and the doctor together?

c Which British character actor played both Sherlock Holmes and Dr Watson in two Hollywood films of the 30s?

d The sage of Baker Street has never lacked opponents worthy of his mettle. Who played Professor Moriarty in SHERLOCK HOLMES AND THE SECRET WEAPON, the 'Spider Woman' in SHERLOCK HOLMES AND THE SPIDER WOMAN and the 'Creeper' in THE PEARL OF DEATH?

e Who imagined that he was Sherlock Holmes in THEY MIGHT BE GIANTS?

161

22 Famous screen villains sometimes played the goodie. In which of his two films below was each actor the goodie?

a Edward G. Robinson in i) THE AMAZING DR CLITTERHOUSE ii) KEY LARGO
b James Cagney in i) EACH DAWN I DIE ii) JOHNNY COME LATELY
c John Garfield in i) DUST BY MY DESTINY b) OUT OF THE FOG
d Richard Widmark in i) PICKUP ON SOUTH STREET ii) PANIC IN THE STREETS
e George Raft in i) MANPOWER ii) SOME LIKE IT HOT

23 Several well-known gangsters and detectives of crime mythology have enjoyed a number of screen incarnations by different actors. Who played
a Philip Marlowe in MARLOWE?
b Charlie Chan in CHARLIE CHAN ON BROADWAY?
c Hercule Poirot in EVIL UNDER THE SUN?
d Al Capone in THE ST VALENTINE'S DAY MASSACRE?
e The Saint in THE SAINT IN NEW YORK?
f Mike Hammer in THE GIRL HUNTERS
g Dillinger in YOUNG DILLINGER?
h Philo Vance in THE CANARY MURDER CASE?
i The Falcon in THE FALCON IN HOLLY-WOOD?
j Bonnie and Clyde in THE BONNIE PARKER STORY?

24 Crime is far too serious a matter to be left entirely to the criminals, and from time to time the humourists have moved in, with varying degrees of success:
a In which Warners film of the 30s is mobster Edward G. Robinson left for dead, then taken in and adopted by a community of monks?
b Name each of THE LADYKILLERS, and their intended victim. What was the cover they used to disguise their meetings to plan a wages snatch?
c Who sent himself up as Spats Columbo in SOME LIKE IT HOT? How did he meet his untimely end?
d Which Launder and Gilliat comedy included a sequence spoofing RIFIFI?
e Who played the white-suited, wildly incompetent Mafia boss, Carmine Ganucci, in EVERY LITTLE CROOK AND NANNY?

This unusual thriller was made by one of the cinema's great directors, who attempted to break new ground in the methods he used in filming. What is the film, who was the director and what was the method in question? The actor at the centre is James Stewart, but can you name the actors either side of him? The characters they are playing were based on real-life characters whose story was also told in a later film – who were the characters, what was the later film, and who played the two young men in that version?

25 Trains, with their fascinatingly enclosed world of compartments and corridors, their ominously insistent rhythms and their lonely whistles in the night, have been a popular setting for stories of mystery and suspense. From the passenger lists below, deduce the 'train' movies:

a Ingrid Bergman, Sean Connery, Vanessa Redgrave

b Margaret Lockwood, Michael Redgrave, Basil Radford

c Margaret Lockwood, Rex Harrison, Naunton Wayne

d Gene Wilder, Jill Clayburgh, Ned Beatty

e Sophia Loren, Richard Harris, Ava Gardner

f Conrad Veidt, Joan Barry, Hugh Williams

g Charles McGraw, Marie Windsor, Jacqueline White

h Yves Montand, Simone Signoret, Jean-Louis Trintignant

i Basil Rathbone, Nigel Bruce, Alan Mowbray

j Jean Kent, Albert Lieven, Derrick De Marney

26 The 1932 classic SCARFACE was remade in 1983:

a Name the directors of both versions

b What was Scarface's name in the original? And in the remake? Who took the title roles in each of the two films?

c The 1932 version boasted an excellent performance from Boris Karloff. On which real-life mobster was his character based?

d Who played Scarface's right-hand man in 1932 and 1983?

e Where was the second version set?

27 Dreams have played an important part in some notable crime films. Name the films in which

a Edward G. Robinson, while admiring a portrait, encounters the model, becomes embroiled in a web of murder and blackmail then discovers it is all a dream

b Mervyn Johns, arriving at a country house party, becomes involved in a terrifying sequence of events including murder. He is relieved to wake up at home and realise it has been a dream, then finds the whole sequence starting over again

c After dreaming of committing murder in a mirrored room, DeDorrest Kelley awakes to find evidence that he was not dreaming. With the help of his policeman brother-in-law, Paul Kelly, he discovers that he had been hypnotised to participate in the crime

d The same story (with a different title) featured Kevin McCarthy as the dreamer and Edward G. Robinson as the policeman

e Robert Cummings plans to flee to Havana with his employer's wife, Michele Morgan. After their arrival she is stabbed to death and he is arrested for her murder, then wakes to find their flight has been a dream

Another of Hollywood's depictions of real-life crime was this violent biography of a notorious female gangster who was head of a sadistic family. What was the film, what was the character's name and who played her? The director was particularly known for exploitation and horror movies – who was he? The central character had several sons in the film, one of whom was played by an actor who went on to become a major star, later portraying the young Marlon Brando in a successful film of the 70s – who is he and what was the film?

28 REAR WINDOW, THE BRIDE WORE BLACK, DEADLINE AT DAWN, NO MAN OF HER OWN and THE LEOPARD MAN are just five of the thrillers based on the writing of one of America's finest exponents of crime fiction – who was he?

29 Young offenders have often been used to tug at the heartstrings and point many a moral tale in the movies:

a In a Don Siegel film of 1956, teenage tearaways Sal Mineo and John Cassavetes found themselves on the run. Name the film, and their companion who grew up to become a famous film director

b What was the theme of Louis Malle's PRETTY BABY?

c Who joined Teddy Boy Laurence Harvey in the dock in I BELIEVE YOU?

d Who was the toughest inhabitant, dramatically reformed by Spencer Tracy, of BOYS' TOWN?

e In which British film of 1949 did Dirk Bogarde and Richard Attenborough find themselves playing a pair of over-age Borstal inmates?

30　Sniff the clues to find the movies, then name the actors:

a　A vagabond drifts into a lunch stand and gas station owned by Nick Smith. Once Frank sees Nick's young wife Cora, however . . .

b　A down-at-heel private eye seeks a missing suburban husband in New York with the help of a call-girl and a tape recorder . . .

c　Insurance agent Walter Neff records how he first met Phyllis Dietrichson and how they plotted a dastardly deed . . .

d　Ex-convict Johnny Clay organises a $2 million racecourse hold-up. He is helped by the cashier, George Peatty . . .

e　America's leading mystery playwright, Sidney Bruhl, invites one of his former students, himself an aspiring playwright, to his country house, with disastrous consequences . . .

31　Murder can play hell with marriage. Name first the murderous, and then the murdered partner in the following films:

a　PINK STRING AND SEALING WAX
b　BORDERTOWN
c　TRAIN OF EVENTS
d　HUMAN DESIRE
e　BODY HEAT

. . . but the best-laid schemes have a distressing habit of falling apart. Name the murderers who failed to carry out their plans, and their threatened spouses, in

f　BEDELIA
g　MIDNIGHT LACE
h　GASLIGHT
i　MONSIEUR VERDOUX
j　SUDDEN FEAR

Two of Hollywood's most popular stars of the 40s teamed as a pair of murderous lovers. Who are they, what was the film and who played the heroine's husband who they murdered? The story's author wrote several books which were turned into *noir* thrillers by Hollywood – who was he? Who directed the 1942 Italian version of the same story, and who played the lovers in the 1981 Hollywood remake?

---

32 The 30s were the heyday of the prison drama, but the genre is still going strong:
a Who played a yellow squealer in THE BIG HOUSE?
b Which Laurel and Hardy film was a parody of THE BIG HOUSE?
c Who was the trusted convict who murdered a stool-pigeon in THE CRIMINAL CODE?
d In which film did Diana Dors find herself in the condemned cell? On which real-life murderer was her character based?
e Who was CONVICT 99?
f Who was COOL HAND LUKE and what did he eat for a bet?
g Who played the prison governor in the following films: EACH DAWN I DIE, CASTLE ON THE HUDSON, RIOT IN CELL BLOCK II, THE LONELINESS OF THE LONG DISTANCE RUNNER, THE LONGEST YARD?
h In which film did convict Tony Curtis escape shackled to another prisoner? Name his fellow escapee and the film's director. The idea was hardly new. Name the British film of 1947 which anticipated Curtis's bid for freedom and the two actors who played similarly manacled fugitives
i In TWO WAY STRETCH, Peter Sellers and his accomplices escape from prison and then return to their cells. Why?
j Alcatraz is the most famous prison in the world. Who effected an ESCAPE FROM ALCATRAZ? Who was the KING OF ALCATRAZ, and what bearing on the prison did the film have?

33 Even the best of police forces have their rotten apples. Name the bent cops in the following films:
a ROGUE COP
b WHERE THE SIDEWALK ENDS
c I WAKE UP SCREAMING
d THE PROWLER
e WHITE LIGHTNING

34 1973's Oscar-winning film was a comedy-thriller concerning one of the most elaborate and entertaining confidence tricks ever perpetrated on screen. Set in Chicago of the 30s, it starred two of Hollywood's biggest names. Who were they, what was the film, who directed it, and whose music was utilised for the background score?

35 Frame-ups and wrongful arrests have placed many an innocent person behind bars. Identify the films in which
a A young woman has her car – and identification – stolen by hitchhikers. She is detained by the police, is raped, and escapes with a criminal. When a pursuing policeman is killed in an accident, they are automatically labelled murderers
b A doctor innocently tends the injured leg of Abraham Lincoln's assassin, John Wilkes Booth, and is sentenced to life imprisonment
c A brassy showgirl takes the rap for a murder she did not commit in a bid to gain personal publicity
d A man is jailed for a crime he did not commit. When a lynch mob burns down the jail, he escapes but is thought to be dead. He sets about plotting revenge on the ringleaders of the lynch mob
e A journalist pretends to be guilty of murder in order to prove the inadequacy of the law and the police. He plants false evidence against himself, is convicted and sent to death row. At this point his publisher – who is supposed to reveal the truth – suddenly dies. Can you complete the story, and name the lead actor?

36 Oddball criminal activity has fascinated film-makers every bit as much as more conventional shootings and stabbings:
a Who tried to take over London's all-in wrestling racket in NIGHT AND THE CITY?
b In which film does a gang of crooks led by Jack Warner communicate with each other by planting messages in a boys' magazine?
c The THOMAS CROWN AFFAIR boasted an unusually elegant insurance investigator. Who?
d Who wrote the unpleasant letters in POISON PEN?
e A young arsonist, released from an institution, fantasises about foiling an imaginary plot to poison his home town's water supply. He enlists the help of a high-school sweetie, who turns out to be a psychopath. A number of murders ensue. What was the film, and who played the arsonist and the all-American cutie?

37 Unscramble the four lists below to match the character, the girl and the director to the appropriate James Cagney movie:
PUBLIC ENEMY
THE ROARING 20s
ANGELS WITH DIRTY FACES
WHITE HEAT
LOVE ME OR LEAVE ME
Eddie Bartlett/Martin Schneider/Tom Powers/Cody Jarrett/Rocky Sullivan
Ann Sheridan/Priscilla Lane/Jean Harlow/Doris Day/Virginia Mayo
Raoul Walsh/Charles Vidor/Michael Curtiz/William Wellman/Raoul Walsh

Buff's Brainteaser

Although each section of this book has contained many questions to test the superbuff, here is a chance for these high flyers to really show off their wide knowledge of the cinema.

1   Kick off with the following mixed bag of questions which range from difficult to very difficult:

a   Which two-time Oscar-winning screenwriter described the Oscar as 'a perfect symbol of the picture business: a powerful athletic body clutching a gleaming sword, with half of his head – that part which held his brains – completely sliced off'? For which films did the speaker win the award?

b   What noted action director made some of the best serials, including DAREDEVILS OF THE RED CIRCLE, SPY SMASHER and ZORRO'S FIGHTING LEGION?

c   Which composer wrote the music for Stanley Kubrick's first four features, and what were they?

d   In what film did Paul Henreid perform a cello concerto? Who, in the film, played the composer of the work, and who actually wrote the music used?

e   What were Cary Grant's initials in NORTH BY NORTHWEST?

f   What does the W.R. in W.R.: MYSTERIES OF THE ORGANISM stand for? Who directed the film? Another of his films had someone say, after stabbing a man in the forehead, 'He had it coming. He cheated at cards'? Name the film

g   Which movie was recorded on a 16-track sound system and had 24 leading characters? Three of the stars had famous parents. Which three? Who wrote the screenplay?

h   Which somewhat unlikely British writer was given the dialogue credit for TARZAN THE APE MAN (1932)?

i   In GONE WITH THE WIND, Scarlett O'Hara eventually marries Rhett Butler, but has already been widowed twice. Who played Scarlett's first two husbands?

j   Who were Victor Hanbury and Joseph Walton?

2   Which films were dedicated to

a   'Monogram Pictures'?

b   'Mr Laurel and Mr Hardy'?

c   'Elias Howe who, in 1846, invented the sewing machine'?

d   'All the funny men and clowns who have made people laugh'?

e   'To the memory of Harry Carey, bright star of the early Western sky'?

3   Can you name the films from which the following lines come, and say who said them?

a   'If you can't sleep at night, it isn't the coffee, it's the bunk'

b   'Gee it's – it's bigger than just a show. Say, it's, it's everybody in the country'

c   'I thought you did it for *me*, Mama!'

d   'Heeeeers Johnny!'

e   'I can find you another two yards'

f   'There can only be one winner, folks, but isn't that the American way?'

g   'Atmosphère, atmosphère!'

h   'Danke schön, already!'

i   'I am *not* Nijinsky. I am *not* Marlon Brando. I am Mrs Hunter's little boy'

4   Who was cast as

a   Bette Davis's niece in NOW VOYAGER?

b   Grace Kelly's sister in HIGH SOCIETY?

c   Dennis Price's mother in KIND HEARTS AND CORONETS?

d   Judy Garland's brother in FOR ME AND MY GAL?

e   Jeff Bridge's father in THE LAST AMERICAN HERO? (aka HARD DRIVER)

5   The thriller, in its multitudinous forms, is perhaps the most durable of movie genres, and shows no signs of abating. Here are five questions specially designed for the superbuff:

a   What was unusual about the sleuth played by Edward Arnold in EYES IN THE NIGHT?

b   Who played the starchy middle-aged schoolmarm Hildegarde Withers in THE PENGUIN POOL MURDER?

c   Name the courtly Chinese scholar-detective Mr Wong in MR WONG IN CHINATOWN

d   Who was the wisecracking sob sister, Torchy Blane, in TORCHY PLAYS WITH DYNAMITE?

e   How many murders did Dennis Price commit on his way to a dukedom in KIND HEARTS AND CORONETS? How did he dispose of his first victim – and his last?

One of many nasty moments from a nasty movie. What was it called, and by what sort of power did the man illustrated lose his head? Who was responsible for the special effects? Who directed the film? One of the leads was the star of a cult TV series of the late 60s. Who is he and what was the series called? What later film did the director make about a cable TV operator? Who played him and who did the special effects on that one?

---

6   Can you supply the cue lines that provoked the following replies? Name the films and identify the speakers of these witty ripostes:

a 'Yes, a case of Scotch'
b 'Oh, my dear, that's something you need never worry about'
c 'Goodness had nothing to do with it'
d 'I *am* big. It's the pictures that got small'
e 'How will you eat? Through a tube?'

7   Sometimes initials give a mysterious ring to a name. Demystify the following by supplying their full names:

a Edward G. Robinson
b H. B. Warner
c D. W. Griffith
d F. W. Murnau
e George C. Scott

8   In which films would you find the following cast lists, and who played the first-named in each case?

a Phroso, Venus, Cleopatra, Hercules
b X27, Lieutenant Kranau, Colonel Kovrin, General von Hindau
c Grusinskaya, Baron Felix von Geigern, Kringelein, Flaemmchen
d Egbert Sousé, Elsie Mae Adele Brunch Sousé, Mrs Hermisillo Brunch, J. Pinkerton Snoopington
e Alfred Kralik, Klara Novak, Matuschek, Ferencz Vadas

167

9 From an acorn comes an oak, from a first film appearance comes a career. Who made their feature film debuts in the films below?
a BONNIE AND CLYDE
b THERE'S ONE BORN EVERY MINUTE
c SINNER'S HOLIDAY (1930)
d THE HAPPENING
e WAR HUNT
f JULIA
g WHAT'S NEW PUSSYCAT?
h FOURTEEN HOURS
i ME NATALIE
j GOODBYE MR CHIPS

10 For what scene and in what movie was the actress given the instruction, 'I want your face to be a blank sheet of paper. I want the writing to be done by every member of the audience. I'd like it if you could avoid blinking your eyes, so that you're nothing but a beautiful mask'? Who was the actress, and the director?

11 Who were known as
a The Dollar Bills?
b The Empress of Emotion?
c The Tsar of all the Rushes?
d 'One-Shot' Woody?
e 'Wild Bill'?

12 In what film did the opening credits represent each leading character as an animal? The three top-billed stars were seen as a fawn, a leopard and a panther. Who were they, and what was particularly distinctive about the film?

13 Much film dialogue is unspeakable, but see if you have a sound knowledge of the following. Which:
a 1952 movie had no dialogue at all?
b western had no dialogue for the first twenty minutes?
c film had a special language created for it?
d film has only one spoken word in it?
e film's dialogue was mostly in pidgin English?
f film had the characters communicating in grunts, groans and shrieks?
g film had no spoken dialogue but ended with a song in gibberish?
h film was made in Esperanto?
i film was made in Latin?

A happy group on a studio lot. Which studio? What year was this picture taken? Name the four stars and the films on which they were each working at the time. Which four directors would they be working with? Each of the films was set in a different country. Name them.

14 Omnibus films i.e. those offering various stories, whether linked or not, and generally each directed by different people, seldom succeed. However, they do provide a showcase for a variety of talents. Answer the questions below:

a The title of ROGOPAG, an Italian film, was derived from the names of its directors. Who were they? Whose episode was banned in Italy, and which actor/director played a director in it?

b Name the three films, each based on several Somerset Maugham short stories. How many stories were treated in all, and which director contributed to all three films?

c Name the four directors involved in TWILIGHT ZONE, THE MOVIE. Which actor was killed during the filming? How was he killed? Who originally conceived the TV series of 'Twilight Zone'?

d How many stories were treated in O. HENRY'S FULL HOUSE? Name the directors of each. Who says 'He called me a lady!' in one of the episodes?

e Edgar Allan Poe was the writer of the three stories adapted for SPIRITS OF THE DEAD. What were the stories called, and who were the male leads in each?

f Name the compendium film in which a group of characters narrate their dreams. Who played
i) two rival golfers ii) a ventriloquist iii) the architect to whom the dreams are told?

15 Almost a one-man film industry, Rainer Werner Fassbinder made over thirty films in twelve years:

a Which of his earliest successes did he describe as 'what's left in the minds of the German people who see a lot of American gangster films'?

b Which American film was the model for FEAR EATS THE SOUL (US: ALI)?

c In which of his films is there a character called Hermann Hermann, and who played him?

d Fassbinder appeared in some of his films, but which one did he narrate, and who wrote the novel from which it was adapted?

e Who played the title roles in THE MARRIAGE OF MARIA BRAUN, THE BITTER TEARS OF PETRA VON KANT, VERONIKA VOSS, LOLA and QUERELLE?

16 In which films did each of the following make their positively last appearance:

a Susan Hayward
b Valentino
c Spencer Tracy
d Joan Crawford
e Natalie Wood
f Carole Lombard
g Alan Ladd
h Gary Cooper
i Jean Harlow
j Humphrey Bogart

17 What do the following groups have in common?
a Princess Marie, Marie de Flor, Nina Maria Azara, Marcia Mornay, Marianne de Beaumanoir
b Rosalind Russell, Deborah Kerr, Audrey Hepburn, Lilli Palmer, Debbie Reynolds
c A NEW LEAF, DAISIES, WANDA, NIGHT GAMES, THE BIGAMIST
d Betty Grable, Romy Schneider, Bebe Daniels, Natalie Wood, Anna May Wong, Elizabeth Taylor
e LA RONDE (1964), LA CURÉE, TOUT VA BIEN, LES FÉLINS, BARBARELLA

18 As people read books in books, or look at paintings in paintings, so characters in films sometimes watch films. From which movies were extracts shown in:
a SUMMER OF '42?
b SUNSET BOULEVARD?
c TWO WEEKS IN ANOTHER TOWN?
d MINNIE AND MOSKOWITZ?
e LA LUNA?
f WORDS AND MUSIC?
g SPIRIT OF THE BEEHIVE?
h VIVRE SA VIE?
i A TOUCH OF CLASS?
j SABOTAGE (US: THE WOMAN ALONE)?

19 'Artistic differences', incompetence, extravagance and death, are some of the reasons why one director sometimes replaces another on a film. Name the film on which, for whatever reason, the first director listed took over from the second named:
a Milos Forman/Robert Altman
b George Cukor/Joseph Strick
c Michael Curtiz/William Keighley
d Rupert Julian/Erich von Stroheim
e Norman Foster/Orson Welles
f Karl Koch/Jean Renoir
g Jack Cardiff/John Ford
h George Cukor/Charles Vidor
i Lewis Milestone/Carol Reed
j Roger Donaldson/David Lean

20 Supporting players often redeem even the poorest movie and add to the delight of a good one. Can you name the performer in each case from the three clues given below, and the films to which each clue refers?
a Prosper Latour; Nicely-Nicely Johnson; a purchaser of a Scottish castle
b Ezra Ounce; Snout; a short-sighted doctor trying to extract a bullet
c Baron Popoff; Marquis de Loiselle; a palaeontologist survivor of a plane crash
d Samuel Peacock; Mr Wiggs; a prosecutor of two brothers accused of a stabbing
e Lilybelle Callahan; Ann Rutledge; The Queen of Marshovia

A scene from a typical thirties tearjerker.
a **Name the film and the stars pictured**
b **What professions were the characters**
c **Why was the film especially significant for the actress?**
d **The film was remade in 1941. What was it called and who took the equivalent roles?**
e **Who directed each version?**

---

21 Name the films and the players involved in the following unusual or bizarre happenings:

a A man arrives at a police station to report his own death
b An actor playing a singer meets himself as the actor who is going to play him!
c The hero tells his story to the director of the film (the story *is* the film)
d The leading character pours glue over girls' heads during the blackouts in wartime England
e Through the intervention of a mysterious power, a husband and wife undergo a change of sex

22 In what films would you find the following unusual credits?
a Miss Hepburn's wardrobe and *perfume*
b Fangs by Dr Ludwig von Krankheit
c Ant consultant
d The Assistant to the Assistant to the Unit Publicist
e Technical Consultant on Vampire Bats

23 What noted film directors played roles in
a CITY FOR CONQUEST?
b THE LADY AND THE MONSTER?
c THE AMERICAN FRIEND?
d CONTEMPT (LE MÉPRIS)?
e THE BATTLE OF THE RIVER PLATE (US: PURSUIT OF THE GRAF SPEE)?

24 Name the films in which the first-listed player portrayed the second as a child:
a Peggy Ann Garner/Joan Fontaine
b Jean Simmons/Valerie Hobson
c Mickey Rooney/Clark Gable
d Natalie Wood/Vanessa Brown
e Ricky Nelson/Farley Granger

25 Before the final fade out, use your movie mastermind on the following few questions:
a Who was the director, the writer and the star of FILM?
b Who were MERTON OF THE MOVIES (in 1924 and 1947) and MOVIE CRAZY?
c In which films did Shemp Howard, Peter Sellers and Buster Keaton play movie projectionists?
d 'Films are smoother than life, they don't just grind to a halt . . . For people like you and me, our happiness lies in the cinema'. Who says this to whom, and in what movie?

Answers

WHAT ARE THESE MOVIES? *Answers to questions on page 1*

1 LADY IN A CAGE
2 THE PINK PANTHER STRIKES AGAIN
3 EL DORADO
4 DIAMONDS ARE FOREVER
5 PLAY MISTY FOR ME
6 POINT BLANK
7 DOGS OF WAR
8 THE RIGHT STUFF

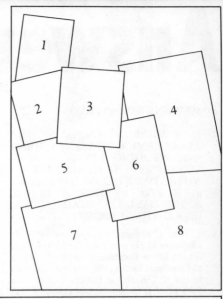

WHO ARE THESE STARS? *Answers to questions on pages 2–3*

1 Elizabeth Taylor
2 Greta Garbo and Melvyn Douglas
3 Marlene Dietrich
4 Marlene Dietrich and Charles Boyer
5 Fatty Arbuckle
6 James Coburn
7 Vivien Leigh and Clark Gable
8 Sophia Loren and Marcello Mastroianni
9 Omar Sharif and Barbra Streisand
10 Gregory Peck
11 Jack Lemmon and Shirley MacLaine
12 Tatum and Ryan O'Neil
13 Michael Sarrazin and Jane Fonda

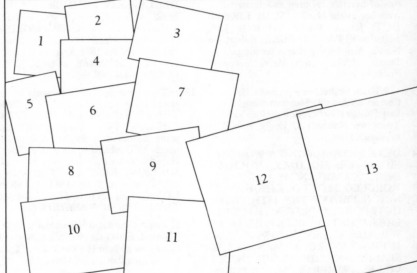

WHERE ARE THESE FILMS LOCATED? *Answers to questions on page 4*

1 THE GUNS OF NAVARONE, which took place on an island in the Aegean
2 THE DEER HUNTER, Vietnam
3 CASABLANCA
4 JEREMIAH JOHNSON, in the Utah mountains
5 SUMMERTIME (G.B. SUMMER MADNESS), which took place in Venice

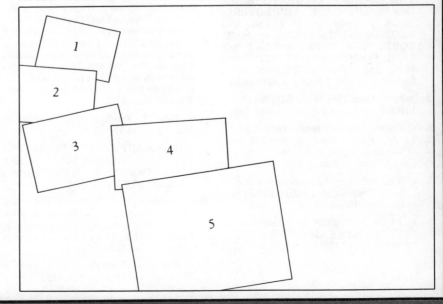

Answers

SOMETHING FOR EVERYONE

1 a) SUMMER MADNESS b) THE APARTMENT c) ROYAL WEDDING (GB: WEDDING BELLS) d) NOW VOYAGER e) THE HUNCHBACK OF NOTRE DAME f) COOL HAND LUKE g) NORTH BY NORTHWEST h) ANNIE HALL i) CAPTAIN COURAGEOUS j) HIGH SOCIETY

2 a) Joan Crawford; her adopted daughter Christina b) He was what the letters stand for, an Extra-Terrestrial; Steven Spielberg c) Elizabeth Taylor; they were all married to her d) DR NO e) George C. Scott for PATTON f) Sophie had to choose which one of her two children should be taken from her by the Nazis g) SOME LIKE IT HOT; Joe E. Brown said it to Jack Lemmon h) RAGING BULL; Robert De Niro i) A divorcing couple personified by Dustin Hoffman and Meryl Streep j) Federico Fellini

3 a) William Shakespeare b) James Hilton c) Charles Dickens d) Somerset Maugham e) Leo Tolstoy f) Robert Bolt g) Gore Vidal h) Tennessee Williams i) Emily Brontë j) Frederick Forsyth

4 DEAR RUTH; HAVING A WONDERFUL TIME; HOLIDAY; HOLIDAY INN; CASABLANCA; AIRPORT; MOROCCO; 12 O'CLOCK HIGH; HIGH NOON; FRIDAY THE 13TH; TAXI; HOTEL; TAXI DRIVER; 8½; DOLLARS; WHAT!; ROBBERY; ROOM AT THE TOP; REAR WINDOW; 10; SUNSET BOULEVARD; WOMAN ON THE BEACH; ON THE BEACH; NASHVILLE; SUMMER OF '42; A PLACE IN THE SUN; DAY FOR NIGHT; DANCING IN THE DARK; THE LOVERS; ROCKY; LOVELY TO LOOK AT; REDS; AUTUMN LEAVES; NEW YORK, NEW YORK; I WANT TO LIVE; COMING HOME; OCTOBER; 1984; HALLOWEEN; WILSON; SINCERELY YOURS; JOHN AND MARY

5 Judy Garland; THE WIZARD OF OZ; L. Frank Baum; Liza Minnelli; Lorna Luft

6 a) Rogers b) Kinski; daughter and father c) Leigh d) Kelly e) Fonda; brother and sister f) Keaten g) Taylor h) Bridges; brothers i) Curtis; father and daughter j) Powell

7 a) Warner Bros. b) Metro-Goldwyn-Mayer c) Radio-Keith-Orpheum d) United Artists e) Universal-International

8 a) LOST HORIZON b) REBECCA c) CITIZEN KANE d) SUPERMAN e) GONE WITH THE WIND

9 a) A steam locomotive b) A World War I fighter plane c) A vintage jalopy d) A river boat e) A racing yacht

10 a) A Japanese POW camp b) A dance palace c) A circus d) A German POW camp e) A nuclear power station f) Again, a Japanese POW camp g) A seaside resort h) Entebbe Airport i) The Beverly Hills Hotel j) A Turkish prison

11 François Truffaut b) Alfred Hitchcock c) Ingmar Bergman d) David Lean e) Werner Herzog f) Jean-Luc Godard g) Martin Scorsese h) Michelangelo Antonioni i) Steven Spielberg j) Fritz Lang

12 a) THE LION IN WINTER b) SUDDENLY LAST SUMMER c) A MAN FOR ALL SEASONS d) AUTUMN SONATA e) SUMMER HOLIDAY (1962) f) SUMMER HOLIDAY (1948) g) SPRING IN PARK LANE h) SUMMER OF '42 i) SUMMER STOCK j) THE FOUR SEASONS

13 a) They were all born in England b) They are all follow-up films – to STAR WARS, THE PINK PANTHER, RAIDERS OF THE LOST ARK c) They were all killed in plane crashes d) They are all films from novels by Daphne Du Maurier e) They all played Indians. Sellers in THE MILLIONAIRESS and THE PARTY (and a cameo in THE ROAD TO HONG KONG), Kingsley in GANDHI, Burton in THE RAINS OF RANCHIPUR

14 a) Brigitte Bardot b) Clark Gable c) John Wayne d) Elvis Presley e) Mary Pickford f) Clara Bow g) Jean Harlow h) Lana Turner i) Ann Sheridan j) Lon Chaney Sr

15 a) Sydney Pollack in his own film b) Lindsay Anderson in Hugh Hudson's film c) Orson Welles in Carol Reed's film d) Paul Bartel in his own film e) Peter Bogdanovich in his own film f) François Truffaut in Steven Spielberg's film g) Roman Polanski – his own film – and John Huston h) Martin Scorsese in his own film i) John Cassavetes in his own film j) Otto Preminger in Billy Wilder's film

16 a) Ballet b) Painting c) Architecture d) Writing e) Music

17 a) ROSEMARY'S BABY b) WHATEVER HAPPENED TO BABY JANE? c) BABY THE RAIN MUST FALL d) BRINGING UP BABY e) BABY DOLL

18 a) Yul Brynner b) Bruce Dern (not Jack Nicholson) c) Elvis Presley d) A giant gorilla e) George Segal f) Charles Chaplin g) Goldie Hawn h) Greta Garbo i) Laurence Olivier j) Joan Crawford

19 a) 2001 b) 55 c) 200 d) Seven, or Two, or Three e) Two f) Five g) 39 h) 633 i) Twelve j) 400

SOMETHING FOR EVERYONE
Answers to Picture Questions

Page 7:
World War II; CASABLANCA with Ingrid Bergman and Humphrey Bogart (right); Paul Henreid is on the left, Claude Rains centre; Bergman is married to Henreid, but involved in a past love affair with Bogart; Dooley Wilson; 'As Time Goes By'

Page 8:
GONE WITH THE WIND; Vivien Leigh and Leslie Howard as Scarlett O'Hara and Ashley Wilkes; Clark Gable; Victor Fleming; Margaret Mitchell; Miss Leigh was married to Laurence Olivier; The American Civil War; Atlanta (the burning of Atlanta)

Page 9:
Sissy Spacek is Jack Lemmon's daughter-in-law; they are in an unnamed Central American country where there is war between right and left-wing factions, searching for Lemmon's son, her husband, a reporter who is MISSING. Costa-Gavras, the director, is a naturalised Frenchman, born in Greece, and his first famous political film was Z. Meryl Streep got the Oscar for SOPHIE'S CHOICE; Spacek received it for COAL MINER'S DAUGHTER in which she starred as country-and-western singer, Loretta Lynn

ALL-SINGING, ALL-DANCING

1 Ad; Bg; Cb; Dh; Ef; Fa; Gk; He; Ic; Jl; Ki; Lj; (Astaire/Rogers: B; C; E; K Garland/Rooney: D; G; H; J MacDonald/Eddy: A; F; I; L)

2 a) No b) Jo Ann Greer c) No d) Laverne Hutchinson e) No f) Marni Nixon g) No h) No i) Betty Wand j) Marni Nixon

3 a) GUYS AND DOLLS; Jean Simmons; Marlon Brando b) SILK STOCKINGS; Cyd Charisse; Fred Astaire c) SUMMER STOCK; Judy Garland; Gene Kelly d) THE BELLE OF NEW YORK; Vera-Ellen; Fred Astaire e) DO YOU LOVE ME?; Maureen O'Hara; Harry James; Dick Haymes

4 a) THE BEST LITTLE WHOREHOUSE IN TEXAS b) PETE KELLY'S BLUES/PAINT YOUR WAGON c) OKLAHOMA! d) GUYS AND DOLLS e) HELLO DOLLY/KING CREOLE f) THE FLEET'S IN g) LOST HORIZON h) ZIEGFELD GIRL i) THE BEST THINGS IN LIFE ARE FREE j) GYPSY

5 a) DADDY LONG LEGS (same title) b) PEPE LE MOKO/CASBAH c) NIGHTS OF CABIRIA/SWEET CHARITY d) THE MATCHMAKER/HELLO DOLLY e) NINOTCHKA/SILK STOCKINGS f) PYGMALION/MY FAIR LADY g) ANNA AND THE KING OF SIAM/THE KING AND I h) SMILES OF A SUMMER NIGHT/A LITTLE NIGHT MUSIC i) GOODBYE MR CHIPS (same title) j) ROMEO AND JULIET/WEST SIDE STORY

172

6 a) SILK STOCKINGS; Cyd Charisse, Fred Astaire b) THE OPPOSITE SEX; June Allyson, Joan Collins, Dolores Gray c) BUNDLE OF JOY; Debbie Reynolds, Eddie Fisher d) YOU CAN'T RUN AWAY FROM IT; June Allyson, Jack Lemmon e) THE GIRL MOST LIKELY; Jane Powell, Keith Andes, Cliff Robertson

7 a) Buchanan b) Cyd Charisse c) Alice Faye d) George Raft e) SATURDAY NIGHT FEVER; GREASE f) Georges Guetary; AN AMERICAN IN PARIS g) LOVE ME TENDER; 1956 h) INCENDIARY BLONDE; THE PERILS OF PAULINE; SOMEBODY LOVES ME; ANNIE GET YOUR GUN i) Rita Moreno; WEST SIDE STORY j) JUPITER'S DARLING

8 a) Omar Sharif/ FUNNY GIRL b) Jean Hagen/SINGIN' IN THE RAIN c) John Travolta/SATURDAY NIGHT FEVER d) Christopher Plummer/THE SOUND OF MUSIC e) Judy Garland/ZIEGFELD FOLLIES

9 Dick Haymes and Jeanne Crain; Vivian Blaine and Dana Andrews; Fay Bainter and Charles Winninger

10 a) Gene Kelly/AN AMERICAN IN PARIS b) Busby Berkeley/GOLDDIGGERS OF 1935 c) Robert Alton/WHITE CHRISTMAS d) Stanley Donen and Gene Kelly/IT'S ALWAYS FAIR WEATHER e) Michael Kidd/SEVEN BRIDES FOR SEVEN BROTHERS

11 a) June Allyson; Kathryn Grayson b) Vera-Ellen; June Haver; Vivian Blaine c) June Allyson; Gloria de Haven; Van Johnson d) Deanna Durbin and an orchestra of 100 led by her father (Adolphe Menjou) e) Kay Francis; Carole Landis; Martha Raye; Mitzi Mayfair

12 a) Frank Sinatra, Gene Kelly, Jules Munshin b) Gene Kelly, Dan Dailey, Michael Kid c) Tony Martin, Vic Damone, Russ Tamblyn d) Gordon MacRae, Gene Nelson, Jack E. Leonard e) Tony Curtis, Gene Nelson, Paul Gilbert

13 G.I. BLUES; Elvis Presley, Juliet Prowse

14 a) THE GAY DIVORCEE b) THE BOY FRIEND c) CAREFREE d) FLYING DOWN TO RIO e) THOROUGHLY MODERN MILLIE

15 a) IN CALIENTE b) THE GANG'S ALL HERE (1943; GB: THE GIRLS HE LEFT BEHIND) c) THE TIME, THE PLACE AND THE GIRL d) MEET ME IN LAS VEGAS (GB: VIVA LAS VEGAS) e) ONE IN A MILLION

16 Michael Jackson; Nipsey Russell; Ted Ross

17 a) Fred Astaire and Rita Hayworth/YOU WERE NEVER LOVELIER b) Gene Kelly and Vera-Ellen/ON THE TOWN c) Bill Robinson and Shirley Temple/THE LITTLEST REBEL d) Tommy Rall and Ann Miller/KISS ME KATE e) John Travolta and Olivia Newton-John/GREASE f) Dan Dailey and Betty Grable/MOTHER WORE TIGHTS g) George

Murphy and Eleanor Powell/BROADWAY MELODY OF 1940 h) Marge and Gower Champion/EVERYTHING I HAVE IS YOURS i) Bob Fosse and Gwen Verdon/DAMN YANKEES j) Donald O'Connor and Peggy Ryan/MR BIG

18 Joan Crawford; DANCING LADY

19 Ac; Ba; Cj; Dh; Ee; Fi; Gf; Hb; Ig; Jd

20 a) Jean Hagen, SINGIN' IN THE RAIN b) Aline MacMahon, GOLDDIGGERS OF 1933 c) Judy Garland, THE PIRATE d) Florence Bates, ON THE TOWN e) Joan McCracken, GOOD NEWS

21 a) HAIR b) FAME c) THE ROCKY HORROR SHOW d) ALL THAT JAZZ e) PHANTOM OF THE PARADISE

22 a) THE SOUND OF MUSIC b) OKLAHOMA! c) THE KING AND I d) SOUTH PACIFIC e) CAROUSEL

23 a) Ira Gershwin b) Johnny Mercer c) Leo Robin d) Ted Koehler e) Ralph Blane

24 a) Juie Andrews, MARY POPPINS b) Doris Day, ROMANCE ON THE HIGH SEAS (GB: IT'S MAGIC) c) Betty Hutton, THE FLEET'S IN d) Jeanette MacDonald, THE LOVE PARADE e) Celeste Holm, THREE LITTLE GIRLS IN BLUE

25 a) Oscar Hammerstein II b) Jerry Stoller c) Adolph Green d) Lorenz Hart e) Gene de Paul f) Andrew Lloyd Webber g) Harry Ruby h) Harry Warren i) Ray Henderson j) Howard Dietz

26 a) TOM SAWYER b) THE MAGIC OF LASSIE c) BEDKNOBS AND BROOMSTICKS d) THE HAPPIEST MILLIONAIRE e) CHARLOTTE'S WEBB

27 Jane Russell and Marilyn Monroe

28 a) ROUSTABOUT b) THE BELLS OF ST MARY'S c) A DATE WITH JUDY d) THE JAZZ SINGER (1980) e) SWING YOUR LADY

29 Peter Palmer (Li'l Abner); Aileen Quinn (Annie)

30 a) Crosby, HOLIDAY INN b) Sinatra, HIGH SOCIETY c) Sinatra, ROBIN AND THE SEVEN HOODS d) Crosby, GOING MY WAY e) Sinatra, GUYS AND DOLLS f) Crosby, ROAD TO MOROCCO g) Crosby, RHYTHM ON THE RANGE h) Sinatra, IT HAPPENED IN BROOKLYN i) Sinatra, HIGHER AND HIGHER j) Crosby, HERE IS MY HEART

31 BYE BYE BIRDIE

32 a) Howard Keel b) Ann Miller c) Tommy Steele d) Sophie Tucker e) Ginger Rogers f) Jane Powell g) Alice Faye h) Mitzi Gaynor i) Dean Martin j) Ethel Merman

33 SUNNYSIDE UP; Janet Gaynor; Charles Farrell

34 Ae; Bc; Cd; Db; Ea

35 a) Michael Curtiz b) Lloyd Bacon c) Walter Lang d) Irving Cummings e) Roy Del Ruth

36 a) ROYAL WEDDING (GB: WEDDING BELLS) b) THE PAJAMA GAME; DAMN YANKEES (GB: WHAT LOLA WANTS) c) THE LITTLE PRINCE d) IT'S ALWAYS FAIR WEATHER e) BEST FOOT FORWARD

37 a) MAD ABOUT MUSIC b) SPRING PARADE c) CHRISTMAS HOLIDAY d) FIRST LOVE e) NICE GIRL? f) ONE HUNDRED MEN AND A GIRL g) CAN'T HELP SINGING h) THAT CERTAIN AGE i) SOMETHING IN THE WIND j) HERS TO HOLD

38 THAT NIGHT IN RIO; Dom Ameche, Alice Faye, Carmen Miranda. ON THE RIVIERA; Danny Kaye, Gene Tierney, Corrine Calvet

39 a) Glenn Miller b) Harry James c) Benny Goodman d) Artie Shaw e) Jimmy Dorsey f) Kay Kyser g) Tommy Dorsey h) Charlie Spivak i) Woody Herman j) Gene Krupa

40 a) ANNIE GET YOUR GUN b) CAROUSEL c) THE BARKLEYS OF BROADWAY d) PRESENTING LILY MARS e) WHITE CHRISTMAS

41 a) Eleanor Powell b) Ilona Massey c) Susanna Foster d) Rise Stevens e) Virginia Bruce

42 YANKEE DOODLE DANDY; THE SEVEN LITTLE FOYS

43 a) 'Shuffle Off To Buffalo', 42ND STREET b) 'I Only Have Eyes For You', DAMES c) 'The Words Are In My Heart'; GOLDDIGGERS OF 1935 d) 'The Shadow Waltz'; GOLDDIGGERS OF 1933 e) 'Don't Say Goodnight'; WONDER BAR

44 WHEN MY BABY SMILES AT ME; Dan Dailey; MOTHER WORE TIGHTS; MY BLUE HEAVEN; CALL ME MISTER

45 Warner Bros. It was the first commercially successful feature-length talkie and starred Al Jolson. He later married Ruby Keeler, female star of 42ND STREET, FOOTLIGHT PARADE, GOLDDIGGERS OF 1933; Busby Berkeley

46 Louis Armstrong

ALL-SINGING, ALL-DANCING
Answers to Picture Questions

Page 11:
Fred Astaire and Judy Garland in EASTER PARADE; Gene Kelly; Irving Berlin; Robert Alton; Charles Walters

Page 12:
LET'S MAKE LOVE; 'My Heart Belongs To Daddy'; George Cukor; Yves Montand; Frankie Vaughan; Milton Berle; Bing Crosby; Gene Kelly

Page 13:
Nanette Fabray and Jack Buchanan, THE BAND WAGON, 'Triplets'; Vincente Minnelli; YOLANDA AND THE THIEF and ZIEGFELD FOLLIES; Cyd Charisse; 'Dancing In The Dark'; Arthur Schwartz and Howard Dietz

Page 14:

THE BEST THINGS IN LIFE ARE FREE; Michael Curtiz; Sheree North and Jacques D'Amboise; Buddy DeSylva, Lew Brown and Ray Henderson; Gordon MacRae, Ernest Borgnine and Dan Dailey; Rod Alexander

Page 15:

John Travolta; SATURDAY NIGHT FEVER; Karen Lynn Gorney; The Bee Gees; John Badham; STAYING ALIVE

Page 16:

WEST SIDE STORY; 'America'; Rita Moreno; George Chakiris; Leonard Bernstein and Stephen Sondheim; Robert Wise and Jerome Robbins; Daniel Fapp; Natalie Wood and Richard Beymer

Page 17:

Catherine Deneuve and Françoise Dorleac; they were real-life sisters; THE YOUNG GIRLS OF ROCHEFORT; Jacques Demy; Michel Legrand (music) and Demy (lyrics); Gene Kelly; THE UMBRELLAS OF CHERBOURG

Page 18:

SINGIN' IN THE RAIN; 'Broadway Rhythm' and 'Broadway Melody'; the producer (Arthur Freed) also wrote the lyrics; Gene Kelly and Cyd Charisse; BRIGADOON; Jean Hagen; Betty Comden and Adolph Green; THE BAND WAGON

Page 19:

Busby Berkeley; GOLDDIGGERS OF 1937; 'All's Fair In Love And War'; Harry Warren and Al Dubin; 'Lullaby Of Broadway'; Lloyd Bacon; Dick Powell and Joan Blondell

MAKE 'EM LAUGH
Answers to Picture Questions

Page 21, right:

THE APARTMENT: Jack Lemmon, he lent the key of his apartment to his (generally married) superiors for the purpose of entertaining their lady friends; Fred MacMurray, Shirley MacLaine; MacLaine (Kubelik), Lemmon (Baxter), MacMurray (Sheldrake)

Page 21, above and left

Cary Grant (above), Tony Curtis, Jack Lemmon (right); Grant can travel home on a troop ship only if he is a woman, Curtis and Lemmon are on the run from gangsters, so they join an all-girl band; a) Lemmon gets engaged to Joe E. Brown b) Grant uses the tail of a horse to make his wig c) Curtis imitates Grant's voice to seduce Marilyn Monroe; I WAS A MALE WAR BRIDE, Howard Hawks; SOME LIKE IT HOT, Billy Wilder; i) THE MOUSE THAT ROARED ii) KIND HEARTS AND CORONETS and THE COMEDIANS iii) VICTOR/VICTORIA iv) THE KREMLIN LETTER v) AT WAR WITH THE ARMY and MONEY FROM HOME

Page 22, right:

a) MON ONCLE b) M. Hulot, Jacques Tati c) Brother-in-law d) M. HULOT'S HOLIDAY, PLAYTIME e) MON ONCLE

Page 22, above:

a) Hyde Park (London) b) Softball c) George Segal, Glenda Jackson d) A TOUCH OF CLASS, LOST AND FOUND e) Melvin Frank

Page 23, above:

M*A*S*H; Mobile Army Surgical Hospital; the Korean War; the characters were Hawkeye Pierce and Trapper John McIntyre played by Donald Sutherland (left) and Elliott Gould (right); Hawkeye played by Alan Alda; Hot Lips

Page 25, above:

THE GENERAL; a railroad steam engine, Keaton played the engine driver; The American Civil War

Page 25, right:

a) Julius, Adolph, Leonard and Herbert b) THE COCOANUTS, 1929 c) Paramount, MGM d) Groucho

Page 25, left:

MY LITTLE CHICKADEE, Mae West and W.C. Fields; a) West b) Fields c) West d) Fields e) West

Page 26, above:

ADAM'S RIB (1949); Judy Holliday is the defendant in a murder case, Hepburn is her lawyer and is married to Tracy, who is prosecuting; WOMAN OF THE YEAR (1942), their first film together, became a Broadway musical in the 70s; KEEPER OF THE FLAME (1942), WITHOUT LOVE (1945), THE SEA OF GRASS (1946), STATE OF THE UNION (1948), PAT AND MIKE (1952), DESK SET (1957), GUESS WHO'S COMING TO DINNER? (1967)

Page 26, right and above right

ANNIE HALL (right), ZELIG; Diane Keaton, Christopher Walken; SLEEPER; PLAY IT AGAIN, SAM; MANHATTAN; LOVE AND DEATH; they are psychiatrists; Mia Farrow; MANHATTAN, STARDUST MEMORIES, BROADWAY DANNY ROSE; INTERIORS, Ingmar Bergman

Page 26, far right:

The title refers to a diamond with a pink glow at its centre; Peter Sellers and Capucine, they play man and wife; Inspector Clouseau; David Niven

Page 28, above:

ARTHUR, Dudley Moore and Liza Minnelli; he is a heavy drinker; John Gielgud, he won his first Oscar (Best Supporting Actor); CHARLIE BUBBLES, Albert Finney

Page 28, right:

Bugs Bunny's; WHAT'S UP, DOC?, Ryan O'Neal, Barbra Streisand; a musicologist; San Francisco; on an airplane; Peter Bogdanovich; THE MAIN EVENT

Page 29, above:

Mel Brooks, BLAZING SADDLES, Warner Bros.; Cleavon Little, he played a black sheriff; Brooks played a Jewish Indian Chief and a territorial governor; Hedley Lamarr; Gene Wilder, Madeline Kahn

Page 31, above left:

Dorothy Lamour, Bob Hope; ROAD TO HONG KONG, Joan Collins and Bing Crosby; Lamour only played a cameo role, whereas in the other 'Road' films, she was the female lead; Sellers repeated the role of an Indian doctor he had played previously in THE MILLIONAIRESS; England

Page 31, above:

Mary Pickford, THE TAMING OF THE SHREW (1929); Elizabeth Taylor and Richard Burton (1967)

Page 31, right:

THE COURT JESTER; he is spitting out what might be poison as he has confused the cups, forgetting that 'the pellet with the poison' was in 'the vessel with the pestle', not 'the flagon with the dragon' or 'the chalice from the palace'

Page 31, left:

Roman Polanski, DANCE OF THE VAMPIRES (also THE FEARLESS VAMPIRE KILLERS); Sharon Tate, they were lovers (and married a year later); REPULSION (a bit part); WHAT?; CHINATOWN; THE TENANT

REACH FOR THE STARS – Page 32

A a) Joel McCrea b) THE SILVER CORD, Laura Hope Crewes, Frances Dee c) GUNFIGHT AT DODGE CITY, WICHITA d) THE MORE THE MERRIER, George Stevens, Jean Arthur, WALK DON'T RUN e) RIDE THE HIGH COUNTRY (GB: GUNS IN THE AFTERNOON), Randolph Scott, Sam Peckinpah

B a) Vanessa Redgrave b) Italian star Franco Nero c) THE SEAGULL, Sidney Lumet d) CAMELOT, Richard Harris e) JULIA, Jane Fonda, Lillian Hellman

C a) Montgomery Clift b) THE SEARCH, RED RIVER; Fred Zinneman, Howard Hawks c) RAINTREE COUNTY; Elizabeth Taylor, Eva-Marie Saint; Johnny Green d) A PLACE IN THE SUN; George Stevens; Phillips Holmes e) THE DEFECTOR; Raoul Levy

D a) Deborah Kerr b) EDWARD MY SON, FROM HERE TO ETERNITY, Fred Zinneman, Burt Lancaster c) THE KING AND I, SEPARATE TABLES, HEAVEN KNOWS MR ALLISON, THE SUNDOWNERS d) THE LIFE AND DEATH OF COLONEL BLIMP; Michael Powell and Emeric Pressburger, Roger Livesey e) THE INNOCENTS, Jack Clayton, 'The Turn Of The Screw' by Henry James

E a) Sylvester Stallone b) PARADISE ALLEY c) F.I.S.T. d) FIRST BLOOD e) STAYING ALIVE

F a) Rod Steiger B) IN THE HEAT OF THE NIGHT; a police officer c) W.C. Fields d) THE SERGEANT e) Claire Bloom

G a) Lana Turner b) THEY WON'T FORGET, Mervyn Leroy c) ZIEGFELD GIRL, Judy Garland and Hedy Lamarr d) THE POSTMAN ALWAYS RINGS TWICE, Jessica Lange e) PEYTON PLACE, Diane Varsi

H a) Robert De Niro b) NEW YORK, NEW YORK c) The young Vito Corleone in THE GODFATHER, PART II d) Monroe Stahr, THE LAST TYCOON e) MEAN STREETS, TAXI DRIVER, THE KING OF COMEDY

I a) Burt Lancaster b) THE SWIMMER c) FROM HERE TO ETERNITY d) THE SWEET SMELL OF SUCCESS e) THE BIRDMAN OF ALCATRAZ

THE LOVE PARADE

1 a) LOVE AFFAIR/AN AFFAIR TO REMEMBER; Irene Dunne/Deborah Kerr b) BACK STREET (all three versions); Irene Dunne/Margaret Sulla-van/Susan Hayward c) WATERLOO BRIDGE/WATERLOO BRIDGE/GABY; Mae Clarke/Vivien Leigh/Leslie Caron d) ROMEO AND JULIET; Norma Shearer/Susan Shentall/Olivia Hussey e) IMITATION OF LIFE (both versions); Claudette Colbert/Lana Turner

2 a) Robert Taylor to Greta Garbo, CAMILLE b) Cyril Raymond to Celia Johnson, BRIEF ENCOUNTER c) Ryan O'Neal to Barbra Streisand, WHAT'S UP DOC? d) Orson Welles about Rita Hayworth, THE LADY FROM SHANGHAI e) Lois Wheeler to Susan Hayward, MY FOOLISH HEART f) Shirley MacLaine to Jack Lemmon, THE APARTMENT g) Bette Davis to Paul Henreid, NOW VOYAGER h) Jessica Lange to Dustin Hoffman, TOOTSIE i) Deborah Kerr to John Kerr, TEA AND SYMPATHY j) Gloria Grahame (alone), IN A LONELY PLACE

3 a) ROMAN HOLIDAY b) THE PRISONER OF ZENDA c) THE STUDENT PRINCE d) ROSALIE e) THE KING AND THE CHORUS GIRL

4 a) Robert Browning; Norma Shearer; THE BARRETTS OF WIMPOLE STREET b) Georges Sand; Cornel Wilde; A SONG TO REMEMBER c) Scott Fitzgerald; Deborah Kerr; BELOVED INFIDEL d) Clark Gable; Jill Clayburgh; GABLE AND LOMBARD e) Nell Gwyn; Cedric Hardwicke; NELL GWYN

5 a) DECEPTION b) THE LETTER c) IN THIS OUR LIFE d) A STOLEN LIFE e) THE GREAT LIE

6 PAID IN FULL; Lizabeth Scott, Diana Lynn

7 a) DARK VICTORY, Bette Davis; STOLEN HOURS, Susan Hayward b) SWEET NOVEMBER, Sandy Dennis c) SENTIMENTAL JOURNEY, Maureen O'Hara; THE GIFT OF LOVE, Lauren Bacall d) INCENDIARY BLONDE, Betty Hutton e) NO SAD SONGS FOR ME, Margaret Sullavan

8 a) Cary Grant b) Wendy Hiller c) Elliott Gould d) Claudette Colbert e) Spencer Tracy

9 a) DARK ANGEL: Ronald Colman, Fredric March

10 Ginger Rogers and Walter Pidgeon; Lana Turner and Van Johnson

11 THE GLASS SLIPPER, Leslie Caron; THE SLIPPER AND THE ROSE; Gemma Craven; CINDERFELLA, Jerry Lewis

12 a) THE GHOST AND MRS MUIR; Gene Tierney, Rex Harrison b) BLITHE SPIRIT; Rex Harrison, Kay Hammond, Constance Cummings, Margaret Rutherford c) PORTRAIT OF JENNIE; Joseph Cotten, Jennifer Jones d) I MARRIED A WITCH; Fredric March, Veronica Lake, Susan Hayward, Cecil Kellaway e) BERKELEY SQUARE; Leslie Howard, Heather Angel; I'LL NEVER FORGET YOU (GB: THE HOUSE IN THE SQUARE): Tyrone Power, Ann Blyth

13 JANE EYRE: Virginia Bruce and Colin Clive, directed by Christy Cabanne; Joan Fontaine and Orson Welles, directed by Robert Stevenson; Susannah York and George C. Scott, directed by Delbert Mann; WUTHERING HEIGHTS: Merle Oberon and Laurence Olivier, directed by William Wyler; Eva Irasema Dilian and Jorge Mistral, directed by Luis Buñuel; Anna Calder-Marshall and Timothy Dalton, directed by Robert Fuest

14 a) Rod Steiger and Claire Bloom b) Jean Simmons and Stewart Grainger c) Rex Harrison and Lilli Palmer d) Elizabeth Taylor and Eddie Fisher e) Janet Leigh and Tony Curtis f) Paul Newman and Joanne Woodward g) Jennifer Jones and Robert Walker h) Charles Bronson and Jill Ireland i) Bobby Darin and Sandra Dee j) Kay Kendall and Rex Harrison

15 LA STRADA; Federico Fellini; Giulietta Masina, Anthony Quinn

16 a) Claudette Colbert; Clark Gable, Spencer Tracy b) Marlene Dietrich; John Wayne, Randolph Scott c) Joan Crawford; Robert Young, Franchot Tone d) Ann Todd; James Mason, Hugh McDermott, Albert Lieven e) Joan Fontaine; George Brent, Dennis O'Keefe, Don DeFore, Walter Abel

17 a) John Barrymore b) Douglas Fairbanks Sr c) Errol Flynn d) Adriano Rimoldi e) Brigitte Bardot

18 a) MILDRED PIERCE c) NORA PRENTISS c) REBECCA d) KITTY e) JANE EYRE

19 a) THE NUN'S STORY; Audrey Hepburn, Peter Finch b) HEAVEN KNOWS, MR ALLISON; Robert Mitchum, Deborah Kerr c) MONSIGNOR, Christopher Reeve, Genevieve Bujold d) WINTER MEETING; Bette Davis, Jim Davis e) A RUNNER STUMBLES; Dick Van Dyke, Kathleen Quinlan

20 a) Bette Davis and Errol Flynn b) Victor Mature and Hedy Lamarr c) Claude Rains and Vivien Leigh d) Gregory Peck and Susan Hayward e) Yul Brynner and Gina Lollobrigida

21 a) Ray Milland and Ginger Rogers b) Gary Cooper and Merle Oberon c) Hedy Lamarr and Robert Walker d) Daniel Gelin and Anne Vernon e) Gena Rowlands and Seymour Cassel

22 PILLOW TALK; LOVER COME BACK; SEND ME NO FLOWERS

23 GILDA; Rita Hayworth, George MaCready, Glenn Ford

24 a) Greta Garbo; QUEEN CHRISTINA b) Barbra Streisand; YENTL c) Renate Muller; VIKTOR UND VIKTORIA; Jessie Matthews; FIRST A GIRL; Julie Andrews; VICTOR/VICTORIA d) Katharine Hepburn; SYLVIA SCARLETT e) Veronica Lake; SULLIVAN'S TRAVELS

25 Ac – THE OLD MAID; Be – WHERE LOVE HAS GONE; Cd – TO EACH HIS OWN; Db – MADAME X; Ea – MILDRED PIERCE

26 BECKY SHARP; Rouben Mamoulian; Miriam Hopkins

27 UN HOMME ET UNE FEMME (A MAN AND A WOMAN); Jean-Louis Trintignant, Anouk Aimée; Deauville; Claude Lelouch, Francis Lai

28 a) LOVE WITH THE PROPER STRANGER b) LOVE IN THE AFTERNOON c) LOVE IS A MANY-SPLENDORED THING d) LOVE LETTERS e) LOVE f) LOVE HAS MANY FACES g) LOVE AND PAIN AND THE WHOLE DAMN THING h) LOVE ON THE DOLE i) LOVE IS NEWS j) A NEW KIND OF LOVE

29 Anthony Dexter, Rudolph Nureyev

30 RANDOM HARVEST; Ronald Colman, Greer Garson; James Hilton

31 a) William Wyler b) George Cukor c) Edmund Goulding d) Anatole Litvak d) Curtis Bernhardt

32 Warner Baxter; Alan Ladd

THE LOVE PARADE
Answers to Picture Questions

Page 34:
Marlene Dietrich; Gary Cooper, MOROCCO; Josef Von Sternberg; THE BLUE ANGEL, DISHONORED, SHANGHAI EXPRESS, BLONDE VENUS, THE SCARLET EMPRESS; THE DEVIL IS A WOMAN; she removes her high (three-inch) heeled shoes as she treks through the windswept desert

Page 36:
BRIEF ENCOUNTER; Celia Johnson and Trevor Howard; Johnson got a piece of grit in her eye and (doctor) Howard removed it; STILL LIFE; Noël Coward; Rachmaninov's 2nd Piano Concerto; Eileen Joyce

Page 37:
Ryan O'Neal and Ali McGraw, LOVE STORY; 'Love Means Never Having To Say You're Sorry'; Erich Segal; OLIVER'S STORY

Page 39:
CAMILLE; Robert Taylor; George Cukor; Lionel Barrymore; Henry Daniell

HOLLYWOOD SCANDAL!

1 a) Joan Crawford b) W.C. Fields c) Robert Taylor d) Cecil B. DeMille e) Alice Faye

2 a) Lewis Stone b) Linda Darnell c) James Dean d) Jayne Mansfield e) Natalie Wood; Robert Wagner; they divorced, then married each other again

3 a) Lupe Velez; Johnny Weissmuller b) Clark Gable and Carole Lombard c) Paul Bern and Jean Harlow d) Douglas Fairbanks Jr; Franchot Tone; Philip Terry; Alfred Steele (chairman of Pepsi Cola) e) They were all married to debonair screenwriter Gene Markey

4 a) The financier Jim Fiske in THE TOAST OF NEW YORK b) Emma Hamilton in LADY HAMILTON c) The multiple murderer Christie in 10 RILLINGTON PLACE d) The crooked financier Stavisky in STAVISKY e) J. Edgar Hoover in THE FILES OF J. EDGAR HOOVER

5 a) He was a VD specialist and the Paramount studio doctor b) Marion Davies, Hearst's lover and protégée. Louella was employed by Hearst's powerful newspaper chain c) Mae West d) SUNSET BOULEVARD e) Joan Bennett f) Paul Drake in the long-running 'Perry Mason' series

6 a) Mae West b) Tallulah Bankhead c) David O. Selznick, Louis B. Mayer's son-in-law d) Rudolph Valentino, because of a story that he asked a favourite restaurant to install a face powder dispenser in the men's room e) Nicholas Ray of Joan Crawford; JOHNNY GUITAR

7 a) Gwili Andre b) George Sanders c) Carole Landis d) Charles Ray e) Gig Young

8 a) Frances Farmer b) RHYTHM ON THE RANGE; Bing Crosby c) It was a thriller on the theme of mental illness d) Leif Erickson e) 'Will There Really Be A Morning?'

9 a) Thelma Todd b) Ramon Novarro c) Sal Mineo d) Mark Frechette e) Sharon Tate

10 a) Wallace Reid b) Barbara La Marr c) Robert Mitchum. He got a two-month jail sentence (which did nothing to harm his career); Lila Leeds; WILD WEED d) Gertrude Michael e) Anthony Perkins

11 a) W.C. Fields b) John Barrymore c) Lee Tracy; VIVA VILLA! d) William Holden e) The house shared by David Niven and Errol Flynn; their landlady, Rosalind Russell

12 a) Judy Garland; bandleader David Rose b) Ingrid Bergman; Roberto Rossellini; STROMBOLI c) Joan Crawford

13 a) Jane Russell; THE OUTLAW; Howard Hughes b) Hedy Lamarr; ECSTACY; Victor Mature c) Janet Leigh d) Margaret Lockwood in THE WICKED LADY e) Julie Andrews; Blake Edwards; S.O.B.

14 a) 'Frankly, my dear, I don't give a damn'; GONE WITH THE WIND; Clark Gable b) NORTH BY NORTHWEST; Cary Grant and Eva Marie Saint c) Georgia was the home of the chain gang, brilliantly portrayed by LeRoy in I AM A FUGITIVE FROM A CHAIN GANG (1932) d) TOWN WITHOUT PITY (1961); Christine Kaufmann e) WATERLOO BRIDGE (1940). The line was changed from 'I have been with other men' to 'I have been with another man'

15 a) Clara Bow b) Mary Astor c) Francis X. Bushman d) Errol Flynn; GENTLEMAN JIM e) David Begelman; Columbia Pictures; Cliff Robertson f) Joan Barry

16 a) Mary Beth Hughes b) Louise Brooks c) Betty Hutton d) Lawrence Tierney e) Neil Hamilton

17 a) Brian Donlevy b) Ray Milland c) Judy Garland d) Maria Montez e) Humphrey Bogart

18 a) John Barrymore b) Clara Bow c) Lupe Velez d) Buster Keaton e) Joan Crawford

19 a) Beery's playful cuffing of co-star Mickey Rooney was drawing blood b) Constance Bennett; THREE FACES EAST c) Joan Crawford; Norma Shearer; THE WOMEN d) Mae West; W.C. Fields; MY LITTLE CHICKADEE e) Clark Gable; Spencer Tracy; TEST PILOT f) George Raft

HOLLYWOOD SCANDAL!
Answers to Picture Questions

Page 40:
The set of CLEOPATRA; Eddie Fisher; BUTTERFIELD 8; DIVORCE HIS, DIVORCE HERS; Richard Burton

Page 41:
Arthur Miller (married to Marilyn Monroe); Simone Signoret and her husband Yves Montand; Frankie Vaughan; LET'S MAKE LOVE directed by George Cukor; THE MISFITS; Joe Di Maggio, the baseball star

Page 42:
IMITATION OF LIFE; Sandra Dee; Lana Turner's daughter, Cheryl Crane; Johnny Stompanato, Lana's boyfriend, who had gangland connections; in Lana's bedroom; in JOHNNY EAGER Lana falls in love with a mobster (Robert Taylor)

Page 44:
Manslaughter (he was acquitted); Virginia Rappe; William R. Goodrich

REACH FOR THE STARS – Page 45

A a) Louise Brooks b) THE BEGGARS OF LIFE (1928); SULLIVAN'S TRAVELS (1941); Joel McCrea, Veronica Lake c) PANDORA'S BOX, Jack The Ripper d) Jean Harlow e) John Wayne

B a) John Barrymore b) Ronald Colman, David Niven; GRAND HOTEL (1932) c) BILL OF DIVORCEMENT; Katharine Hepburn d) TOO MUCH, TOO SOON (1957); the autobiography of his daughter Diana Barrymore e) Richard III (SHOW OF SHOWS, 1929 – plus Gloucester' 'Ambition' Soliloquy from 'Henry VI, Part 3'!); Hamlet (PLAYMATES), 1941)

C a) Rita Hayworth b) BLOOD AND SAND, Tyrone Power c) YOU'LL NEVER GET RICH, YOU WERE NEVER LOVELIER d) Orson Welles; THE LADY FROM SHANGHAI; he cut her hair and dyed it blonde e) GILDA, 'Put The Blame On Mame', Glenn Ford, Charles Vidor

D a) June Allyson b) Dick Powell; RIGHT CROSS, THE REFORMER AND THE REDHEAD c) THE GLENN MILLER STORY; James Stewart; THE STRATTON STORY, STRATEGIC AIR COMMAND d) GIRL CRAZY; 'Treat Me Rough'; Mickey Rooney e) LITTLE WOMEN; Elizabeth Taylor, Janet Leigh, Margaret O'Brien; Katharine Hepburn, Joan Bennett, Frances Dee, Jean Parker

TORSOS AND TOGAS – THE EPIC

1 a) SAMSON AND DELILAH b) SAMSON AND DELILAH c) THE TEN COMMANDMENTS; ADAM'S RIB, FORBIDDEN FRUIT d) Claudette Colbert; CLEOPATRA e) Blount f) JOAN THE WOMAN (1916) g) KING OF KINGS h) Charlton Heston i) Victor Mature; SAMSON AND DELILAH – C.B.'s first epic wholly in Technicolor j) THE GREATEST SHOW ON EARTH, Charlton Heston

2 a) Richard Widmark in THE LONG SHIPS b) Fredric March in THE SIGN OF THE CROSS c) Charlton Heston in THE WAR LORD d) Flora Robson in CAESAR AND CLEOPATRA e) Hugh Griffith in BEN HUR (1959)

3 a) Rouben Mamoulian b) Caesar: Peter Finch, Rex Harrison. Anthony: Stephen Boyd, Richard Burton c) Anthony Mann d) Charles Brabin, George Walsh; Fred Niblo, Ramon Novarro e) Yul Brynner; Tyrone Power – he died of a heart attack after filming a strenuous duel with George Sanders; it was one of Yul's rare appearances sporting a head of hair

4 a) Michael Jayston and Janet Suzman b) Nikolai Cherkasov c) Edmund Purdom d) Elana Eden e) Anthony Quinn f) Marlene Dietrich g) Richard Burton h) Mohammed did not appear in the film (portrayals not permitted by Muslim religion) i) Lionel Barrymore and Ethel Barrymore j) Burt Lancaster

5 a) THE HISTORY OF THE WORLD PART I b) THE THREE AGES c) ROMAN SCANDALS d) MONTY PYTHON'S LIFE OF BRIAN e) MONTY PYTHON AND THE HOLY GRAIL

6 EL CID; Charlton Heston, Sophia Loren, John Fraser, Genevieve Page; Miklos Rozsa: Anthony Mann

7 a) ALEXANDER THE GREAT b) CLEOPATRA (1934) c) LAND OF THE PHARAOHS d) BEN HUR (1925) e) QUO VADIS

8 a) JUPITER'S DARLING, Marge Champion, Gower Champion b) SPARTACUS, Peter Ustinov c) CAESAR AND CLEOPATRA, Vivien Leigh d) THE LONG SHIPS, Richard Widmark e) THE TEN COMMANDMENTS, Anne Baxter, Charlton Heston f) BEN HUR, Stephen Boyd g) KING RICHARD AND THE CRUSADERS, Virginia Mayo (to George Sanders) h) LAND OF THE PHARAOHS, William Faulkner (to Howard Hawks) i) THE TEN COMMANDMENTS, Adolph Zukor (to Cecil B. DeMille) when confronted with the plans for the silent version j) THE CHARGE OF THE LIGHT BRIGADE (1936), director Michael Curtiz during shooting

9 a) Miklos Rozsa b) Franz Waxman c) Bernard Herrmann d) Maurice Jarre e) Alex North

10 a) Howard Gaye b) H.B. Warner c) Max von Sydow d) Ted Neeley e) Cameron Mitchell

11 a) Steve Reeves and Gordon Scott b) Rory Calhoun c) Mickey Hargitay and Jayne Mansfield d) Broderick Crawford e) Reg Park (Mr Universe), Fay Spain

12 a) Best Costume Design/Best Art Direction/Set Decoration; Franklin J. Schaffner; Irene Worth b) Sergei Eisenstein; Stalin disapproved of it — it was shown five years after his death in 1958; Sergei Prokofiev c) Lana Turner; Walter Hampden; THE EGYPTIAN (1954) d) 20th Century-Fox; Henry Koster, THE ROBE; Stuart Whitman e) Christopher Fry (with Diego Fabbri, Ivo Perilli and Nigel Balchin); Arthur Kennedy; THE SHOES OF THE FISHERMAN f) George Bernard Shaw; Jeanne Moreau; Peter O'Toole g) Jean Anouilh; King Henry II, Peter O'Toole; Louis VII h) Anthony Quinn; Irene Papas i) John Barrymore; to avoid a libel action by Youssoupoff (he sued MGM anyway); Christopher Lee, Tom Baker j) Anthony Burgess; Bill Lancaster, Burt's son; Anthony Quayle

13 a) Raoul Walsh, ESTHER AND THE KING, Joan Collins, Richard Egan b) Eugene Pallette c) Lillian Gish d) Billy Bitzer e) The Ku Klux Klan

14 a) THE VIKINGS b) THE LONG SHIPS c) SPARTACUS d) THE TEN COMMANDMENTS (1956) e) LAND OF THE PHARAOHS

15 a) Kirk Douglas b) Fredric March c) Rossano Brazzi d) Steve Reeves e) Honor Blackman

16 a) Herbert Lom b) Rod Steiger c) Charles Boyer d) Marlon Brando e) Dennis Hopper

17 a) John P. Fulton b) Arnold Gillespie c) Willis O'Brien d) Gordon Jennings e) Ray Harryhausen

18 a) Dino de Laurentiis b) John Huston c) THE BIBLE d) The first 22 chapters of the Book of Genesis e) George C. Scott, John Huston, Ava Gardner, Michael Parks, Richard Harris, Peter O'Toole

19 Ae; Ba; Ch; Di; Eb; Fg; Gj; Hf; Id; Jc

20 a) Alec Guinness b) Charles Laughton c) Jay Robinson d) Timothy West e) Cornel Wilde

21 a) Mark Anthony b) Andrew Jackson c) John the Baptist d) Michelangelo e) General Gordon

22 a) Susan Hayward b) Rhonda Fleming c) Anouk Aimée d) Susan Hayward e) Rita Hayworth; this time she danced to *save* the head of John the Baptist

TORSOS AND TOGAS
Answers to Picture Questions

Page 46:
Joseph L. Mankiewicz, JULIUS CAESAR; Cinecitta Studios, Rome; 20th Century-Fox; Roddy McDowell

Page 48:
Filmed in Spain, but set in Russia; DOCTOR ZHIVAGO; Boris Pasternak wrote the novel and Robert Bolt the screenplay; Omar Sharif as Zhivago, Julie Christie as Lara; Sir Alec Guinness and Sir Ralph Richardson; David Lean

Page 49:
WAR AND PEACE (1956); Mel Ferrer, Prince Andrei; None; King Vidor; Russia; Sergei Bondarchuk

Page 50:
a) Ben Kingsley, BETRAYAL; Harold Pinter b) Richard Attenborough, YOUNG WINSTON (Churchill) c) Candice Bergen (Edgar's daughter); photo-journalist Margaret Bourke-White; Bergen is, herself, a sometime photo-journalist

Page 51:
a) False — it is LAWRENCE OF ARABIA b) False — David Lean directed c) True d) False — it was Robert Bolt e) True

Page 52:
THE SIGN OF THE CROSS, (1 to r) Charles Laughton, Claudette Colbert, Fredric March; Nero; Poppaea; she is taking a bath — in asses' milk

Page 53:
BEN HUR, Charlton Heston; Francis X. Bushman in 1925, who was maimed for life in the chariot race, and Stephen Boyd in 1959 who was killed in it; Haya Harareet, Esther; McAvoy was an extra in 1959; Cathy O'Donnell (foreground centre), Martha Scott (background centre)

THE WAY OF THE WEST

1 a) Jean Arthur, Frances Farmer, Jane Russell, Yvonne De Carlo, Doris Day b) Gene Tierney, Jane Russell c) Barbara Stanwyck, Betty Hutton d) Barbara Stanwyck e) Marlene Dietrich f) Brigitte Bardot g) Mari Blanchard h) Joan Crawford i) Jane Fonda j) Jane Fonda

2 Aa; Be; Ch; Df; Eg; Fd; Gj; Hc/Hi; Ic/Ii; Jb

3 a) Fonda (bad) Bronson (good) b) Cotten (good) Peck (bad) c) Fonda (good) Douglas (bad) d) Fonda (bad) Stewart (good) e) Widmark (bad) Taylor (good)

4 a) THE SHOOTIST; John Wayne – he was himself dying of cancer b) HIGH NOON; Gary Cooper, Grace Kelly c) TRUE GRIT; John Wayne, Kim Darby; Wayne won his only Oscar d) GOIN' SOUTH; Mary Steenburgen, Jack Nicholson – He also directed e) WAY OUT WEST; Laurel and Hardy, 'Commence To Dancing' and 'The Trail Of The Lonesome Pine'

5 a) The incident was the lynching of three innocent men; Henry Fonda, Dana Andrews, William Wellman b) The name of a roller-skating rink; Kris Kristofferson, Michael Cimino c) Honorary name given to white man adopted by the Cheyennes; Dustin Hoffman, Arthur Penn d) A coveted rifle fought over; James Stewart, Anthony Mann e) The headwaters of the Missouri river in Montana; Marlon Brando, Arthur Penn f) The railroad linking east and west; Joel McCrea, Cecil B. DeMille g) Double-meaning, referring to Joanne Woodward taking over the playing of a poker game for her ailing husband; Henry Fonda, Fielder Cook h) The transcontinental train; George O'Brien, John Ford i) A specially armoured stage coach; John Wayne, Kirk Douglas, Burt Kennedy j) A group of men searching for 10 years to find white girl kidnapped by Indians; John Wayne, John Ford

6 a) James Stewart b) Gary Cooper c) Kirk Douglas d) Burt Reynolds e) John Wayne – not James Stewart who thought he had f) Randolph Scott g) Richard Harris h) Robert Mitchum i) Terence Hill j) Clint Eastwood as he was known in his 'spaghetti' westerns

7 a) THE FRISCO KID (Gene Wilder) b) THERE WAS A CROOKED MAN (Hume Cronyn and John Randolph) c) LITTLE BIG MAN (Robert Little Star) d) BLAZING SADDLES (Mel Brooks) e) BLAZING SADDLES (Cleavon Little) f) RED SUN (Toshiro Mifune) g) RUGGLES OF RED GAP (Charles Laughton)/FANCY PANTS (Bop Hope) h) THE SHERIFF OF FRACTURED JAW (Kenneth More) i) MISSOURI BREAKS (Marlon Brando) j) THE GUNSLINGER (Beverly Garland)

8 Ah; Bb; Ci; Df; Ej; Fc; Gg; Ha; Ie; Jd

9 Ab; Bc; Ci; Dd; Ef; Fg; Ga; Hh; Ij; Je

10 a) Joel McCrea b) Randolph Scott c) Andy Devine d) Charles Bronson e) Audie Murphy f) Glenn Ford g) Lee Marvin

11 a) McCrea made FOREIGN CORRE-SPONDENT with Hitchcock, and several, including SULLIVAN'S TRAVELS, for Preston Sturges b) Scott appeared in ROBERTA and FOLLOW THE FLEET c) Devine was the voice of Little John in ROBIN HOOD d) Bronson, actually born Bunchinsky, used those names e) Murphy played himself in TO HELL AND BACK f) Ford played Superman's adopted father g) Marvin won an Oscar for CAT BALLOU

12 William Wyler; Gregory Peck, Jean Simmons and Carroll Baker; Charlton Heston, Burl Ives; Jerome Moross

13 a) RASHOMON (Akira Kurosawa) b) KISS OF DEATH (Henry Hathaway) c) HIGH SIERRA (Raoul Walsh) d) HOUSE OF STRANGERS (Joseph Mankiewicz) e) THE SEVEN SAMURAI (Akira Kurosawa)

14 1939, United Artist's, Paramount's, Universal's, NORTHWEST PASSAGE, Young, Brennan, New England, Indians, 18th

15 John Wayne; John Wayne; George Montgomery; DAVY CROCKETT, KING OF THE WILD FRONTIER and DAVY CROCKETT AND THE RIVER PIRATES; the word 'fesse' in French means a buttock

16 a) THE UNFORGIVEN b) HOUR OF THE GUN c) MONTE WALSH d) CAT BALLOU e) CANYON PASSAGE f) THREE YOUNG TEXANS g) TWO MULES FOR SISTER SARA and THE SHEEPMAN h) GUNFIGHT IN ABILENE i) STAGECOACH (1966) and RHYTHM ON THE RANGE j) THEY CAME TO CORDURA and THE WRATH OF GOD

17 a) Billy the Kid (Paul Newman) b) Wild Bill Hickock (Gary Cooper) c) Wyatt Earp (Henry Fonda) and Doc Holliday (Victor Mature) d) Wild Bill Hickock (Howard Keel) e) Wyatt Earp (Burt Lancaster) and Doc Holliday (Kirk Douglas)

18 a) Tyrone Power, Henry Fonda b) Audie Murphy, Richard Long c) James Keach, Stacy Keach d) Henry Fonda (Jesse is dead, but seen being shot at film's opening in a clip from JESSE JAMES viz Tyrone Power) e) John Ireland pretends to be Jesse; Reed Hadley was Frank James

19 Ab; Be; Cd; Dc; Ea

20 Ac (sympathetic); Ba (sympathetic); Cd (sympathetic); Db (unsympathetic); Ee (both)

21 a) i) THE HORSE SOLDIERS ii) RIO GRANDE iii) THE SEARCHERS iv) FORT APACHE v) THE SEARCHERS and THE MAN WHO SHOT LIBERTY VALANCE b) James Stewart and Richard Widmark c) Althea Gibson d) Francis Ford e) Victor McLaglen, Andrew McLaglen

22 a) SHANE b) THE NAKED SPUR c) THE TALL MEN d) ONE-EYED JACKS e) THE HANGING TREE f) THE GUNFIGHTER g) SHOWDOWN h) THE GOOD GUYS AND THE BAD GUYS i) THE GOOD, THE BAD AND THE UGLY j) THE MAGNIFICENT SEVEN

23 THE MAGNIFICENT SEVEN: Horst Buchholz, James Coburn, Robert Vaughan, Charles Bronson, Yul Brynner, Steve McQueen, Brad Dexter; THE WILD BUNCH: Warren Oates, William Holden, Edmond O'Brien, Ben Johnson, Ernest Borgnine, Robert Ryan (Lee Van Cleef and Jordan Christopher were in remakes of THE MAGNIFICENT SEVEN)

24 a) Warren Beatty, Julie Christie b) John Wayne c) Clint Eastwood d) Clint Eastwood, Lee Van Cleef, Eli Wallach e) Steve McQueen f) William Holden g) Jack Beutel h) Jason Robards i) Robert Redford j) Robert Blake

25 a) The Marx Brothers in GO WEST b) Buster Keaton in GO WEST c) Dean Martin and Jerry Lewis in PARDNERS d) Abbott and Costello in THE WISTFUL WIDOW OF WAGON GAP e) Sidney James, Kenneth Williams et al in CARRY ON COWBOY

26 a) PALEFACE (a winner) b) CALAMITY JANE (a winner) c) BUTCH CASSIDY AND THE SUNDANCE KID (a winner) d) CANYON PASSAGE e) THE ALAMO f) SINGING GUNS g) SON OF PALE-FACE h) THE YOUNG LAND i) HIGH NOON (a winner) j) THE LIFE AND TIMES OF JUDGE ROY BEAN

27 a) GIRL OF THE GOLDEN WEST (1938) b) RED GARTERS c) OKLA-HOMA! d) PAINT YOUR WAGON e) RIO RITA f) THE GAY DESPERADO g) CALAMITY JANE h) THE HARVEY GIRLS i) ANNIE GET YOUR GUN j) HIGH, WIDE AND HANDSOME

28 a9; b3; c1; d5; e10; f7; g6; h4; i8; j2

29 a) They all starred Clint Eastwood b) All directed by Sergio Leone c) All directed by Cecil B. DeMille d) They are all about real events e) They all starred Kris Kristoffer-son f) They all starred Gary Cooper g) They all starred one Fonda – Jane, Peter, Henry respectively h) They are all about real historical figures

30 a) Gary Cooper; THE VIRGINIAN b) THREE GODFATHERS; John Wayne, Pedro Armendariz, Harry Carey Jr c) VERA CRUZ; Robert Aldrich d) THE IRON MISTRESS; THE ALAMO e) Montgomery Clift; Howard Hawks; John Wayne f) Sterling Hayden; THE LAST COMMAND g) It featured four sets of real brothers: two Guests, three Carradines, two Quaids, two Keaches h) James Mitchum, Alana Ladd, Jody McCrea; Pat Wayne i) Sean Connery; HIGH NOON j) Henry Hathaway, John Ford, George Marshall; Spencer Tracy was the narrator and all the others appeared except Angie Dickinson

THE WAY OF THE WEST
Answers to Picture Questions

Page 54:
The title is the name of the town; Anthony Quinn; he's shooting at Henry Fonda, and doesn't survive; Cecil B. DeMille; VIVA ZAPATA and LUST FOR LIFE

Page 56:
Claire Trevor and John Carradine; she was a 'woman of easy virtue' and he was a gambler; Donald Meek and Thomas Mitchell are missing, Andy Devine was the driver; Monument Valley; The Ringo Kid

Page 58:
a) EL DORADO b) Robert Mitchum, John Wayne; James Caan c) RIO BRAVO d) Dean Martin, John Wayne, Ricky Nelson e) Mitchum

Page 59:
FORTY GUNS; Barbara Stanwyck, she was a rancher; John Erickson, Barry Sullivan

Page 60:
a) A MAN CALLED HORSE b) THE RETURN OF A MAN CALLED HORSE c) The Sioux d) Dame Judith Anderson, better known as Mrs Danvers in REBECCA e) Richard Harris, MAJOR DUNDEE

Page 61:
a) APACHE b) Burt Lancaster c) Jean Peters d) Robert Aldrich e) JIM THORPE – ALL AMERICAN (GB: MAN OF BRONZE)

DRAMA AND SUSPENSE
Answers to Picture Questions

Page 62, above:
ONE FLEW OVER THE CUCKOO'S NEST, Ken Kesey; Jack Nicholson; a mental institution; Kirk Douglas; his son Michael Douglas produced the film; Louise Fletcher, Milos Forman, Laurence Hauben and Bo Goldman

Page 62, right:
ALL ABOUT EVE, Joseph L. Mankie-wicz; Bette Davis, Claudette Colbert; Margo Channing; SLEUTH; George Sanders, Addison de Witt (theatre critic); Marilyn Monroe; Anne Baxter; George Sanders (Best Supporting Actor)

Page 62, above right:
A PLACE IN THE SUN, Montgomery Clift, Shelley Winters; AN AMERICAN TRAGEDY, Theodore Dreiser, Sylvia Sidney, Phillips Holmes, Frances Dee; Josef von Sternberg (1931), George Stevens (1951)

Page 64, above:
Kim Hunter, Vivien Leigh, Marlon Brando; Hunter and Brando, Elia Kazan; Stella (Hunter) is married to Stanley Kowalski (Brando) and Blanche DuBois (Leigh) is her sister; the film, of course, is A STREETCAR NAMED DESIRE

Page 64, right:
a) THE SPY WHO CAME IN FROM THE COLD, John Le Carré b) Martin Ritt c) Richard Burton, Peter Van Eyck d) East Germany e) Claire Bloom, THE MAN BETWEEN

Page 65, above:
They have made ten films together; WHO'S AFRAID OF VIRGINIA WOOLF?, Edward Albee; Mike Nichols (director), George Segal, Sandy Dennis; Taylor has won two Oscars, one for this film and one for BUTTERFIELD 8; Burton, nominated many times, has never won

Page 67, above left:
THE TIN DRUM; David Bennent, Günter Grass; Volker Schlöndorff a) MICHAEL KOHLHAAS b) THE LOST HONOUR OF KATHARINA BLU c) YOUNG TÖRLESS d) SWANN IN LOVE; Margarethe von Trotta

Page 67, above:
Peter Ustinov, Alec Guinness, Richard Burton; THE COMEDIANS by Graham Greene; Haiti, Elizabeth Taylor; OUR MAN IN HAVANA; Truffaut's DAY FOR NIGHT

Page 67, left:
The same story is told from four different points of view, RASHOMON; Akira Kurosawa, Toshiro Mifune; a samurai and a bandit; Machiko Kyo, THE TEAHOUSE OF THE AUGUST MOON

Page 69, above left:
ALL THE PRESIDENT'S MEN; Carl Bernstein and Bob Woodward, *The Washington Post*; Jason Robards as Ben Bradlee; DEEP THROAT was the nickname given to the newshounds' unknown informant

Page 69, above:
The title of the film is BELLE DE JOUR, which was also the character's nickname; Catherine Deneuve; a brothel, during the afternoon (she is a housewife who enjoys spending her free afternoons in this way); Louis Buñuel, French; TRISTANA

Page 69, left:
a) The custody of their son; they are in divorce proceedings in KRAMER VS KRAMER b) Dustin Hoffman, Robert Benton, Meryl Streep (Jane Alexander was also nominated) c) All of them d) THE TIGER MAKES OUT (THE GRADUATE was his first major role)

Page 70, above:
Bibi Andersson (left), Liv Ullmann (right) in PERSONA, directed by Ingmar Bergman; Ullmann played a psychiatric patient unable, or unwilling, to speak, Andersson her nurse – they take on each other's identity in the course of the film; THE TOUCH (Gould, Bibi Andersson), THE SERPENT'S EGG (Carradine, Liv Ullmann), AUTUMN SONATA (Bergman, Liv Ullmann)

Page 70, right:
Anita Ekberg; LA DOLCE VITA, Rome, Federico Fellini; BOCCACCIO '70, THE CLOWNS; Giulietta Masina, six

REACH FOR THE STARS – Page 71

A a) Meryl Streep b) JULIA, Jane Fonda, Vanessa Redgrave, Jason Robards c) MANHATTAN d) 'Holocaust' e) Harold Pinter, THE FRENCH LIEUTENANT'S WOMAN; Jeremy Irons

B a) Alan Bates b) THE FIXER; John Frankenheimer; Julie Christie; John Schlesinger; Thomas Hardy d) A DAY IN THE DEATH OF JOE EGG; Janet Suzman e) KING OF HEARTS

C a) Mary Pickford b) POLLYANNA c) The first close-up d) Little Lord Fauntleroy e) Pickfair

D a) Shelley Winters b) A PLACE IN THE SUN, THE DIARY OF ANNE FRANK, A PATCH OF BLUE, THE POSEIDON ADVENTURE c) Shirley Schrift, Vittorio Gassman d) NEXT STOP GREENWICH VILLAGE e) SASKATCHEWAN

E a) Marcello Mastroianni b) THE PRIEST'S WIFE; Sophia Loren; a pop singer c) CASANOVA 70 d) Jeanne Moreau; Antonioni e) LA GRANDE BOUFFE (BLOW OUT)

CHILDHOOD MEMORIES

1 a) Walt Disney himself; Clarence 'Ducky' Nash; THE WISE LITTLE HEN (1934), though was first *called* Donald Duck in ORPHANS' BENEFIT (1934) b) They were respectively the first Disney film in Technicolor, CinemaScope and Technirama 70mm c) THREE LITTLE PIGS; 'Who's Afraid Of The Big Bad Wolf?'; Frank E. Churchill and Ann Ronell d) Dopey, Doc, Sleepy, Grumpy, Bashful, Sneezy, Happy e) Bach, Tchaikovsky, Beethoven, Stravinsky, Dukas, Ponchielli, Moussorgsky and Schubert; Leopold Stokowski f) A fox, a lion and a bear; Sir Hiss, Terry-Thomas g) i) PINOCCHIO ii) MAKE MINE MUSIC iii) MELODY TIME iv) THE JUNGLE BOOK v) THE ARISTOCATS h) i) DUMBO ii) PINOCCHIO iii) SNOW WHITE AND THE SEVEN DWARFS iv) THE JUNGLE BOOK v) CINDERELLA i) Experimental Prototype Community of Tomorrow j) i) CINDERELLA ii) DUMBO iii) SONG OF THE SOUTH iv) LADY AND THE TRAMP v) 101 DALMATIANS

2 a) Margaret O'Brien b) Lionel Barrymore c) Lionel Barrymore again d) Mary Astor while making MEET ME IN ST LOUIS e) Vincente Minnelli during the making of MEET ME IN ST LOUIS

3 THOROUGHBREDS DON'T CRY; NATIONAL VELVET; Shirley Williams; Nanette Newman; INTERNATIONAL VELVET; THE BLACK STALLION, THE BLACK STALLION RETURNS

4 a) Miss Brodie in THE PRIME OF MISS JEAN BRODIE, Maggie Smith b) Mr Chipping in GOODBYE MR CHIPS, Robert Donat; Donat won the Oscar in the year Gable was nominated for GONE

WITH THE WIND c) GREASE II d) THE BLACKBOARD JUNGLE; Paul Mazursky e) MÄDCHEN (CHILDREN) IN UNIFORM, Leontine Sagan; Lilli Palmer, Romy Schneider f) THE BELLES OF ST TRINIANS and BLUE MURDER AT ST TRINIANS; Alastair Sim g) ZERO DE CONDUIT, Jean Vigo h) IF . . . , Lindsay Anderson, Rudyard Kipling i) TOM BROWN'S SCHOOLDAYS; Freddie Bartholomew, John Howard Davies j) TO SIR WITH LOVE; Sidney Poitier, Judy Geeson

5 a) THE MAJOR AND THE MINOR, to save paying the full train fare b) YOU'RE NEVER TOO YOUNG, for the same reason. It was a remake of the above c) SYLVIA SCARLETT, in order to get sympathy and beg d) MONKEY BUSINESS, after inventing a youth serum e) THE BAND WAGON, for the number 'Triplets'

6 a)Jackie Coogan, Tommy Kelly, Johnny Whitaker b) Mickey Rooney, Eddie Hodges, Jeff East c) The Mauch Twins, Sean Scully, Mark Lester d) Mary Pickford, Haley Mills e) Mary Pickford, Freddie Bartholomew, Rickie Schroder

7 a) OLIVER TWIST, GREAT EXPECTATIONS, Alec Guinness, Francis L. Sullivan b) Mark Lester, Jackie Coogan, Dickie Moore, John Howard Davies, Richard Charles; 'A Christmas Carol' became SCROOGE, 'The Old Curiosity Shop' became MR QUILP c) THE SIMPLE THINGS, 1952; Bob Cratchit, Scrooge's nephew, Mrs Cratchit, Marley's ghost d) W.C. Fields (Micawber), Lionel Barrymore (Peggoty), Freddie Bartholomew (the boy David), Frank Lawton (David as a man), Roland Young (Heep), Basil Rathbone (Murdstone), Lewis Stone (Wickfield), Hugh Williams (Steerforth), Lennox Pawle (Dick), Hugh Walpole (the Vicar) e) Charles Laughton, Elsa Lanchester

8 Male collies coats are fuller and healthier; Pal; Roddy McDowall; Elizabeth Taylor; Larry Kert; Yorkshire and Scotland after World War I; SON OF LASSIE, COURAGE OF LASSIE, CHALLENGE TO LASSIE, LASSIE'S GREAT ADVENTURE, THE MAGIC OF LASSIE; THE SUN COMES UP; KISS ME KATE in the number 'I Hate Men'

9 a) Donkey in AU HASARD BALTHAZAR/BALTHAZAR b) Horse in MY FRIEND FLICKA c) Chimpanzee in BONZO GOES TO COLLEGE and BEDTIME FOR BONZO d) Parrot in SALUDOS AMIGOS and THE THREE CABALLEROS e) Horse in NATIONAL VELVET f) Chimpanzee in many 'Tarzan' movies g) Cat in RHUBARB h) rabbit in BAMBI i) Otter in TARKA THE OTTER j) Double-ended llama in DR DOLITTLE

10 a) BICYCLE THIEVES, Vittorio de Sica; a bicycle; SHOESHINE b) THE 400 BLOWS, François Truffaut; Jean-Pierre Léaud, Antoine Doinel; a freeze as the boy runs to the sea; L'ENFANT SAUVAGE (WILD CHILD) c) GERMANY, YEAR ZERO, Roberto Rossellini; EUROPA '51 d) LES JEUX INTERDITS (FORBIDDEN GAMES), René Clément; Brigitte Fossey e) LOS OLVIDADOS (THE YOUNG AND THE DAMNED), Luis Buñuel

11 a) Tommy Rettig b) Brandon de Wilde c) Bobby Driscoll d) Judy Garland e) Jackie Coogan

12 a) 20th Century-Fox b) Dorothy in THE WIZARD OF OZ c) BRIGHT EYES, CURLY TOP, DIMPLES d) FORT APACHE, ADVENTURE IN BALTIMORE, John Agar e) i) MR BELVEDERE GOES TO COLLEGE ii) THE BACHELOR AND THE BOBBYSOXER (GB: BACHELOR KNIGHT) iii) I'LL BE SEEING YOU iv) A KISS FOR CORLISS v) SINCE YOU WENT AWAY f) BRIGHT EYES, CURLY TOP, STAND UP AND CHEER g) i) HEIDI ii) SUSANNAH OF THE MOUNTIES iii) THAT HAGEN GIRL h) Shirley Temple Black, US Representative to the UN and US ambassador to Ghana i) Bill 'Bojangles' Robinson; four movies; DIMPLES j) i) COLONEL, PRINCESS ii) REBEL iii) MARKER, BROADWAY iv) GIRL v) RICH GIRL

13 a) Kathryn Grant b) Arlene Dahl c) Janet Leigh d) Lucille Ball e) Debbie Reynolds f) Joanna Moore g) Harriet Hilliard h) Rachel Kempson i) Mary Martin j) Simone Signoret

14 a) Humpty Dumpty, The Mock Turtle, The White Knight, The Mad Hatter; Peter Sellers b) BOYS' TOWN; Spencer Tracy and Mickey Rooney c) W.C. Fields of Baby LeRoy d) Shirley Temple e) THE MUPPET MOVIE f) LE SOUFFLE AU COEUR (MURMUR OF THE HEART); PRETTY BABY; Brooke Shields; Louis Malle g) THE RAILWAY CHILDREN, THE AMAZING MR BLUNDEN, THE WATER BABIES h) Patty McCormack; Bonita Granville i) They were members of 'Our Gang' (Pete was the dog); Hall and Gorcey were members of 'The Dead End Kids', later 'The East Side Kids' and 'The Bowery Boys' j) They are connected through ANNIE. Gray wrote the original comic strip 'Little Orphan Annie', Roosevelt appears as a character, and Strouse wrote the music

CHILDHOOD MEMORIES
Answers to Picture Questions

Page 72:
a) Leslie Caron b) LILI, Paul Gallico c) Mel Ferrer d) 'Hi Lili, Hi Lo' e) 'Carnival'

Page 75:
Shirley Temple; WEE WILLIE WINKIE; Rudyard Kipling; the hero was changed from a boy to a girl; John Ford; C. Aubrey Smith; Victor McLaglen; India

Page 76:
Jody Foster; BUGSY MALONE; Tallulah, speakeasy queen; the child prostitute in TAXI DRIVER; THE LITTLE GIRL WHO LIVED DOWN THE LANE; her elder sister; FREAKY FRIDAY (they changed places for a day)

Page 77:
E.T. – The Extra-Terrestrial; Los Angeles; Elliott, Henry Thomas; they are trying to make a machine so that E.T. can 'phone home'; Steven Spielberg, John Williams; THE QUIET MAN; he created the creature

THE GENERATION GAP

1 a) It's the date James Dean was killed in an auto accident b) THEOREM/TEOREMA c) Connie Francis d) BREEZY e) YOUNG AND INNOCENT; Hitchcock; THE YOUNG ONE and THE YOUNG AND THE DAMNED (LOS OLVIDADOS), Buñuel f) THE YOUNG ONES; THE YOUNG SAVAGES; YOUNG AT HEART g) Debbie Reynolds and Leslie Nielsen; Sandra Dee and Peter Fonda h) PINK FLOYD – THE WALL; Gerald Scarfe i) Roger Daltrey, Elton John, Tina Turner and Eric Clapton j) FOOTLOOSE; Kevin Bacon

2 a) DINER b) PORKY'S c) THE LAST PICTURE SHOW d) SPLENDOR IN THE GRASS e) SUMMER OF '42

3 a) Freemont High in FAST TIMES AT FREEMONT HIGH b) Delta House in NATIONAL LAMPOON'S ANIMAL HOUSE c) Harvard Law School in THE PAPER CHASE; John Houseman d) i) CLASS OF '44 ii) CLASS OF 1984 iii) CLASS e) i) France ii) Israel iii) Canada

4 a) PANIC IN NEEDLE PARK b) THE TRIP c) I LOVE YOU, ALICE B. TOKLAS d) CHRISTIANE F e) TRASH

5 Stanley Kubrick; Stanley Kubrick; England; The Droogs; Malcolm McDowell; Beethoven; 'I was cured all right'

6 Frankie Avalon and Annette Funicello; BINGO and WILD BIKINI

7 a) Hopper (REBEL and GIANT), Baker (GIANT), Ives (EDEN), Taylor (GIANT), Mineo (REBEL and GIANT b) REBEL WITHOUT A CAUSE c) EAST OF EDEN; Julie Harris, Raymond Massey and Richard Davalos d) REBEL WITHOUT A CAUSE; a test of bravery to see who could drive furthest towards a cliff e) REBEL WITHOUT A CAUSE; Jim Backus was the voice of 'Mr Magoo'

8 AMERICAN GRAFFITI; the film was set in 1962, but made in 1973; Richard Dreyfuss, Ronny Howard, Paul Le Mat, Charles Martin Smith; Dreyfuss was not in MORE AMERICAN GRAFFITI; he was reported missing in Vietnam

9 a) MONTREAL POP b) GIMME SHELTER c) WOODSTOCK d) THE LAST WALTZ e) LET IT BE

10 a) Bob Dylan b) Sting c) David Bowie d) Roger Daltrey e) Neil Diamond f) Mick Jagger

11 a) Ruth Gordon b) Dick Powell c) Vivien Leigh d) Curt Jurgens e) Peter Finch and Glenda Jackson f) Melvyn Douglas g) Joanne Woodward h) Barry Sullivan i) Dirk Bogarde j) Eva Marie Saint

12 THEY LIVE BY NIGHT; Farley Granger and Cathy O'Donnell; it was the director Nicholas Ray's first feature film; THIEVES LIKE US; Robert Altman; Keith Carradine and Shelley Duvall

13 a) ORDINARY PEOPLE b) BREAKING AWAY c) TRIBUTE d) THE GREAT SANTINI e) FRIENDLY PERSUASION

14 They were all based on novels by S.E. Hinton and starred Matt Dillon; TEX, directed by Tim Hunter, is the odd one out – the other two were directed by Francis Ford Coppola

15 THE BLUE LAGOON; Brooke Shields and Christopher Atkins; GREASE and SUMMER LOVERS

16 a) Liza Minnelli b) Sandra Dee c) Lynn Redgrave d) Natalie Wood e) Brooke Shields

17 a) Michelangelo Antonioni; ZABRISKIE POINT; an orgy; the film ends with consumer goods exploding into the air; Mark Frechette; he was jailed for drugs and was killed in a prison brawl b) GETTING STRAIGHT; Candice Bergen; Bergman cast Gould in THE TOUCH c) The title is based on a university Dean's statement that the students were against the war in the same way as they liked strawberries; Bruce Davison and Kim Darby d) ALICE'S RESTAURANT; Woody Guthrie; Arthur Penn e) HAIR; Twyla Tharp

18 a) i) WEST SIDE STORY ii) THE OUTSIDERS b) THE WARRIORS c) QUADROPHENIA d) ANGELS WITH DIRTY FACES; he does it for the Dead End Kids who idolize him, to disillusion them into believing that he's a coward e) THE WANDERERS

19 a) G.I. BLUES b) IT HAPPENED AT THE WORLD'S FAIR c) FUN IN ACAPULCO d) DOUBLE TROUBLE e) HARUM SCARUM f) BLUE HAWAII and PARADISE HAWAIIAN STYLE g) VIVA LAS VEGAS h) KISSIN' COUSINS i) KING CREOLE j) CLAMBAKE

20 a) SUGARLAND EXPRESS b) TWO-LANE BLACKTOP c) BADLANDS d) DIRTY MARY, CRAZY LARRY e) ALICE IN THE CITIES

21 a) David Essex b) Marianne Faithbull c) Peter Fonda and Nancy Sinatra d) DIVA; Wilhelminia Wiggins Fernandez, Jean-Jacques Beineix e) ORPHEUS (ORPHÉE)

22 Plastics; Dustin Hoffman; Katherine Ross; Anne Bancroft; she was referred to throughout only as Mrs Robinson; Simon and Garfunkel; 'Mrs Robinson' and 'The Sound Of Silence'; Buck Henry

THE GENERATION GAP
Answers to Picture Questions

Page 78:

a) JAILHOUSE ROCK b) Third film c) Judy Tyler d) 'Treat Me Nice' e) GIRLS! GIRLS! GIRLS!, GIRL HAPPY, THE TROUBLE WITH GIRLS

Page 80:

GIANT; Jett Rink; Elizabeth Taylor and Rock Hudson; Texas; he had to play a man in his fifties; Rocky Graziano in SOMEBODY UP THERE LIKES ME

Page 81:

a) THE WILD ONE, the leader of a motorcycle gang b) A string of bike movies c) Mary Murphy, Lee Marvin d) LES GIRLS and STEELYARD BLUES e) A STREETCAR NAMED DESIRE, ON THE WATERFRONT, THE FUGITIVE KIND

Page 83, top:

TAKING OFF; they are playing strip poker; children taking off (running away) from home; Ike and Tina Turner; Milos Forman; it was his first American film; BLACK PETER (GB: PETER AND PAVLA), LOVES OF A BLONDE (GB: A BLONDE IN LOVE)

Page 83, bottom:

Peter Fonda (right) and Dennis Hopper, EASY RIDER; New Orleans; Jack Nicholson; Fonda (producer), Hopper (director); Terry Southern; both Fonda and Hopper are killed

GUESSING GAMES

1 a) Tony Curtis and Piper Laurie b) John Garfield and Lana Turner c) Joan Crawford and Jeff Chandler d) Anne Bancroft and Mel Brooks e) John Wayne and Lauren Bacall f) Veronica Lake and Fredric March g) William Holden and Peter Finch h) Fred Astaire and Joan Fontaine i) Kirk Douglas and Cyd Charisse j) Woody Allen and Diane Keaton

2 a) Gene Kelly and Debbie Reynolds in SINGIN' IN THE RAIN b) Gary Cooper and Claudette Colbert in BLUEBEARD'S EIGHTH WIFE c) Marilyn Monroe and Tom Ewell in THE SEVEN YEAR ITCH d) Trevor Howard and Celia Johnson in BRIEF ENCOUNTER e) Ginger Rogers and Fred Astaire in TOP HAT f) Ursula Andress and Sean Connery in DR NO g) Robert Taylor and Vivien Leigh in WATERLOO BRIDGE (1940 h) Ryan O'Neal and Ali McGraw in LOVE STORY i) Isabelle Huppert and Miou-Miou in AT FIRST SIGHT (COUP DE FOUDRE/ENTRE NOUS) j) Christopher Reeve and Margot Kidder in SUPERMAN

3 aE; bC; cD; dA; eB

4 a) Robert De Niro in KING OF COMEDY; Betty Hutton in THE MIRACLE OF MORGAN'S CREEK; Rudy Vallee in THE PALM BEACH STORY; Marilyn Monroe in SOME LIKE IT HOT; Jack Nicholson in THE LAST DETAIL b) Percy Kilbride and Marjorie Main; THE EGG AND I c) Eric Rohmer; MY NIGHT WITH MAUD, CLAIRE'S KNEE, PAULINE AT THE BEACH d) BREAKFAST AT TIFFANY'S, TEAHOUSE OF THE AUGUST MOON, DRAGON SEED, BLACK NARCISSUS, GAMBIT, LOVE IS A MANY SPLENDORED THING e) HAMMETT, Wim Wenders, Frederic Forrest f) Jeremy Irons in THE FRENCH LIEUTENANT'S WOMAN g) Erich von Stroheim h) Alfred Hitchcock i) Woody Allen in EVERYTHING YOU'VE ALWAYS WANTED TO KNOW ABOUT SEX j) THE END, Burt Reynolds as actor-director

5 a) THE EXORCIST II b) PIRANHA II c) HALLOWEEN III d) DR STRANGELOVE e) DANCE OF THE VAMPIRES (US: THE FEARLESS VAMPIRE KILLERS) f) JAWS g) SALO h) SCARFACE (1932) i) AMITYVILLE II j) SMASH-UP

6 a) THE CANDIDATE b) THE SEDUCTION OF JOE TYNAN c) THE BEST MAN d) ADVISE AND CONSENT e) STATE OF THE UNION and THE LAST HURRAH

7 *La Nouvelle Vague*; Claude Chabrol; LE BEAU SERGE; Alain Resnais, HIROSHIMA MON AMOUR and François Truffaut, LES QUATRE CENTS COUPS (THE 400 BLOWS); Jean-Luc Godard; A BOUT DE SOUFFLE (BREATHLESS); *Cahiers du Cinéma*

8 a) BULLITT, Peter Yates; THE HOT ROCK (GB: HOW TO STEAL A DIAMOND IN FOUR EASY LESSONS), MOTHER JUGS AND SPEED b) THE ITALIAN JOB c) THE CHASE, Robert Redford, Marlon Brando d) Orson Welles by Joseph Cotten in THE THIRD MAN e) Fredric March and Charles Laughton (1935), Michael Rennie and Robert Newton (1952), Jean Gabin and Bernard Blier (1957)

9 Andrzej Wajda; Zbigniew Cybulski; he was killed running for a train; EVERYTHING FOR SALE; MAN OF MARBLE; MAN OF IRON; DANTON

10 a) Joyce Redman in TOM JONES b) Jack Nicholson in FIVE EASY PIECES c) THE DISCREET CHARM OF THE BOURGEOISIE (LE CHARME DISCRET DE LA BOURGEOISIE); Buñuel and Jean-Claude Carrière d) Marcello Mastroianni, Philippe Noiret, Michel Piccoli, Ugo Tognazzi in LA GRANDE BOUFFE (BLOW-OUT) e) The sole of the boot; a nail and shoe-laces; he executes a dance with the rolls on forks f) EATING RAOUL; Paul Bartel and Mary Woronov; Robert Beltran g) Bette Davis serves Joan Crawford in WHATEVER HAPPENED

TO BABY JANE? h) LOCAL HERO i) Andre Gregory in MY DINNER WITH ANDRE directed by Louis Malle

11 a) THE CHANT OF JIMMY BLACKSMITH, Fred Schepisi b) MY BRILLIANT CAREER, Gillian Armstrong; Judy Davis c) PICNIC AT HANGING ROCK, Peter Weir d) THE LAST WAVE, Peter Weir, Richard Chamberlain e) MAD MAX and MAD MAX II, George Miller

12 a) Morphine, Katharine Hepburn b) Drink, Ray Milland c) Heroin, Frank Sinatra d) Gambling, Jeanne Moreau e) Drink, Jack Lemmon and Lee Remick

13 a) THE SEVENTH SEAL, Max von Sydow b) Gloria Swanson as Norma Desmond in SUNSET BOULEVARD c) Jack Nicholson in FIVE EASY PIECES d) Dick Powell in IT HAPPENED TOMORROW e) Dennis Weaver in DUEL f) Ann Todd, THE SEVENTH VEIL, James Mason g) Spencer Tracy, Elizabeth Taylor; Joan Bennett h) Anne Baxter as Eve in ALL ABOUT EVE i) Peter O'Toole as Henry II in BECKET and THE LION IN WINTER j) Robert Redford; daredevil flying; TARNISHED ANGELS and THE GYPSY MOTHS

14 a) Vittorio de Sica, THE GARDEN OF THE FINZI-CONTINIS; Dominique Sanda, Helmut Berger; Manuel de Sica, the director's son b) Nino Rota, THE GODFATHER PART II c) OSSESSIONE, Luchino Visconti; THE POSTMAN ALWAYS RINGS TWICE d) THE DECAMERON, THE CANTERBURY TALES, THE ARABIAN NIGHTS (US: A THOUSAND AND ONE NIGHTS); Giotto in the first e) Fellini's CASANOVA, 1900 – Bertolucci (Sutherland); THE LEOPARD and CONVERSATION PIECE – Visconti, 1900 (Lancaster); 1900 (De Niro); HANDS OVER THE CITY and LUCKY LUCIANO – Rosi (Steiger); THE RED DESERT – Antonioni (Harris)

15 a) It was a vintage car b) He never appears c) It is the name of a nightclub d) It is merely a song sung by Elizabeth Taylor as an academic joke e) He is the corpse that is constantly dug up f) Colin Clive; Boris Karloff plays the Monster g) It is a lost dog h) He is an imaginary 6ft white rabbit seen by James Stewart when drunk i) She is Laurence Olivier's dead wife j) 'Mr Goodbar' is synonymous with 'Mr Right', for whom Diane Keaton is searching in the singles' bars

16 a) Columbia, 40s b) MGM, 20s c) 20th Century-Fox, 50s d) Paramount, 40s e) Ealing, 40s f) United Artists, 20s g) Republic, 40s h) RKO, 30s i) Warner Bros., 50s j) Universal, 30s

17 a) LAST TANGO IN PARIS b) MOMMIE DEAREST c) A NIGHT AT THE OPERA d) PSYCHO e) FROM HERE TO ETERNITY

18 a) Mickey Rooney b) Bette Davis c) Bert Lahr d) Robin Williams e) Candice Bergen

GUESSING GAMES
Answers to Picture Questions

Page 85:

Rex Harrison and Kay Kendall; THE RELUCTANT DEBUTANTE, Vincente Minnelli, Sandra Dee; William Douglas Home; THE CONSTANT HUSBAND; ONCE MORE WITH FEELING

Page 86:

a) She has stolen $40,000 which she has in her bag. The man at the car window is a traffic cop b) Martin Balsam; he is stabbed to death c) Saul Bass d) It guaranteed to refuse admission after projection began e) Anthony Perkins and Vera Miles

Page 88:

FIDDLER ON THE ROOF, Tevye, the milkman and his wife Golde; Topol and Norma Crane; Molly Picon; in a Ukrainian village in 1905; in England (interiors) and Yugoslavia (exteriors); Isaac Stern; Sholom Aleichem

REACH FOR THE STARS – Page 89

A a) Sophia Loren b) TWO WOMEN c) DESIRE UNDER THE ELMS; Burl Ives, Anthony Perkins d) Scicolone e) BOY ON A DOLPHIN (Ladd); THE PRIDE AND THE PASSION (Sinatra & Grant); HOUSEBOAT (Grant); EL CID (Heston); A COUNTESS FROM HONG KONG (Brando)

B a) Paul Newman b) Oscar-nominated for CAT ON A HOT TIN ROOF, THE HUSTLER, HUD, COOL HAND LUKE, THE VERDICT c) Roy Bean (THE LIFE AND TIMES OF JUDGE ROY BEAN); Billy The Kid (THE LEFT-HANDED GUN); Rocky Graziano (SOMEBODY UP THERE LIKES ME); Butch Cassidy (BUTCH CASSIDY AND THE SUNDANCE KID); Buffalo Bill (BUFFALO BILL AND THE INDIANS) d) THE PRIZE (Sommer); THE SECRET WAR OF HARRY FRIGG (Koscina); THE MACKINTOSH MAN (Sanda) e) RACHEL, RACHEL; THE EFFECT OF GAMMA RAYS ON MAN-IN-THE-MOON MARIGOLDS; Joanne Woodward

C a) Charles Chaplin b) United Artists; Mary Pickford, Douglas Fairbanks, D.W. Griffith c) A WOMAN OF PARIS d) Eugene O'Neill, Oona O'Neill, Geraldine Chaplin e) THE GREAT DICTATOR; Paulette Goddard

D a) Cary Grant b) SUSPICION with Joan Fontaine; NOTORIOUS with Ingrid Bergman; TO CATCH A THIEF with Grace Kelly; NORTH BY NORTHWEST with Eva Marie Saint c) NIGHT AND DAY, 'based on the career' of Cole Porter d) I WAS A MALE WAR BRIDE with Ann Sheridan and BRINGING UP BABY with Katharine Hepburn, both directed by Howard Hawks e) WALK, DON'T RUN; Charles Walters

E a) Jennifer Jones b) LOVE IS A MANY SPLENDORED THING, William Holden c) CARRIE (1952), William Wyler d) DUEL IN THE SUN, Gregory Peck

THIS SPORTING LIFE

1 aH; bG; cA; dC; eD; fE; gB; hF

2 Ae; Bd; Ca; Dc; Eb

3 THE RING (Hitchcock), THE CHAMP (Vidor) GOLDEN BOY (Mamoulian), FAT CITY (Huston), ROCCO AND HIS BROTHERS (Visconti), WALKOVER (Skolimowsky), THE CHAMP (Zeffirelli)

4 a) GREGORY'S GIRL, Dee Hepburn b) PERSONAL BEST, Mariel Hemingway and Patrice Donnelly c) ALL THE MAR-BLES (GB: CALIFORNIA DOLLS), Vicki Frederick and Laurene Landon, Peter Falk d) IT'S ALWAYS FAIR WEATHER, Cyd Charisse e) THE OTHER SIDE OF THE MOUNTAIN (A WINDOW ON THE SKY), Marilyn Hassett, Beau Bridges f) TAKE ME OUT TO THE BALL GAME, Esther Williams, Gene Kelly g) DANGEROUS WHEN WET, Esther Williams h) SUN VALLEY SERENADE, Sonja Henie i) PAT AND MIKE, Katharine Hepburn, Spencer Tracy j) BOBBY DEERFIELD, Marthe Keller, Al Pacino

5 Kung Fu means simply technique or skill; Bruce Lee; RETURN OF THE DRAGON (US: WAY OF THE DRAGON) and ENTER THE DRAGON; BILLY JACK, THE TRIAL OF BILLY JACK and BILLY JACK GOES TO WASHING-TON

6 a) GENTLEMAN JIM b) THE KID FROM BROOKLYN c) THE IRON MAN d) HARD TIMES (GB: THE STREETFIGHTER) e) THE HARDER THEY FALL, Jeff Chandler lost his fight

7 a) Henry Winkler in THE ONE AND ONLY b) Arnold Schwarzenegger in PUMPING IRON c) Anthony Quinn in REQUIEM FOR A HEAVYWEIGHT (GB: BLOOD MONEY) d) James Earl Jones in the GREAT WHITE HOPE e) Sylvester Stallone in ESCAPE TO VICTORY

8 a) Farley Granger in STRANGERS ON A TRAIN; Ray Milland in DIAL M FOR MURDER b) Vijay Amritraj in OCTO-PUSSY c) Dean-Paul Martin in PLAYERS d) BLOW-UP, David Hemmings e) SCHOOL FOR SCOUNDRELS, Alastair Sim f) Bill Cosby and Gloria Gifford at the Beverley Hills Hotel in CALIFORNIA SUITE g) Katharine Hepburn in PAT AND MIKE h) Jacques Tati in M. HULOT'S HOLIDAY i) COME TO THE STABLE j) Sally Forrest, Ida Lupino

9 a) Horse racing b) Body-building c) Sailing d) Basketball e) Cricket f) Baseball g) Foot-ball h) The shot-put i) Amateur wrestling j) Motor-cycle racing

10 THE HARDER THEY FALL; Humphrey Bogart – it was his last role; Rod Steiger; 'Jersey' Joe Walcott and Max Baer

11 Tatum O'Neal, Walter Matthau, Bill Lancaster (Burt's son); Michael Ritchie, SEMI-TOUGH; THE BAD NEWS BEARS IN BREAKING TRAINING and THE BAD NEWS BEARS GO TO JAPAN

12 CHARIOTS OF FIRE; Ben Cross and Ian Charleston; they had to be able to run fast; Abrahams encountered anti-semi-tism and Liddell refused to run on a Sunday for religious reasons; Colin Welland, the writer of the screenplay, at the Oscar ceremonies

13 A) a) BANG THE DRUM SLOWLY b) THE GANG THAT COULDN'T SHOOT STRAIGHT c) RAGING BULL B) a) DOWNHILL RACER b) LITTLE FAUSS AND BIG HALSEY c) a) THE WORLD'S GREATEST ATHLETE b) BIG WEDNESDAY D) a) THE WIN-NING TEAM b) KNUTE ROCKNE – ALL AMERICAN (GB: A MODERN HERO) E) a) FEAR STRIKES OUT b) TALL STORY F) a) TOP SPEED b) YOU SAID A MOUTHFUL c) SIT TIGHT d) POLO JOE e) SIX DAY BIKE RIDER G) a) A DAY AT THE RACES b) HORSE FEATHERS H) a) THE HUSTLER b) WINNING c) THE STING I) a) THE CROWD ROARS b) WINNER TAKE ALL, THE IRISH IN US, CITY FOR CONQUEST J) a) THAT'S MY BOY b) MONEY FROM HOME

14 a) THE GAMES; the Olympic Marathon, Athol Compton b) GRAND PRIX; the Grand Prix motor race at Monza, James Garner c) SPELLBOUND; he remembers killing his younger brother accidentally when they were children d) CADDY-SHACK e) THE FORTUNE COOKIE (GB: MEET WHIPLASH WILLIE); he was a TV cameraman who was knocked unconscious by a massive halfback while standing on the sidelines

15 Marlon Brando to Rod Steiger in ON THE WATERFRONT; RAGING BULL

16 a) He was the champion in ROCKY, Carl Weathers b) William Holden, Barbara Stanwyck c) Busby Berkeley; BODY AND SOUL d) The bullfighter in Bizet's opera 'Carmen' became a boxer in CARMEN JONES e) The 'Dynamite Hands' spoof in Stanley Donen's MOVIE MOVIE; Harry Hamlin and George C. Scott

17 a) Leni Riefenstahl b) Four hours c) Part one concentrates on the track events in the Olympic stadium, while the second deals with the preparations in the Olympic Village, and ranges a little around other Olympic sporting events in Berlin, such as the horse trials etc d) TRIUMPH OF THE WILL, the 1934 Nuremberg Rally e) THE BLUE LIGHT; Riefenstahl herself played the lead

18 a) Amateur boxing, Jon Voight b) Football, Tony Curtis c) Stock car racing, Jeff Bridges d) Baseball, Tom Ewell e) Foot-ball, Elroy 'Crazylegs' Hirsch played himself

19 a) LET'S DO IT AGAIN, Sidney Poitier b) THE MAGIC CHRISTIAN, Peter Sellers c) BATTLING BUTLER, Buster Keaton d) HERE COMES MR JORDAN, Robert Montgomery e) THE MAIN EVENT, Ryan O'Neal

20 a) Wayne Morris (boxing) b) Elvis Presley (boxing) c) Eddie Cantor (bullfighting) d) Bob Hope (horse racing) e) Billy Chapin (baseball)

21 a) Fishing (or women) b) A gambling joint where wrestling matches were held c) THE LONGEST YARD (GB: THE MEAN MACHINE), football, Burt Reynolds, the cons won d) He (Dennis Christopher) pretended to be Italian because he identified with the Italians in relation to his sporting interest viz cycling; BREAKING AWAY e) Rugby League

THIS SPORTING LIFE
Answers to Picture Questions

Page 90:
ROCKY III (he did not win the championship in ROCKY, so he would not be wearing the belt); Rocky Balboa; Burgess Meredith; Stallone directed ROCKY II and III; ROCKY III; ROCKY II

Page 92:
Because the team won by playing dirty; The Charlestown Chiefs; SLAP SHOT; George Roy Hill, BUTCH CASSIDY AND THE SUNDANCE KID and THE STING; LOVE STORY and ICE CASTLES; John Wayne, Keir Dullea

Page 93:
James Caan; ROLLERBALL; American football, motor-cycling and roller-derby; Ralph Richardson; RED LINE 7000 and THE GAMBLER

Page 94:
The story is a version of the Faust legend: a man sells his soul to the Devil in order to play first-class baseball; Tab Hunter and Gwen Verdon; she, an agent of the Devil, is attempting to seduce him (and failing); Ray Walston (the Devil); Verdon was then the wife of Bob Fosse

Page 95:
a) THE CINCINNATI KID b) Stud Poker c) (l to r) Steve McQueen, Karl Malden, Edward G. Robinson d) The Depression, in New Orleans e) Cab Calloway

FOR KING AND COUNTRY

1 Robert Watson, Richard Basehart, Luther Adler, Charles Chaplin, Alec Guinness

2 a) McHALE'S NAVY, Ernest Borgnine b) THE PRIVATE NAVY OF SERGEANT O'FARRELL, Bob Hope c) THE PRIVATE WAR OF MAJOR BENSON, Charlton Heston d) SEE HERE, PRIVATE HARGROVE, Robert Walker e) PRIVATE ANGELO, Peter Ustinov

3 a) THE GREAT DICTATOR b) MRS MINIVER c) FOREIGN CORRESPONDENT d) SINCE YOU WENT AWAY e) DESPERATE JOURNEY

4 HIROSHIMA MON AMOUR, Alain Resnais; Marguerite Duras; Emmanuelle Riva and Eiji Okada; architect; a) NIGHT AND FOG (NUIT ET BROUILLARD) b) MURIEL c) THE WAR IS OVER (LA GUERRE EST FINIE)

5 a) Lost an eye and a leg in Vietnam b) Had his legs amputated, Vietnam c) Was blinded in World War II d) A serious heart attack, World War II e) Confined to a wheelchair, Vietnam f) Arms and legs amputated, World War I g) Paralysed from the waist down, World War II h) Lost both hands, World War II i) Lost right hand, Vietnam j) Lost a leg, World War I

6 a) OH, WHAT A LOVELY WAR!; Richard Attenborough; IN WHICH WE SERVE, Noel Coward b) James Whale, ACES HIGH c) PATHS OF GLORY; Kirk Douglas, Stanley Kubrick; KING AND COUNTRY d) A FAREWELL TO ARMS; Gary Cooper and Helen Hayes; Rock Hudson and Jennifer Jones e) King Vidor, Renée Adorée

7 a) 'Hurray for the next man that dies!', Howard Hawks – it was his first sound film; Barthelmess dies; Errol Flynn and David Niven b) WINGS, Gary Cooper c) Jean Harlow, Ben Lyon, HELL'S ANGELS, Howard Hughes d) John Philip Law and Don Stroud; he gave up directing e) Ursula Andress, THE BLUE MAX

8 Af; Be; Cb; Dc; Eh

9 a) AIR FORCE, Howard Hawks b) Sydney Greenstreet, Humphrey Bogart, ACROSS THE PACIFIC, John Huston; THE MALTESE FALCON, Mary Astor c) TORA! TORA! TORA!, Richard Fleischer, Special Visual Effects d) MIDWAY, Henry Fonda e) Tyrone Power, Fritz Lang; General Douglas MacArthur f) OBJECTIVE BURMA!; it did not give credit to the British participation in the Burma campaign; a prologue extolled the British contribution g) THIRTY SECONDS OVER TOKYO; Mervyn LeRoy, Blake Edwards h) Jeff Chandler; Sam Fuller, Burma i) THE PURPLE HEART, Lewis Milestone; they were all executed j) *Variety*

10 a) John Wayne, THE GREEN BERETS b) D.W. Griffith c) HEARTS OF THE WORLD, Erich von Stroheim d) Lewis Milestone, ALL QUIET ON THE WESTERN FRONT e) FOR WHOM THE BELL TOLLS

11 'God Bless America'; Michael Cimino; one (THUNDERBOLT AND LIGHTFOOT): Christopher Walken; John Cazale; Robert De Niro – prisoners of the Viet Cong are forced to play Russian Roulette

12 THE DESERT FOX, THE DESERT RATS; THE BLUE MAX, CROSS OF IRON

13 a) Dirk Bogarde b) Carl Reiner c) Albert Lieven d) Gregory Peck e) Otto Kruger f) Otto Preminger g) Cedric Hardwicke h) Robert Young i) Erich von Stroheim j) Laurence Olivier

14 aE; bB; cA; dD; eC

15 a) Jack Hawkins b) John Wayne c) Kenneth More d) David Niven e) Richard Todd

16 a) BUCK PRIVATES, AT WAR WITH THE ARMY, UP IN ARMS b) JUMPING JACKS, SAILOR BEWARE; SAD SACK, WHICH WAY TO THE FRONT?, DON'T GIVE UP THE SHIP c) YOU'RE IN THE ARMY NOW, Phil Silvers and Jimmy Durante d) Laurel and Hardy e) SOLDIER ARMS, Edna Purviance, Sydney Chaplin (Charlie's half-brother) f) Danny Kaye, ON THE DOUBLE g) SUPPOSE THEY GAVE A WAR AND NOBODY CAME?, Don Ameche h) William Hartnell, Ian Carmichael i) WHAT DID YOU DO IN THE WAR, DADDY?, Blake Edwards j) THE WACKIEST SHIP IN THE ARMY; OPERATION MAD BALL, Ernie Kovacs

17 a) Spanish Civil War, Gary Cooper b) The Korean War, Humphrey Bogart c) World War II, after Pearl Harbor, John Wayne d) The Boer War, Edward Woodward e) World War I, Victor McLaglen (1926), James Cagney (1952)

18 a) i) A tunnel is dug under a vaulting horse ii) An escape is made with a crowd after a football match iii) A dummy stands in at roll-call for any escaped prisoners iv) One of the POWs impersonates the camp commandant b) They dealt with Germans escaping from British POW camps; Hardy Kruger c) THE GREAT ESCAPE; the fifty who escaped were shot by the Gestapo d) THE PASSWORD IS COURAGE e) Tom Conti; 'The Seed And The Sower', Laurens van der Post; Nagisa Oshima; David Bowie – he kisses the commandant f) THE PASSENGER; Andrzej Munk, one hour g) WHERE EAGLES DARE, the Bavarian Alps h) Virginia MacKenna and Peter Finch, A TOWN LIKE ALICE, Nevil Shute i) a) THE COLDITZ STORY b) STALAG 17 c) THE CAMP ON BLOOD ISLAND j) i) SOPHIE'S CHOICE ii) KING RAT iii) PRISONER OF WAR iv) KAPO v) THE CAPTIVE HEART

19 a) THE TRAIN b) THE BATTLE OF THE RIVER PLATE (US: PURSUIT OF THE GRAF SPEE) c) THE ENEMY BELOW d) THE BEST OF ENEMIES e) HELL IN THE PACIFIC

20 a) THE CAINE MUTINY b) MR ROBERTS c) RUN SILENT RUN DEEP d) TUNES OF GLORY e) VON RYAN'S EXPRESS

21 a) THE CRANES ARE FLYING; Russian, Mikhail Kalatozov, Tatiana Samoilova b) THE BURMESE HARP, Japanese, Kon Ichikawa c) CLOSELY OBSERVED TRAINS, Czechoslovakian, Jiří Menzel d) A GENERATION, Polish, Andrzej Wajda; KANAL and ASHES AND DIAMONDS e) SHOP ON THE HIGH STREET (US: SHOP ON MAIN STREET), Czechoslovakian, Jan Kadar (with Elmar Klos), Ida Kaminska

22 a) TAPS, Jim and Timothy Hutton b) THE LONG GRAY LINE, Tyrone Power, Maureen O'Hara c) WEST POINT STORY (GB: FINE AND DANDY), BEST FOOT FORWARD d) THE STRANGE ONE (GB: END AS A MAN), 'End As A Man'; YOUNG TÖRLESS e) Franc Roddam; AN OFFICER AND A GENTLEMAN, Richard Gere, Debra Winger, Lou Gossett Jr; he was the first black to win the award

23 a) ME AND THE COLONEL b) SERGEANT PEPPER'S LONELY HEARTS CLUB BAND c) PRIVATES ON PARADE d) THE SERGEANT e) THE LIEUTENANT WORE SKIRTS f) THE DIARY OF MAJOR THOMPSON g) THE GENERAL DIED AT DAWN h) GENERAL DELLA ROVERE i) THE LIFE AND DEATH OF COLONEL BLIMP j) THE ELUSIVE (VANISHING) CORPORAL (LE CAPORAL ÉPINGLÉ)

24 Ernst Lubitsch; Sig Ruman of Jack Benny (to Benny who is in disguise); it is the signal for his rendezvous with Benny's wife backstage; Robert Stack; 'Hath not a Jew eyes?' from 'The Merchant Of Venice'; Carole Lombard; Mel Brooks and Anne Bancroft; Bronski; 'Sweet Georgia Brown'

25 Walter Pidgeon, Hitler b) They are all about disturbed Vietnam veterans in civilian life c) No-one. It implies an ordinary soldier d) Arnhem; Bernhard Wicki; THE BRIDGE AT REMAGEN; THE BRIDGES AT TOKO-RI and BRIDGE ON THE RIVER KWAI e) Colour prejudice f) Nicaragua, The Lebanon g) Fritz Lang, Bertolt Brecht, Hans Eisler h) THE GUNS OF NAVARONE; Irene Papas, Gia Scala i) Rainer Werner Fassbinder; Grigori Chukrai j) Matthew Broderick, WAR GAMES

FOR KING AND COUNTRY
Answers to Picture Questions

Page 96:
PRIVATE BENJAMIN, Goldie Hawn; Armand Assante; in an army training camp a) SKIRTS AHOY b) KEEP YOUR POWDER DRY c) HERE COME THE WAVES – Hutton played the double role of twin sisters

Page 97:
FROM HERE TO ETERNITY, Fred Zinnemann, Frank Sinatra, Donna Reed, Daniel Taradash, Burnett Guffey; Burt Lancaster, Deborah Kerr; they are lovers; she broke away from her usual 'well-bred lady' roles to become sexy; Pearl Harbor just before the attack in 1941

Page 98:
a) ALL QUIET ON THE WESTERN FRONT, Lewis Milestone b) Lew Ayres c) German, French d) The German side, World War I e) Ayres is killed while reaching for a butterfly; that moment was photographed later, and Milestone's own hand was used

Page 100:
Alec Guinness and Sessue Hayakawa; colonels; prisoner of war and prison commander; soon after the bridge is complete, it is blown up; 'Madness, madness . . .' says James Donald

Page 101:
LA GRANDE ILLUSION, Jean Renoir; Erich von Stroheim, the commandant of a POW camp; he was injured in an air accident. FIVE GRAVES TO CAIRO and NAPOLEON (1955); Jean Gabin, Marcel Dalio, Pierre Fresnay

Page 103:
Lee Marvin, Charles Bronson; they are attacking a stately home held by the Nazis; they were convicts serving life sentences, or from the death cell; Cassavetes, Walker, Savalas, Brown

Page 104:
GALLIPOLI, Australia, Peter Weir; Mel Gibson; he runs messages, and was an athlete in civilian life; THE YEAR OF LIVING DANGEROUSLY

Page 105:
APOCALYPSE NOW; Kurtz, Marlon Brando; they are there to greet the arrival of Martin Sheen's boat; Cambodia (Sheen has crossed over from Vietnam); 'Heart Of Darkness' by Joseph Conrad, Francis Ford Coppola

SPINETINGLERS
Answers to Picture Questions

Page 106, above:
THE NIGHT OF THE HUNTER (1955), Robert Mitchum, Shelley Winters and Lillian Gish; Charles Laughton

Page 106, right:
Clint Eastwood, Jessica Walter, PLAY MISTY FOR ME (1971); he plays a local disc jockey of a popular request programme and Miss Walter first makes contact with him by phoning in with this request.

Page 106, far right:
Piper Laurie and Sissy Spacek; CARRIE (1976), Brian De Palma; Amy Irving, Nancy Allen, John Travolta

Page 108, above:
WAIT UNTIL DARK, Alan Arkin; a housewife in whose home, unbeknown to her, is a drug-filled doll which Arkin is after; Audrey Hepburn; she was blind

Page 108, right:
Gregory Peck, SPELLBOUND (1945) with Ingrid Bergman, THE PARADINE CASE (1948) with Ann Todd and Alida Valli; THE OMEN (1976), Harvey Stephens; Peck is the boy's stepfather, and has become convinced that the child is the 'anti-Christ' who has been responsible for a number of horrible deaths

Page 108, far right:
Olivia de Havilland, LADY IN A CAGE (illustrated), HUSH, HUSH, SWEET CHARLOTTE; Rafael Campos, James Caan

Page 110, above:
Elsa Lanchester and Boris Karloff, THE BRIDE OF FRANKENSTEIN (1935); Colin Clive, Valerie Hobson; James Whale; FRANKENSTEIN (1931), THE OLD DARK HOUSE (1932), THE INVISIBLE MAN (1933)

Page 111, above:
DR JEKYLL AND MR HYDE (1931), Fredric March (Oscar winner) and Miriam Hopkins; Robert Louis Stevenson, Spencer Tracy and Ingrid Bergman

Page 111, left:
I WALKED WITH A ZOMBIE (1942), Val Lewton, RKO; Jacques Tourneur, CAT PEOPLE (1942), THE LEOPARD MAN (1943); his father was silent film director Maurice Tourneur

Page 112, above:
Klaus Kinski; NOSFERATU, Werner Herzog; 1922, F.W. (Friedrich) Murnau, Max Schreck

Page 112, right:
DR X (1932), THE RETURN OF DR X (1939) (illustrated); Bogart is actually returned from the dead – a vampire – and needs blood to survive, so uses it to extract blood for this purpose

Page 113, above:
DRACULA (1931), Bela Lugosi and Helen Chandler; THE CURSE OF FRANKENSTEIN (1957), THE REVENGE OF FRANKENSTEIN (1958), DRACULA (1958; US: HORROR OF DRACULA), THE MUMMY (1959); the two stars were Christopher Lee and Peter Cushing, both of whom appeared in three of the four pictures – Cushing alone was in THE REVENGE OF FRANKENSTEIN

Page 113, right:
Filmed as THE PHANTOM OF THE OPERA in 1926 starring Lon Chaney; in 1943 with Claude Rains (illustrated); in 1962 starring Herbert Lom; the most recent, rock version was retitled THE PHANTOM OF THE PARADISE (1974) and starred William Finley. The 1943 version won Oscars for Best Colour Cinematography and also for Best Colour Art Direction

Page 114, above:
a) THEATRE OF BLOOD (1973) b) DIARY OF A MADMAN (1963) c) HOUSE OF WAX (1953) d) THE RAVEN (1962)

Page 114, right:
a) Constance Towers in THE NAKED KISS (1964) b) Jean Peters in PICKUP ON SOUTH STREET (1953) c) Angie Dickinson in CHINA GATE (1957)

REACH FOR THE STARS – Page 115

A a) Michael Caine b) ZULU (1964) c) HURRY SUNDOWN, BILLION DOLLAR BRAIN, SLEUTH d) DEATHTRAP, Christopher Reeve and Dyan Cannon e) EDUCATING RITA, Julie Walters

B a) Peter Lorre b) Luis Buñuel c) THE VERDICT; Sidney Greenstreet; Don Siegel d) NINOTCHKA (1939); SILK STOCKINGS e) It was Mike Todd's short-lived experiment in Smell-O-Vision; Elizabeth Taylor – Todd's wife at the time

C a) Burt Reynolds b) GATOR c) HOOPER d) AT LONG LAST LOVE, Peter Bogdanovich, Cybill Shepherd e) LUCKY LADY

D a) Mia Farrow b) Frank Sinatra and André Previn c) ROSEMARY'S BABY; Ruth Gordon d) SECRET CEREMONY; Robert Mitchum, Joseph Losey e) A DANDY IN ASPIC (Harvey); FOLLOW ME (US: THE PUBLIC EYE) (Topol); JOHN AND MARY (Hoffman); DOCTEUR POPAUL (US: HIGH HEELS, GB: SCOUNDREL IN WHITE) (Belmondo)

E a) Jane Wyman b) JOHNNY BELINDA; Jean Negulesco c) 'In the Cool, Cool, Cool of the Evening'; Bing Crosby; HERE COMES THE GROOM d) Ronald Reagan; President of the United States

LUST FOR LIVES

1 a) Woody Guthrie, David Carradine b) John F. Kennedy, Cliff Robertson c) Charles Lindbergh, James Stewart d) Joan Crawford, Faye Dunaway e) Sol Hurok, David Wayne f) Lon Chaney, James Cagney g) Modigliani, Gerard Philipe h) Ferdinand de Lesseps, Tyrone Power i) Diana Barrymore, Dorothy Malone j) Annette Kellerman, Esther Williams

2 a) BONNIE AND CLYDE b) THE AGONY AND THE ECSTASY c) THE MUSIC LOVERS d) THE BARRETTS OF WIMPOLE STREET (1934) e) MARIE ANTOINETTE (Norma Shearer) f) RASPUTIN AND THE EMPRESS g) LUST FOR LIFE h) GANDHI i) VALENTINO j) THE STORY OF ALEXANDER GRAHAM BELL

3 a) Diana Ross as Billie Holiday in LADY SINGS THE BLUES b) Susan Hayward as Jane Froman in WITH A SONG IN MY HEART c) Susan Hayward as Lillian Roth in I'LL CRY TOMORROW d) Frank Sinatra as Joe E. Lewis in THE JOKER IS WILD e) John Hurt as Bob Champion in CHAMPIONS f) Eleanor Parker as Marjorie Lawrence in INTERRUPTED MELODY g) Patty Duke as Helen Keller in THE MIRACLE WORKER h) James Stewart as Monty Stratton in THE STRATTON STORY i) Anthony Perkins as Jim Piersall in FEAR STRIKES OUT j) John Hurt as John Merrick in THE ELEPHANT MAN

4 SILKWOOD, Meryl Streep; that the dangers at the nuclear facility were being covered up; she was killed (murdered?) in a car accident; Cher, and Kurt Russell; THE CHINA SYNDROME

5 a) Anna Neagle in NURSE EDITH CAVELL, THEY FLEW ALONE (Amy Johnson), THE LADY WITH A LAMP (Florence Nightingale) b) Tony Curtis in HOUDINI, THE OUTSIDER (Ira Hayes), LEPKE c) Charlton Heston in KHARTOUM (General Gordon), THE FAR HORIZONS (Bill Clark), THE BUCCANEER (Andrew Jackson) d) Ava Gardner in THE NAKED MAJA (The Duchess of Alba), MAYERLING (Empress Elizabeth), THE LIFE AND TIMES OF JUDGE ROY BEAN (Lily Langtry) e) Gary Cooper in THE ADVENTURES OF MARCO POLO, SERGEANT YORK (Alvin York), THE COURT-MARTIAL OF BILLY MITCHELL (GB: ONE MAN MUTINY) f) Paul Muni in JUAREZ, HUDSON'S BAY (Pierre Radisson), A SONG TO REMEMBER (Joseph Elsner) g) Susan Hayward in I WANT TO LIVE (Barbara Graham), THE PRESIDENT'S LADY (Rachel Jackson), DAVID AND BATHSHEBA h) Fredric March in CHRISTOPHER COLUMBUS, THE BARRETTS OF WIMPOLE STREET (Robert Browning), THE ADVENTURES OF MARK TWAIN i) Jose Ferrer in CYRANO DE BERGERAC (and CYRANO ET D'ARTAGNAN), I ACCUSE (Alfred Dreyfus), MOULIN ROUGE (Toulouse-Lautrec) j) Alec Guinness in HITLER, THE LAST TEN DAYS, THE FALL OF THE ROMAN EMPIRE (Marcus Aurelius), CROMWELL (Charles I)

6 a) THE RIGHT STUFF b) Professional lookalikes for Richard Nixon and Queen Elizabeth II c) NASTY HABITS was an allegory of Watergate set in a convent; Jackson played the Nixon role d) Broderick Crawford e) Hitler and Mussolini in THE GREAT DICTATOR, Charles Chaplin and Jack Oakie f) The Jackal, played by Edward Fox in THE DAY OF THE JACKAL g) Che Guevara and Fidel Castro in CHE!, played by Omar Sharif and Jack Palance h) Winston Churchill (Simon Ward) in YOUNG WINSTON i) Pancho Villa in VIVA VILLA! (Beery) and VILLA RIDES! (Palance) j) They conspired to assassinate President Kennedy in EXECUTIVE ACTION

7 a) THE MAGNIFICENT REBEL (Karl-Heinz Boehm as Beethoven) b) THE GREAT WALTZ (Fernand Gravet as Johann Strauss) c) SONG OF SCHEHEREZADE (Jean-Pierre Aumont as Rimsky-Korsakov) d) SONG OF LOVE (Katharine Hepburn as Clara Schumann) e) THE GREAT CARUSO (Mario Lanza)

8 The stars appeared as themselves in all of them a) Muhammed Ali b) George Raft c) Audie Murphy

9 a) Queen Elizabeth I; ELIZABETH AND ESSEX and THE VIRGIN QUEEN (Davis); MARY, QUEEN OF SCOTS (Jackson); FIRE OVER ENGLAND and THE SEA HAWK (Robson) b) Napoleon; DESIREE (Brando); WATERLOO (Steiger); THE ADVENTURES OF GERARD (Wallach) c) Cleopatra; CLEOPATRA (Colbert); CAESAR AND CLEOPATRA (Leigh); SERPENT OF THE NILE (Fleming) d) Abraham Lincoln; YOUNG MR LINCOLN (Fonda); ABE LINCOLN IN ILLINOIS and HOW THE WEST WAS WON (Massey); ABRAHAM LINCOLN (Huston) e) Queen Victoria; VICTORIA THE GREAT and SIXTY GLORIOUS YEARS (US: QUEEN OF DESTINY) (Neagle); THE MUDLARK (Dunne); THE GREAT McGONAGALL (Sellers) f) Henry VIII; THE PRIVATE LIFE OF HENRY VIII and YOUNG BESS (Laughton); A MAN FOR ALL SEASONS (Shaw); ANNE OF THE THOUSAND DAYS (Burton) g) Lenin; LENIN IN OCTOBER and LENIN IN 1918 (Shchukin); LENIN IN POLAND – and innumerable other appearances as Lenin (Straukh); OCTOBER (Nikadrov) h) Catherine the Great; THE SCARLET EMPRESS (Dietrich); GREAT CATHERINE (Moreau); CATHERINE THE GREAT (Bergner) i) Benjamin Disraeli; DISRAELI (Arliss); THE PRIME MINISTER (Gielgud); THE MUDLARK (Guinness) j) Julius Caesar; CAESAR AND CLEOPATRA (Rains); CLEOPATRA (Harrison); JULIUS CAESAR (Calhern)

10 a) Boxers; SOMEBODY UP THERE LIKES ME, Rocky Graziano (Newman); GENTLEMAN JIM, Jim Corbett (Flynn); RAGING BULL, Jake La Motta (De Niro) b) Soldiers; PATTON, General George S. Patton (Scott); MACARTHUR, General Douglas MacArthur (Peck); THE DESERT FOX (GB: ROMMEL – DESERT FOX) and THE DESERT RATS, Field Marshal Rommel (Mason) c) Film actresses; HARLOW, Jean Harlow (Baker); FRANCES, Frances Farmer (Lange); JEANNE EAGELS (Novak) d) Songwriters; TILL THE CLOUDS ROLL BY, Jerome Kern (Walker); RHAPSODY IN BLUE, George Gershwin (Alda); WORDS AND MUSIC, Richard Rodgers (Drake) e) Painters; REMBRANDT (Laughton); EL GRECO (Ferrer); THE NAKED MAJA, Goya (Franciosa) f) Composers; SONG WITHOUT END, Liszt (Bogarde); LUDWIG, Richard Wagner (Howard); SONG OF SCHEHEREZADE, Rimsky-Korsakov (Aumont) g) Opera singers; MELBA, Dame Nellie Melba (Munsel); THE GREAT CARUSO (Lanza); SO THIS IS LOVE (GB: THE GRACE MOORE STORY), Grace Moore (Grayson) h) US Presidents; SUNRISE AT CAMPOBELLO, Franklin D. Roosevelt (Bellamy), THE PRESIDENT'S LADY and THE BUCCANEER, Andrew Jackson (Heston); THE WIND AND THE LION, Theodore Roosevelt (Keith) i) Scientists; THE STORY OF LOUIS PASTEUR (Muni); EDISON THE MAN, Thomas Edison (Tracy); MADAME CURIE, Pierre Curie (Pidgeon) j) Comedians; LENNY, Lenny Bruce (Hoffman); W.C. FIELDS AND ME (Steiger); THE EDDIE CANTOR STORY (Brasselle)

11 aD (LADY CAROLINE LAMB); bJ (NIJINSKY); cE (BEAU BRUMMELL); dG (CLIVE OF INDIA); eI (MELVIN AND HOWARD); fB (LADY WITH RED HAIR); gA (GAILY GAILY/GB: CHICAGO, CHICAGO); hC (THE YOUNG MR PITT); iF (BONNIE PRINCE CHARLIE); jH (ROB ROY, THE HIGHLAND ROGUE)

12 a) i) Bette Davis (THE STAR) ii) biopic: Ruth Gordon, Jean Simmons (THE ACTRESS) iii) biopic: Gertrude Lawrence, Julie Andrews (STAR!) b) i) Jean Harlow (BLONDE BOMBSHELL) ii) biopic: Texas Guinan, Betty Hutton (INCENDIARY BLONDE) iii) Marlene Dietrich (BLONDE VENUS) c) i) biopic: Edwin Booth, Richard Burton (PRINCE OF PLAYERS) ii) biopic: Moss Hart, George Hamilton (ACT ONE) iii) Susan Strasberg (STAGE STRUCK) d) i) biopic: William Friese-Greene, Robert Donat (THE MAGIC BOX) ii) Anthony Hopkins (MAGIC) iii) biopic: Richard Wagner, Alan Badel (MAGIC FIRE) e) i) biopic: Evelyn Nesbitt Thaw, Joan Collins (THE GIRL IN THE RED VELVET SWING) ii) Jane Powell (THE GIRL MOST LIKELY) iii) biopic: Eva Tanguay, Mitzi Gaynor (THE 'I DON'T CARE' GIRL)

13 a) GABLE AND LOMBARD b) THE DOLLY SISTERS c) JULIA (as Lillian Hellman and Dashiell Hammett) d) Frieda and D.H. Lawrence in PRIEST OF LOVE e) GILBERT AND SULLIVAN f) Gertrude Lawrence and Noël Coward in STAR! g) Sheilah Graham and F. Scott Fitzgerald in BELOVED INFIDEL h) STANLEY AND LIVINGSTONE i) BUTCH CASSIDY AND THE SUNDANCE KID j) BUTCH AND SUNDANCE: THE EARLY DAYS

14 a) William Randolph Hearst, Orson Welles b) Julius and Ethel Rosenberg's son, Timothy Hutton c) Sean O'Casey, Rod Taylor d) Paul Gaugin, George Sanders e) Aristotle Onassis, Anthony Quinn f) Huey Long, Broderick Crawford g) Jack Johnson, James Earl Jones h) Christopher Isherwood, Michael York i) Bix Beiderbecke, Kirk Douglas j) Janis Joplin, Bette Midler

15 a) Larry Parks b) Donald O'Connor c) Gary Busey d) James Stewart e) Ray Danton f) Ann Blyth g) It was a documentary h) Fred Astaire and Ginger Rogers i) Gary Cooper j) Will Rogers Jr

16 a) GANDHI b) THE GREAT ZIEGFELD c) LOVE ME OR LEAVE ME (Ruth Etting) d) THE BABE RUTH STORY e) SCOTT OF THE ANTARCTIC

17 a) A SONG TO REMEMBER (Cornel Wilde as Chopin) b) THE MAGIC BOW (Stewart Granger as Paganini) c) THE ASSASSINATION OF TROTSKY (Richard Burton as Trotsky) d) QUEEN CHRISTINA (Garbo as Christina) e) THE GREATEST STORY EVER TOLD (Max von Sydow as Christ)

18 a) Peter Finch (THE TRIALS) and Robert Morley (THE TRIALS) c) THE OSCAR WILDE d) John Fraser and Yvonne Mitchell in THE TRIALS and John Neville and Phyllis Calvert in OSCAR WILDE e) Edward Carson QC (Mason in THE TRIALS)

19 James Mason in MADAME BOVARY, Christopher Plummer in THE MAN WHO WOULD BE KING, Herbert Marshall in THE MOON AND SIXPENCE and THE RAZOR'S EDGE

20 a) Glenda Jackson as Sarah Bernhardt in THE INCREDIBLE SARAH b) Rudolph Nureyev as VALENTINO c) Richard Burton as ALEXANDER THE GREAT d) Anthony Quinn as ATTILA e) Greer Garson as MADAME CURIE f) Cornel Wilde as OMAR KHAYYAM g) Clark Gable as PARNELL h) Montgomery Clift as FREUD I) Edward G. Robinson as Dr Paul Ehrlich in DR EHRLICH'S MAGIC BULLET j) Jean Seberg as SAINT JOAN

21 a) Cole Porter in NIGHT AND DAY b) Michelangelo in THE AGONY AND THE ECSTASY c) Lorenz Hart in WORDS AND MUSIC d) LAWRENCE OF ARABIA e) TCHAIKOVSKY

22 ROSE OF WASHINGTON SQUARE, Alice Faye; Barbra Streisand, FUNNY GIRL; FUNNY LADY; Omar Sharif, James Caan; 'My Man'; THE GREAT ZIEGFELD

23 a) Heroine of adventure film serials, Betty Hutton, THE PERILS OF PAULINE b) Wartime air ace who had lost both legs, Kenneth More, REACH FOR THE SKY c) Political writer, Warren Beatty, REDS d) Sculptor, Scott Anthony, SAVAGE MESSIAH e) *Playboy* magazine model, Mariel Hemingway, STAR 80 f) Mayor of New York, Bob Hope, BEAU JAMES g) Baseball player, Gary Cooper, THE PRIDE OF THE YANKEES h) War journalist, Burgess Meredith, THE STORY OF G.I. JOE i) Beat-generation writer, John Heard, HEART BEAT j) Couturière, Marie-France Pisier, CHANEL SOLITAIRE

24 a) Emily, Charlotte and Anne Brontë in DEVOTION b) Victor Hugo's daughter; Isabelle Adjani, François Truffaut c) Marilyn Miller; in TILL THE CLOUDS ROLL BY (Garland), LOOK FOR THE SILVER LINING d) MAGNIFICENT DOLL (Dolly Madison) and HARLOW (with Carol Lynley as Jean Harlow – the Carroll Baker version was made the same year) e) Julie Andrews in THE SOUND OF MUSIC as Maria von Trapp f) BRIDE OF FRANKENSTEIN; Elsa Lanchester played Mary Shelley in the prologue g) LADY CAROLINE LAMB, Robert Bolt h) Louise Bryant and Emma Goldman in REDS

LUST FOR LIVES
Answers to Picture Questions

Page 116:

LUST FOR LIFE, Kirk Douglas, Vincente Minnelli; Irving Stone, Vincent Van Gogh; Anthony Quinn as Paul Gaugin

Page 118, top:

a) COAL MINER'S DAUGHTER b) Sissy Spacek, Loretta Lynn c) She did her own singing d) Tommy Lee Jones e) NASHVILLE

Page 118, bottom:

Peter Ilyich Tchaikovsky, Richard Chamberlain, THE MUSIC LOVERS; MAHLER (Robert Powell), LISZTOMANIA (Liszt – Roger Daltrey); Glenda

Jackson, she played Tchaikovsky's wife; WOMEN IN LOVE

Page 121:

GYPSY; June Havoc and Gypsy Rose Lee; Louise, Natalie Wood; she is part of an act called Baby June (Havoc) and the Newsboys; as Gypsy Rose Lee, she perfected the art of striptease; it was used as the accompaniment to all the 'Baby June' acts, and then by Gypsy for her striptease; Rosalind Russell

Page 122:

Vanessa Redgrave as Isadora Duncan; ISADORA (aka THE LOVES OF ISADORA); in Russia in the 20s; she married Paris Singer, the sewing-machine millionaire, played by Jason Robards Jr; MARY, QUEEN OF SCOTS, JULIA, AGATHA

Page 123:

a) LENNY, Lenny Bruce, Dustin Hoffman b) Valerie Perrine c) Bob Fosse d) ALL THAT JAZZ

BEHIND THE SCENES

1 a) Walter Matthau to Barbra Streisand on the set of HELLO DOLLY b) Laurence Harvey to Capucine on the set of WALK ON THE WILD SIDE c) Tony Curtis about Marilyn Monroe after making SOME LIKE IT HOT d) Otto Preminger on Marilyn Monroe in RIVER OF NO RETURN e) Billy Wilder on Marilyn Monroe f) John Simon writing on Elizabeth Taylor in THE TAMING OF THE SHREW g) David Puttnam on Dustin Hoffman after AGATHA h) Dustin Hoffman on David Puttnam after AGATHA i) Producer Joe Pasternak of Doris Day

2 E.T; $44,809,658; STAR WARS i) JAWS ii) GREASE iii) THE EXORCIST iv) THE GODFATHER v) SUPERMAN vi) THE SOUND OF MUSIC vii) THE STING viii) CLOSE ENCOUNTERS ix) GONE WITH THE WIND x) SATURDAY NIGHT FEVER

3 a) Charles Laughton b) Marlon Brando c) Sylvester Stallone d) Sean Connery e) Vanessa Redgrave f) Alec Guinness g) Peter O'Toole h) Martin Sheen i) Julie Walters j) Joan Collins

4 a) Lou Costello sued Bud Abbott b) Jeanette MacDonald on SAN FRANCISCO c) Vivien Leigh during GONE WITH THE WIND d) Errol Flynn during ELIZABETH AND ESSEX e) JINXED, Bette Midler

5 HEAVEN'S GATE (Michael Cimino) and ONE FROM THE HEART (Francis Ford Coppola); 1941; INCHON, The Reverend Sun Moon

6 a) THREE COMRADES b) i) Raymond Chandler (co-wrote) ii) William Faulkner (co-wrote) iii) John Steinbeck iv) Gore Vidal (co-wrote) v) Dashiell Hammett c) THE YAKUZA, TAXI DRIVER, OBSESSION d) William Goldman e) Billy Wilder, Vittorio de Sica, Luchino Visconti, Woody Allen

7 a) Puerto Rica b) Belgium c) Russia d) Wales e) Sweden f) India g) Japan h) Hungary i) England j) Australia (Tasmania)

8 a) The slicked-down hair-style b) Baggy pants, man's jacket, shirt and tie c) The Afro hair-style for whites d) He wore no undershirt e) The natural look, less make-up and unplucked eyebrows f) Jeans and a windcheater g) Wide-shouldered dresses h) The gamine look i) Platinum blonde hair j) The 'peek-a-boo' hair-style

9 aB; bE; cC; dA; eD

10 a) CLEOPATRA, Elizabeth Taylor b) Hedy Lamarr, Edith Head for SAMSON AND DELILAH c) Adrian d) GIGI, ON A CLEAR DAY YOU CAN SEE FOR-EVER, MY FAIR LADY e) BONNIE AND CLYDE f) THE GREAT GATSBY g) Helen Rose h) JEZEBEL i) Walter Plunkett j) LADY IN THE DARK

11 Marlon Brando for SUPERMAN; about $10 million each; James Stewart, WINCHESTER '73 (1950); Lillian Gish, WAY DOWN EAST (1920)

12 a) Hattie McDaniel (GONE WITH THE WIND) – Best Supporting Actress b) Peter Finch (NETWORK) c) Douglas Fairbanks Sr d) Henry Fonda (ON GOLDEN POND) e) Walter Brennan (COME AND GET IT!) and Gale Sondergaard (ANTHONY ADVERSE) f) Clark Gable and Claudette Colbert in IT HAPPENED ONE NIGHT g) De Sica's SHOE SHINE (Italy) – Special Award 1947; (Fellini's LA STRADA, 1956, established category) h) James Cagney (YANKEE DOODLE DANDY) i) Luise Rainer (THE GREAT ZIEGFELD – 1936, THE GOOD EARTH – 1937), Katharine Hepburn (GUESS WHO'S COMING TO DINNER? – 1967, THE LION IN WINTER – 1968) j) Amazingly, none of them ever won a best acting Oscar

13 a) Harold Lloyd b) Herbert Marshall c) Peter Falk d) Van Johnson e) Montgomery Clift f) Margaret Dumont (the Marx Brothers' stooge) g) Judy Garland for THE WIZARD OF OZ h) Jeffrey Hunter for KING OF KINGS i) George Raft j) Robert Donat

14 a) IN OLD CALIFORNIA (1910) directed by D.W. Griffith b) LA SORTIE DES OUVRIERS DE L'USINE LUMIÈRE (WORKERS LEAVING THE LUMIÈRE FACTORY), exhibited in March 1895 c) THE ROBE (1953) d) HOUSE OF WAX (1953) e) THE BROADWAY MELODY (1929) f) EARTHQUAKE (1974) g) ARIZONA (1913) released six months before DeMille's THE SQUAW MAN, usually credited as the first feature western h) Hungary i) LIGHTS OF NEW YORK (1928) j) Hitchcock's BLACKMAIL (1929)

15 aB; bH; cA; dF; eJ; fE; gD; hI; iG; jC

16 a) THE ILLUSTRATED MAN; Rod Steiger b) THE BRIDE OF FRANKEN-STEIN c) PLANET OF THE APES d) GREYSTOKE e) LITTLE BIG MAN (he played a 121-year-old man) and TOOTSIE (he played a man disguised as a woman) f) THE LADYKILLERS g) The first three all played the PHANTOM OF THE OPERA; Williams starred in the rock-opera remake, PHANTOM OF THE PARADISE h) Jack Pierce; Karloff's legs were stiffened by steel struts i) Marlon Brando in THE GODFATHER

17 Cedric Gibbons; her uncle Oscar; about $150, 13½ inches; 1928, WINGS, Frank Borzage (SEVENTH HEAVEN), Emil Jannings, Janet Gaynor; TERMS OF ENDEARMENT, James L. Brooks, Robert Duvall, Shirley MacLaine

18 a) Director of photography b) Sound engineer c) Art director d) Screenwriter e) Musical director f) Hairstylist g) Colour consultant h) Choreographer i) Director j) Special effects technician

BEHIND THE SCENES
Answers to Picture Questions

Page 125:
THIS IS CINERAMA; Fred Waller, director of special effects at Paramount; it used three projectors and three screens to cover 140 degrees; HOW THE WEST WAS WON

Page 126:
The first American manned space flight on February 20, 1962; Vice-President Lyndon Johnson (left), astronaut John Glenn, and the Speaker of the House of Representatives; THE RIGHT STUFF, Tom Wolfe; a) The Watergate affair b) The Israeli raid on Entebbe airport c) The military take-over in Indonesia in 1965 d) The last days of the Somoza regime in Nicaragua

Page 127:
MACBETH, Roman Polanski; Jon Finch; HAMLET, Sarah Bernhardt in a three-minute version of the duel scene in 1900 (Forbes-Robertson played in the fullest early version in 1913); THE TAMING OF THE SHREW (1929)

Page 128:
a) (l to r) Charles 'Buddy' Rogers, Richard Arlen, Gary Cooper b) WINGS, William Wellman c) He was an ace pilot during World War I with the Lafayette Escadrille d) It was the first to win a Best Picture Oscar e) Howard Hughes's HELL'S ANGELS

REACH FOR THE STARS – Page 129

A a) Jean Simmons b) Stewart Granger, Richard Brooks c) GIVE US THE MOON d) DESIREE, GUYS AND DOLLS

B a) Robert Taylor b) Spangler Arlington Brugh c) CAMILLE (1936) d) A YANK AT OXFORD e) Billy the Kid in the film of the same name

C a) Shirley MacLaine b) THE TROUBLE WITH HARRY c) THE CHILDREN'S HOUR (GB: THE LOUDEST WHIS-PER), William Wyler, Audrey Hepburn d) Warren Beatty

D a) Robert Mitchum b) TWO FOR THE SEESAW, WHAT A WAY TO GO c) NIGHT OF THE HUNTER d) FARE-WELL MY LOVELY, THE BIG SLEEP (remakes) e) RYAN'S DAUGHTER

E a) Sidney Poitier b) A PATCH OF BLUE, Elizabeth Hartman; THE SLENDER THREAD, Anne Bancroft c) GUESS WHO'S COMING TO DINNER, Katharine Houghton d) IN THE HEAT OF THE NIGHT e) DUEL AT DIABLO

ADVENTURE PLAYGROUND

1 a) They were trapped upside-down in a capsized luxury liner b) The *Titanic* sank c) AVALANCHE d) THE HURRICANE (1937), HURRICANE (1979) e) He defused the bomb in JUGGERNAUT f) Paul Newman, Fred Astaire g) EARTH-QUAKE (Walter Matthau billed under his real name) h) ORCA – KILLER WHALE i) Peter Benchley j) Roy Scheider

2 a) Gary Cooper in MOROCCO, Clive Brook in SHANGHAI EXPRESS, Vittorio de Sica in THE MONTE CARLO STORY b) William Holden c) THE TREASURE OF THE SIERRA MADRE (Huston), CASABLANCA (Bergman), PASSAGE TO MARSEILLE (Morgan), TOKYO JOE (Marly), SAHARA (Bridges) d) Rosa-lind Russell in THEY MET IN BOMBAY, Sophia Loren in IT HAPPENED IN NAPLES, Jean Harlow in CHINA SEAS e) Tyrone Power starred in CAPTAIN FROM CASTILE, KING OF THE KHYBER RIFLES and SUEZ

3 a) THE FLIGHT OF THE PHOENIX; James Stewart, Ernest Borgnine, George Kennedy, Dan Duryea (American); Richard Attenborough, Ian Bannen, Ronald Fraser, Peter Finch (British); Hardy Kruger (German); Christian Marquand (French) b) LEGEND OF THE LOST; Sophia Loren c) SANDS OF THE KALAHARI; Stuart Whitman d) THE LOST PATROL; Victor McLaglen, Boris Karloff e) FIVE GRAVES TO CAIRO; Akim Tamiroff and Anne Baxter, Billy Wilder f) DESERT LEGION; Arlene Dahl g) ICE COLD IN ALEX; Sylvia Sims; a German disguised as a South African; the longing for an ice cold beer in Alexandria h) OASIS; Yves Allegret i) PLAY DIRTY; Michael Caine j) THE FLYING DEUCES; Laurel and Hardy

4 Dead soldiers at their posts around a fort open the film; Ronald Colman and Noah Beery (1926), Gary Cooper and Brian Donlevy (1939), Guy Stockwell and Telly Savalas (1966); O'Connor appeared as Beau Geste as a child in the 1939 version; Ray Milland and Robert Preston; Marty Feld-man; Gary Cooper (scenes from the 1939 version were intercut into the film)

5 a) KING SOLOMON'S MINES b) Sir Cedric Hardwicke (Livingstone) in STANLEY AND LIVINGSTONE; Tracy was Stanley c) A lion in BORN FREE d) Animals for zoos in HATARI e) THE LION

6 John Huston, Peter Ustinov; a white whale, Terence Stamp; Gregory Peck, Peter Ustinov; Richard Basehart, Robert Ryan; Orson Welles; *The Pequod, The Rights Of Man*; Ray Bradbury and John Huston, Ireland; Terence Stamp

7 a) Errol Flynn and Claude Rains b) Errol Flynn and Anthony Quinn c) Alan Ladd and Howard Da Silva d) Alan Ladd and James Mason e) Alec Guinness and Dirk Bogarde

8 LOST HORIZON; 'Be Kind'; James Hilton; Frank Capra; Ronald Colman, H.B. Warner, Sam Jaffe; Peter Finch, John Gielgud, Charles Boyer – it was a musical version

9 a) viii; iv; ix; v; i; vii; x; ii; iii; vi b) LIVE AND LET DIE, THE MAN WITH THE GOLDEN GUN, THE SPY WHO LOVED ME, MOONRAKER c) LIVE AND LET DIE, YOU ONLY LIVE TWICE d) THE MAN WITH THE GOLDEN GUN (Lee), THE SPY WHO LOVED ME (Jurgens), OCTOPUSSY (Jourdan), GOLDFINGER (Frobe), DR NO (Wiseman) e) David Niven, CASINO ROYALE

10 a) MODESTY BLAISE b) Matt Helm c) MATA HARI d) Moyzich in FIVE FINGERS (operating as 'Cicero') e) Harry Palmer f) Flint g) James Bond in ON HER MAJESTY'S SECRET SERVICE h) Napoleon Solo i) Violette Szabo in CARVE HER NAME WITH PRIDE j) Odette Churchill in ODETTE V.C.

11 a) SECRET AGENT b) SABOTAGE (US: THE WOMAN ALONE) c) THE 39 STEPS d) THE MAN WHO KNEW TOO MUCH e) NORTH BY NORTHWEST

12 a) FAMILY PLOT b) TORN CURTAIN c) TOPAZ d) THE TROUBLE WITH HARRY e) THE MAN WHO KNEW TOO MUCH (1934) f) MR AND MRS SMITH g) SECRET AGENT h) FOREIGN CORRESPONDENT i) RICH AND STRANGE (US: EAST OF SHANGHAI) j) THE PARADINE CASE

13 a) 'It was Beauty killed the Beast', Robert Armstrong b) She is being directed for a screen test, Fay Wray c) Skull Island, The Empire State Building d) 18 inches, Willis O'Brien; 40 feet e) Max Steiner; John Barry f) True g) Merian C. Cooper and Ernest B. Schoedsack – they can be seen for a few seconds as the pilots of the plane trying to shoot Kong on the Empire State h) 'King Kong Died For Our Sins' i) Edgar Wallace j) . . . KONG, . . . GODZILLA, . . . JOE YOUNG; MORGAN – A SUITABLE CASE FOR TREATMENT

14 a) b) f) i) Montez; c) e) h) j) de Carlo; d) Mari Blanchard; g) Maureen O'Hara

15 a) Elliott Gould and Donald Sutherland b) Richard Burton c) Laurence Harvey d) Roger Moore e) Conrad Veidt

16 Ae (shot in Sherwood Forest); Bc; Cd; Da; Eb

17 a) Alan Hale, ROBIN HOOD (1922), THE ADVENTURES OF ROBIN HOOD (1938), ROGUES OF SHERWOOD FOREST (1950) b) Cornel Wilde, John Derek c) She actually played Robin Hood's daughter, disguised as his son (the title refers to her) d) ROBIN AND THE SEVEN HOODS; Chicago e) THE TIME BANDITS

18 a) JOURNEY TO THE CENTRE OF THE EARTH; James Mason b) EARTHQUAKE c) THE WORLD, THE FLESH AND THE DEVIL; Harry Belafonte, Inger Stevens, Mel Ferrer d) THE LIGHT AT THE EDGE OF THE WORLD; Samantha Eggar e) THE WORLD OF APU; Satyajit Ray f) AROUND THE WORLD IN EIGHTY DAYS g) EARTH h) THE WORLD IN HIS ARMS; Gregory Peck, Ann Blyth i) AROUND THE WORLD UNDER THE SEA; Shirley Eaton j) THE WORLD OF SUZIE WONG; William Holden, Nancy Kwan

19 a) Klaus Kinski in AGUIRRE – THE WRATH OF GOD, FITZCARRALDO, WOYZECK b) Peter Finch in THE NUN'S STORY, ELEPHANT WALK, A BEQUEST TO THE NATION (US: THE NELSON AFFAIR) c) Glenda Jackson in A BEQUEST TO THE NATION, MARY, QUEEN OF SCOTS, THE MARAT-SADE d) Burt Reynolds in SMOKEY AND THE BANDIT, SHARK!, DELIVERANCE e) Jon Voight in DELIVERANCE, THE ODESSA FILE, CONRACK

20 a) Sam Jaffe as GUNGA DIN; Rudyard Kipling, Douglas Fairbanks Jr, Cary Grant, Victor McLaglen b) THE MAN WHO WOULD BE KING, Sean Connery, Michael Caine c) THE FOUR FEATHERS; STORM OVER THE NILE; Zoltan Korda (1939), Zoltan Korda and Terence Fisher (1955); Robert Powell d) THE SUN NEVER SETS, Virginia Field e) LIVES OF A BENGAL LANCER, Richard Cromwell

21 a) Lancelot; KNIGHTS OF THE ROUND TABLE (Taylor), LANCELOT AND GUINEVERE (aka SWORD OF LANCELOT) (Wilde), CAMELOT (Nero), LANCELOT DU LAC (Simon) b) IVANHOE, Elizabeth Taylor and Joan Fontaine; QUENTIN DURWARD, Kay Kendall c) Merlin, John Boorman d) i) THE SWORD IN THE STONE ii) LORD OF THE RINGS e) JABBERWOCKY

22 a) SCALAWAG b) ANNE OF THE INDIES c) SAVAGE ISLANDS d) DOUBLE CROSSBONES e) BLACKBEARD'S GHOST

23 a) Burt Lancaster b) Robert Shaw c) Graham Chapman d) Robert Newton e) Douglas Fairbanks Sr

24 John Ford, MOGAMBO; RED DUST; Kenya; Victor Fleming, Clark Gable, Jean Harlow, Mary Astor; Clark Gable; Ava Gardner (Best Actress), Grace Kelly (Best Supporting Actress)

25 a) 'Me Tarzan, You Jane'; Bo Derek b) GREYSTOKE c) A riverboat; Ursula Andress, Susan Hayward, Dorothy Lamour d) Jungle Jim, Bomba the Jungle Boy e) THE MACOMBER AFFAIR, THE SNOWS OF KILIMANJARO

26 a) THE DUELLISTS b) SCARAMOUCHE c) PRINCE VALIANT d) THE BLACK SHIELD OF FALWORTH e) THE COURT JESTER

ADVENTURE PLAYGROUND
Answers to Picture Questions

Page 130:
Johnny Weissmuller – he was a five times Olympic swimming gold-medallist; Maureen O'Sullivan, Mia Farrow; false – it was the first sound version

Page 132:
a) FIRE OVER ENGLAND b) Flora Robson, THE SEA HAWK c) Laurence Olivier and Vivien Leigh d) They were lovers, but not yet married e) LADY HAMILTON (US: THAT HAMILTON WOMAN)

Page 134:
FROM RUSSIA WITH LOVE; Lotte Lenya as Rosa Klebb; she had a flick knife which sprang from the toe of her shoe; the composer Kurt Weill

Page 135:
RAIDERS OF THE LOST ARK, Steven Spielberg; Harrison Ford; Indiana Jones, archaeologist; during 1936 in Egypt

Page 136:
Errol Flynn; CAPTAIN BLOOD; Warner Bros.; black and white; Guy Kibbee

Page 137:
THE LADY VANISHES, Alfred Hitchcock; on a train; Paul Lukas; Michael Redgrave and Margaret Lockwood, Elliott Gould and Cybill Shepherd; Dame May Whitty, Angela Lansbury

REACH FOR THE STARS – Page 138

A a) Rock Hudson b) GIANT c) Doris Day d) *McMillan And Wife* e) AVALANCHE

B a) Dirk Bogarde b) *A Postillion Struck By Lightning, Snakes And Ladders* c) THE SERVANT, James Fox d) DEATH IN VENICE e) Julie Christie, John Schlesinger

C a) Alain Delon b) PLEIN SOLEIL (PURPLE NOON) – based on 'The Talented Mr Ripley' c) THE YELLOW ROLLS ROYCE d) ROCCO AND HIS BROTHERS, THE LEOPARD e) SWANN IN LOVE, Jeremy Irons, Ornella Muti

D a) Alec Guinness b) THE MAN IN THE WHITE SUIT c) THE CARD (US: THE PROMOTER) d) THE SCAPEGOAT e) A MAJORITY OF ONE; a Japanese

E a) Carole Lombard b) Clark Gable c) GABLE AND LOMBARD, Jill Clayburgh and James Brolin d) MY MAN GODFREY, William Powell e) Jane Alice Peters

F a) Theda Bara b) Hibernian societies objected to a Jewish girl playing an Irish colleen c) Greta Garbo and Mary Pickford d) THE HUNCHBACK OF NOTRE DAME e) A FOOL THERE WAS; 'Kiss me, my fool' she ordered.

G a) Richard Gere b) REPORT TO THE COMMISSIONER (GB: OPERATION UNDERCOVER) c) LOOKING FOR MR GOODBAR; Diane Keaton d) AMERICAN GIGOLO; a male prostitute e) John Schlesinger; YANKS

H a) Barbara Stanwyck b) DOUBLE INDEMNITY; Billy Wilder; Fred MacMurray, Edward G. Robinson c) Robert Taylor; THIS IS MY AFFAIR (GB: HIS AFFAIR), THE NIGHT WALKER d) LADY OF BURLESQUE (GB: STRIP-TEASE LADY); William Wellman; 'Take it off the E-String, Play it on the G-String'; e) GOLDEN BOY; William Holden

I a) Catherine Deneuve b) BELLE DE JOUR, TRISTANA c) Roger Vadim, Marcello Mastroianni d) REPULSION e) Françoise Dorléac – she was killed in a car crash

J a) Lon Chaney Sr b) Greta Garbo c) OLIVER TWIST (1922) – Coogan was in the title role and Chaney played Fagin d) He was armless; Joan Crawford e) James Cagney, MAN OF A THOUSAND FACES (1957)

OUT OF THIS WORLD

1 a) Los Angeles b) London c) Ottawa d) Rome e) New York

2 a) William Cameron Menzies, Ralph Richardson; its score was the first to be commercially recorded b) George Sanders c) Burt Lancaster; ISLAND OF LOST SOULS, Charles Laughton d) Bert I. Gordon; it caused giant growth in wasps, worms, chickens and rats e) TIME AFTER TIME, Malcolm McDowell; Jack the Ripper

3 a) With their explosive vintage wine c) Up a huge ramp c) The rocket was fired from a monster cannon d) An anti-gravity device e) On board meteorites

4 a) Alex Raymond's b) Ming the Merciless; Charles Middleton, Priscilla Lawson c) Dr Zarkov (Frank Shannon), Dale Arden (Jean Rogers), Happy (Donald Kerr) d) Buck Rogers e) Sam Jones, Max von Sydow

5 a) STAR WARS b) WESTWORLD c) FRANKENSTEIN MEETS THE SPACE MONSTER (GB: DUEL OF THE SPACE MONSTERS) d) 2001: A SPACE ODYSSEY e) GODZILLA VERSUS MEGALON

6 a) A deadly dust called 'The Purple Death' dropped into the atmosphere b) A vegetation-destroying virus created by pollution c) Materialised thought d) A monster bird from outer space e) Two super-computers with evil intentions

7 They are all set in a post-nuclear holocaust world

8 a) Helmut Dantine in STRANGER FROM VENUS (US: IMMEDIATE DISASTER) b) Paul Birch in NOT OF THIS EARTH c) Patricia Laffan in DEVIL GIRL FROM MARS d) Jane Fonda in BARBARELLA e) Leonard Nimoy in STAR TREK: THE MOTION PICTURE and STAR TREK: THE WRATH OF KHAN

9 a) CONQUEST OF THE EARTH; Wolfman Jack, AMERICAN GRAFFITI b) Heroin c) TWILIGHT ZONE – THE MOVIE d) The Martians were Christians e) Water

10 a) . . . THE BIKINI MACHINE (or . . . THE GIRL BOMBS, which was a sequel) b) . . . CONQUERS THE MARTIANS c) . . . OF THE MOON d) . . . OR IT BECAME NECESSARY TO DESTROY THE WORLD IN ORDER TO SAVE IT e) . . . ON MARS

11 a) Claude Rains b) E.E. Clive as the policeman (PC Jaffers) c) His footsteps appear in the snow d) Vincent Price – to clear himself of a murder charge e) Jon Hall, Ilona Massey f) John Carradine g) John Barrymore h) Robby the Robot i) THE INVISIBLE RAY j) By taking control of the bodies of the dead

12 a) It was immobilised by Steve McQueen's fire extinguisher and dumped in the Arctic. (It made a disappointing come-back in BEWARE! THE BLOB, directed by Larry Hagman of 'Dallas' fame.) b) It was given a monster electric shock of 9 million volts c) IT – a statue brought to life by mad museum curator Roddy McDowell – was the target of a nuclear strike, which failed even to make it miss a stride as it plodded thoughtfully off into the sea d) It (ie intelligent radioactive mud) was trapped and blown up in a web of radar waves e) The Triffids were melted by being doused with sea water

13 a) A strange device implanted on their necks; Leif Erickson and Hillary Brooke; a green disembodied head in a glass sphere with two tentacle-like arms sprouting from its shoulders b) Don Siegel (director), Dana Wynter and Kevin McCarthy; it grew 'blanks' of its human victims and then took them over while they were asleep; with McCarthy standing on the edge of a freeway yelling 'You're next!' at the passing cars; Donald Sutherland, Brooke Adams; the first film was set in a small town, the remake in San Francisco; Don Siegel appeared as a taxi-driver, and Kevin McCarthy was still asking for help from passing cars c) Gloria Talbott d) On the edge of a small town in the Arizona desert e) Sigourney Weaver

14 a) Steve McQueen b) Sylvester Stallone c) Clint Eastwood d) Joan Crawford e) Bela Lugosi f) Mickey Rooney g) Bette Davis h) Gene Autry i) Humphrey Bogart j) Jack Nicholson

15 a) Boris Karloff b) Hans Conried c) Howard Vernon d) Albert Dekker e) George Zucco f) Ray Milland g) Alec Guinness h) Sam Jaffe i) Ernest Thesiger j) Walter Pidgeon

16 Ac; Be; Ca; Db; Ed

17 a) Grant Williams b) Lily Tomlin c) Allison Hayes d) Virginia Bruce e) Glenn Langan

18 a) John Dykstra b) Douglas Trumbull c) Ray Harryhausen d) Rick Baker e) A jet-propelled giant turtle f) A monster shrimp g) An armour-plated chicken from outer space h) A pterodactyl i) A giant jelly-fish

19 a) Rod Taylor b) In a time-warp just before the attack on Pearl Harbor c) In Ancient Rome d) In California in the 60s e) Anton Diffring's; THE MAN IN HALF MOON STREET, Nils Asther

20 a) It was the agent of invisibility b) It enabled Fred MacMurray to defy gravity c) A few drops soaked into pipe tobacco and cheerfully puffed by the unsuspecting Arthur Franz turned him into a homicidal neanderthal man d) It enabled you to lock mentally into someone's nervous system, with explosive results e) Freely applied to his face, it transformed Preston Foster into the Moon Monster

21 a) He duplicated her b) Brian Donlevy; Andrew Keir c) Bryan Forbes d) Westminster Abbey e) MOON ZERO TWO

22 a) CLOSE ENCOUNTERS OF THE THIRD KIND b) THE ENTITY c) THE 27TH DAY d) THE DAY THE EARTH CAUGHT FIRE e) LOGAN'S RUN

23 a) Ants b) A 30ft queen wasp c) Locusts d) An outsize caterpillar e) Bees

24 a) KING OF THE ROCKET MEN b) Linda Stirling and Charles Quigley c) Kirk Alyn d) Mars e) With a robot army

25 a) FORBIDDEN PLANET b) SPACE-HUNTER: ADVENTURES IN THE FORBIDDEN ZONE c) NOT OF THIS EARTH d) THIS ISLAND EARTH e) FLASH GORDON

26 a) VIDEODROME, Debbie Harry b) To blow up unstable asteroids – it was destroyed by one of its own talking bombs c) She had come to find some husky male earthlings as breeding stock for her Martian matriarchy d) To save money, Harryhausen made it a quintopus (fewer tentacles than an octopus!) e) SOYLENT GREEN f) Robert Duvall, George Lucas g) Four (Gary Lockwood and the three crewmen in suspended animation) h) SOLARIS i) THE THING (FROM ANOTHER WORLD)

OUT OF THIS WORLD
Answers to Picture Questions

Page 140:
PLANET OF THE APES (illustrated), BENEATH THE PLANET OF THE APES, ESCAPE FROM THE PLANET OF THE APES, CONQUEST OF THE PLANET OF THE APES, BATTLE FOR THE PLANET OF THE APES; Charlton Heston and Linda Harrison, Kim Hunter; he was an astronaut; by coming upon The Statue of Liberty, the hero (Heston) discovers that the planet of the apes is, in fact Earth (he has been in a time warp)

Page 141:
Luke Skywalker (Mark Hamill), Princess Leia Organa (Carrie Fisher), Chewbaca (Peter Mayhew), Han Solo (Harrison Ford) – STAR WARS, THE EMPIRE STRIKES BACK, RETURN OF THE JEDI; Darth Vader; David Prowse, James Earl Jones; Ben Obi Wan Kenobi, Alec Guinness

Page 142:
1984, George Orwell, 1948; Michael Anderson (director), Edmond O'Brien, Jan Sterling; Winston Smith continues to defy Big Brother – in the book he recants and denies his love

Page 144, above:
a) BLADE RUNNER b) Los Angeles, 40 years hence (ie 2020) c) Sean Young, Harrison Ford d) A robot or 'replicant' e) Ridley Scott, ALIEN

Page 144, below:
FAHRENHEIT 451, Montag, Oskar Werner; he was a fireman trained to seek out and destroy books; Julie Christie (far right); François Truffaut, CLOSE ENCOUNTERS OF THE THIRD KIND; Nicholas Roeg; Ray Bradbury's – the title is the temperature at which books burn

Page 145:
THE DAY THE EARTH STOOD STILL, Gort; Michael Rennie – to save the world from self-destruction; 'Klaatu Barada Nikto', uttered by the robot's captive (played by Patricia Neal); he stopped all machinery and power plants on Earth for half-an-hour

Page 146:
On board the submarine *Nautilus* in 20,000 LEAGUES UNDER THE SEA; (l to r) James Mason, Kirk Douglas, Peter Lorre, Paul Lukas; Captain Nemo; Richard Fleischer, Disney; a giant squid

Page 147:
DR STRANGELOVE OR HOW I LEARNED TO STOP WORRYING AND LOVE THE BOMB, the War Room in the Pentagon; the President of the United States speaking to the Soviet General Secretary to warn him that a rogue US nuclear bomber is flying into Russian airspace; Peter Sellers, the title role and an RAF officer; Peter Bull, the Russian Ambassador; Keenan Wynn, Sterling Hayden; 'We'll Meet Again', Vera Lynn

SILENCE
Answers to Picture Questions

Page 149, above:
The 'business' was the selling of Christmas trees, but 'business' also being the term for the mechanics of comedy (or other) routines, the 'big business' of this film embraced the actions of the plot. The actors are, of course, Laurel (left) and Hardy (right), with James Finlayson; the comedy duo are destroying Finlayson's house, while he retaliates by destroying their car; the car; Leo McCarey, George Stevens

Page 149, left:
a) THE FRESHMAN (1923) – MAD WEDNESDAY (aka THE SIN OF HAROLD DIDDLEBOCK, 1947) re-used the same sequence b) HORSE FEATHERS (1932) c) HEAVEN CAN WAIT (1978) d) M*A*S*H (1970) e) SEMI-TOUGH (1977)

Page 149, above left:
United Artists of which Fairbanks was one of the original co-founders; THE BLACK PIRATE was the first major length feature film to be shot entirely in the then new two-strip Technicolor process

Page 150, above:
Patricia Kelly, a convent girl, became a 'queen' by marrying a prince; Seena Owen is taking the whip to Gloria Swanson whom she has caught in the prince's bedroom and whom she is attacking for flirting with him; Joseph Kennedy, father of the future American president; SUNSET BOULEVARD (1950)

Page 150, right:
Mae Murray, John Gilbert; Clark Gable; Jeanette MacDonald and Maurice Chevalier directed by Ernst Lubitsch (1934), Lana Turner and Fernando Lamas directed by Curtis Bernhardt (1952); Joseph Cotten in SHADOW OF A DOUBT (1943)

Page 151, above:
a) False – the film is THE EAGLE b) False – he was born in Castellaneta, Italy c) True d) True e) True f) False – he died at 31

Page 151, left:
Louise Brooks, PANDORA'S BOX (1928), THE DIARY OF A LOST GIRL (1929); she started as a dancer, appearing for George White in his 'Scandals' and Florenz Ziegfeld in his 'Follies'; BEGGARS OF LIFE (1928)

Page 153, above:
Producer/star Gloria Swanson, director/co-star Raoul Walsh, SADIE THOMPSON (1928); Joan Crawford in RAIN (1932), Rita Hayworth in MISS SADIE THOMPSON (1952)

Page 153, left:
A DOG'S LIFE (1918); a) M. VERDOUX (1947) b) THE GREAT DICTATOR (1940) c) A KING IN NEW YORK (1957); A WOMAN OF PARIS (1924)

Page 153, below:
BLIND HUSBANDS (1919); Sam de Grasse; FOOLISH WIVES (1922), THE WEDDING MARCH (1926)

Page 154, right:
THE CABINET OF DR CALIGARI directed by Robert Wiene; Conrad Veidt as the somnambulist Cesare. Here he is kidnapping the heroine, Jane (Lil Dagover) but, pursued by townspeople, he drops her and runs off; both stories are told from the point of view of someone who is mad, although the 1962 film is *not* a remake

Page 154, below:
Abel Gance, St Just; Antonin Artaud; Cinerama, in its use of a triple screen

Page 154, above right (pic on p155):
a) MIGHTY b) EARTH c) THINGS d) REVENGE e) ON f) PANIC g) ONE h) LOST i) IT j) STAR; METROPOLIS directed by Fritz Lang

Page 154, right (pic on p155):
D.W. Griffith's INTOLERANCE; it intercut four different stories set during four different eras (ancient Babylon, biblical Palestine at the time of Christ, medieval France under Charles IX, and a contemporary American story); Italy, CABIRIA (1913) directed by Giovanni Pastrone

CRIME AND PUNISHMENT

1 a) MURDER BY DEATH; Elsa Lanchester, James Coco, David Niven and Maggie Smith, Peter Falk, Peter Sellers b) Agatha Christie, Margaret Rutherford c) Scenes from vintage films were cut in to DEAD MEN DON'T WEAR PLAID d) Edward Ellis; William Powell became famous, The Thin Man's real name was Nick Charles, Myrna Loy played Powell's wife e) Marlon Brando, Al Pacino; the word 'mafia' was never used f) THE MALTESE FALCON (1931, 1941), SATAN MET A LADY (1936) g) Gloria Grahame h) All blonde, they were all cast in major starring roles by Alfred Hitchcock i) Joan Bennett, Fritz Lang j) Fay Helm, Robert Siodmak

2 Ac; Ba; Ca; Dc; Ea; Fb; Gb

3 a) THE VERDICT; Paul Newman, James Mason b) IN THE HEAT OF THE NIGHT; Sidney Poitier, Rod Steiger c) FRENCH CONNECTION II, Gene Hackman; Fernando Rey d) SLEUTH; Laurence Olivier; Michael Caine e) PICKUP ON SOUTH STREET; Richard Widmark; Jean Peters; Thelma Ritter

4 a) I AM A FUGITIVE FROM A CHAIN GANG b) DEAD RECKONING c) LADY IN THE LAKE d) LITTLE CAESAR e) ROXIE HART

5 THE CONVERSATION, Francis Ford Coppola; BLOW-OUT, Brian De Palma

6 a) STRAIGHT TIME b) CHARLEY VARRICK c) TAKE THE MONEY AND RUN d) BUNNY O'HARE e) DOG DAY AFTERNOON

7 LA BALANCE; Philippe Leotard, Nathalie Baye

8 a) Herbert Marshall and Miriam Hopkins b) George C. Scott c) THE LADY EVE; Barbara Stanwyck and Charles Coburn, THE BIRDS AND THE BEES d) A 'talking' dog e) In small towns in Missouri and Kansas Garner puts negro Gossett up for sale as his slave, then rescues him after money has changed hands

9 a) SPELLBOUND; Gregory Peck, Ingrid Bergman, Leo G. Carroll b) MIRAGE;

Gregory Peck, Diane Baker, Walter Matthau c) HANGOVER SQUARE; Laird Cregar, Linda Darnell, George Sanders d) BLACK ANGEL; Dan Duryea, Constance Dowling, June Vincent, Peter Lorre e) SOMEWHERE IN THE NIGHT; John Hodiak, Lloyd Nolan, Nancy Guild, Richard Conte

10 a) Robert Siodmak b) Samuel Fuller c) Claude Chabrol d) Sidney Lumet e) Joseph H. Lewis

11 Ae, A DOUBLE LIFE; Bc, THE BIG CLOCK; Ch, THE WICKED LADY; Di, STRANGERS ON A TRAIN; Eg, THE ASSASSINATION OF TROTSKY; Fa, THE SPIRAL STAIRCASE; Gb, CONFLICT; Hj, POSSESSED; Id, NO WAY TO TREAT A LADY; Jf, TEMPTATION

12 Sidney Greenstreet, Peter Lorre, Geraldine Fitzgerald; Jean Negulesco; John Huston

13 Ad, THE BOSTON STRANGLER; Bh, BABY FACE NELSON; Cj, THE LODGER; Db, TEN RILLINGTON PLACE; Ec, THE EXECUTIONER'S SONG; Fi, DR CRIPPEN; Ge, BLUEBEARD; Ha, BIRDMAN OF ALCATRAZ; If, A BULLET FOR PRETTY BOY; Jg, CELL 2455, DEATH ROW

14 a) Robert Taylor b) Dick Powell c) Henry Silva d) Dan Duryea e) Tyrone Power

15 a) Dirk Bogarde b) Peter Lorre c) Sydney Greenstreet d) Noël Coward e) In a lunatic asylum

16 a) Orson Welles, THE STRANGER b) Agnes Moorehead, DARK PASSAGE c) Norman Lloyd, SABOTEUR d) Joseph Cotten, NIAGARA e) Joan Fontaine, IVY

17 a) Richard Widmark b) Bob Steele c) Earl Holliman and Lee Van Cleef d) William Bendix; Alan Ladd e) Neville Brand, Luther Adler

18 a) COTTON COMES TO HARLEM b) TOUCH OF EVIL c) FREEBIE AND THE BEAN d) THE NAKED CITY e) THE FOUR JUST MEN

19 a) MURDER AT THE GALLOP b) MURDER BY DEATH c) MURDER INC d) MURDER AT THE VANITIES e) MURDER IN THE MUSIC HALL

20 a) With the aid of a Howitzer cannon b) A casino in Reno, Nevada c) TOPKAPI; a bird which has flown in during the robbery sets off an alarm; to steal the Romanoff jewels from the Kremlin d) HOT ROCK (GB: HOW TO STEAL A DIAMOND IN FOUR UNEASY LESSONS)

21 a) Raymond Massey, Basil Rathbone, Robert Stephens; Christopher Lee b) THE SEVEN PER CENT SOLUTION; Nicol Williamson, Alan Arkin – Freud was attempting to cure Holmes of his addiction to cocaine c) Reginald Owen (he played Watson in the 1932 SHERLOCK HOLMES and a year later graduated to Holmes in A STUDY IN SCARLET) d) Lionel Atwill, Gale Sondergaard, Rondo Hatton e) George C. Scott

22 a) THE AMAZING DR CLITTERHOUSE b) Both c) DUST BE MY DESTINY d) PANIC IN THE STREETS e) MANPOWER

23 a) James Garner b) Warner Oland c) Peter Ustinov d) Jason Robards Jr e) Louis Hayward f) Mickey Spillane g) Nick Adams h) William Powell i) Tom Conway j) Dorothy Provine and Jack Hogan

24 a) BROTHER ORCHID b) Alec Guinness, Cecil Parker, Herbert Lom, Peter Sellers, Danny Green; Katie Johnson; they pretended to be a string quintet c) George Raft; a huge birthday cake opened up to reveal a hitman with a sub-machine gun d) BLUE MURDER AT ST TRINIANS e) Victor Mature

25 a) MURDER ON THE ORIENT EXPRESS b) THE LADY VANISHES c) NIGHT TRAIN TO MUNICH (US: NIGHT TRAIN) d) SILVER STREAK e) THE CASSANDRA CROSSING f) ROME EXPRESS g) THE NARROW MARGIN h) THE SLEEPING CAR MURDERS i) TERROR BY NIGHT j) SLEEPING CAR TO TRIESTE

26 a) Howard Hawks, Brian De Palma b) Tony Camonte (1932); Tony Montana (1983); Paul Muni, Al Pacino c) Bugs Moran d) George Raft, Steve Bauer e) Florida

27 a) THE WOMAN IN THE WINDOW b) DEAD OF NIGHT c) FEAR IN THE NIGHT d) NIGHTMARE e) THE CHASE (1947)

28 Cornell Woolrich (aka William Irish)

29 a) CRIME IN THE STREETS, Mark Rydell b) Child prostitution c) Joan Collins d) Mickey Rooney e) THE BOYS IN BROWN

30 a) THE POSTMAN ALWAYS RINGS TWICE (1946): Cecil Kellaway, John Garfield, Lana Turner/THE POSTMAN ALWAYS RINGS TWICE (1981): John Colicos, Jack Nicholson, Jessica Lange b) KLUTE: Donald Sutherland, Robert Milli, Jane Fonda c) DOUBLE INDEMNITY: Fred MacMurray, Barbara Stanwyck d) THE KILLING: Sterling Hayden, Elisha Cook Jr e) DEATHTRAP: Michael Caine, Christopher Reeve

31 a) Googie Withers, Gary Marsh b) Bette Davis, Eugene Pallette c) Peter Finch, Mary Morris d) Broderick Crawford, Gloria Grahame e) Kathleen Turner, Richard Crenna f) Margaret Lockwood, Ian Hunter g) Rex Harrison, Doris Day h) Anton Walbrook, Diana Wynyard (1939) /Charles Boyer, Ingrid Bergman (1944) i) Charles Chaplin, Martha Raye j) Jack Palance, Joan Crawford

32 a) Robert Montgomery b) PARDON US c) Boris Karloff d) YIELD TO THE NIGHT (US: BLONDE SINNER), Ruth Ellis e) Will Hay f) Paul Newman, 50 hardboiled eggs – one after the other g) George Bancroft, Pat O'Brien, Emile Meyer, Michael Redgrave, Eddie Albert h) THE DEFIANT ONES; Sidney Poitier, Stanley Kramer; MY BROTHER'S KEEPER,

Jack Warner and George Cole i) The better to conceal the proceeds of a jewel robbery j) Clint Eastwood; J. Carrol Naish; absolutely none – it was set on a passenger ship

33 a) Robert Taylor b) Dana Andrews c) Laird Cregar d) Van Heflin e) Ned Beatty

34 Paul Newman, Robert Redford; THE STING; George Roy Hill; Scott Joplin

35 a) JACKSON COUNTY JAIL b) THE PRISONER OF SHARK ISLAND c) ROXIE HART d) FURY e) BEYOND A REASONABLE DOUBT; his fiancée sets out to prove his innocence, and finds the necessary evidence. But in an unguarded moment he reveals that he is, in fact, the killer. She tells another journalist, who informs the governor just as he is about to sign the pardon; Dana Andrews

36 a) Richard Widmark b) HUE AND CRY c) Faye Dunaway d) Flora Robson e) PRETTY POISON; Anthony Perkins, Tuesday Weld

37 PUBLIC ENEMY: Tom Powers, Jean Harlow, William Wellman; THE ROARING 20s: Eddie Bartlett, Priscilla Lane, Raoul Walsh; ANGELS WITH DIRTY FACES: Rocky Sullivan, Ann Sheridan, Michael Curtiz; WHITE HEAT: Cody Jarrett, Virginia Mayo, Raoul Walsh; LOVE ME OR LEAVE ME: Martin Schneider (aka The Gimp), Doris Day, Charles Vidor

CRIME AND PUNISHMENT
Answers to Picture Questions

Page 156:
BONNIE AND CLYDE; Faye Dunaway and Warren Beatty, Gene Hackman and Estelle Parsons; Arthur Penn, Robert Benton and David Newman, Burnett Guffey

Page 158:
M; Fritz Lang, Peter Lorre; it concerned a child molester and murderer; Joseph Losey, David Wayne

Page 160:
The film was THE SCARFACE MOB. It became the TV series 'The Untouchables', based on the true-life experiences of Eliot Ness. The star is Robert Stack

Page 161:
Edward G. Robinson, Jean Arthur, THE WHOLE TOWN'S TALKING, John Ford

Page 162:
ROPE, Alfred Hitchcock; he used continuous takes of ten-minute duration; Farley Granger and John Dall; Leopold and Loeb, COMPULSION, Dean Stockwell and Bradford Dillman

Page 163:
BLOODY MAMA, Ma Barker, Shelley Winters; Roger Corman; Robert De Niro, THE GODFATHER PART II

Page 164:
Lana Turner and John Garfield, THE POSTMAN ALWAYS RINGS TWICE, Cecil Kellaway; James M. Cain; Luchino Visconti, Jack Nicholson and Jessica Lange

BUFF'S BRAINTEASER

1 a) Frances Marion; THE BIG HOUSE (1930), THE CHAMP (1931) b) William Witney c) Gerald Fried; FEAR AND DESIRE, KILLER'S KISS, THE KILLING, PATHS OF GLORY d) DECEPTION; Claude Rains, Erich Wolfgang Korngold e) R.O.T. (Roger O. Thornhill) f) Wilhelm Reich; Dusan Makavejev; MONTENEGRO g) NASHVILLE; Geraldine Chaplin, Keith Carradine, Keenan Wynn; Joan Tewkesbury h) Ivor Novello i) Rand Brooks, Carroll Nye j) They were pseudonyms of Joseph Losey for THE SLEEPING TIGER and THE INTIMATE STRANGER (the McCarthy witch-hunt prevented him from working under his own name)

2 a) BREATHLESS (À BOUT DE SOUFFLE) b) THE GREAT RACE c) HELP! d) SULLIVAN'S TRAVELS e) THREE GODFATHERS (1948)

3 a) CHRISTMAS IN JULY, (a slogan invented by) Dick Powell b) BABES IN ARMS, Mickey Rooney c) GYPSY, Natalie Wood d) THE SHINING, Jack Nicholson e) CHARIOTS OF FIRE, Ian Holm f) THEY SHOOT HORSES, DON'T THEY?, Gig Young g) HÔTEL DU NORD, Arletty h) ONE, TWO, THREE, James Cagney i) THE BAND WAGON, Fred Astaire

4 a) Bonita Granville b) Lydia Reed c) Audrey Fildes d) Richard Quine e) Art Lund

5 a) He was blind b) Edna May Oliver c) Boris Karloff d) Jane Wyman e) Six, eight members of the D'Ascoyne family stood between Price and the dukedom, but one of them – the Admiral – obligingly sank himself at sea, while another Lord D'Ascoyne – succumbed to a heart attack on learning that he had succeeded to the dukedom. Price's first victim – Ascoyne D'Ascoyne – was propelled over a weir; the last – the Duke – was caught in one of his own mantraps and then despatched with both barrels of his shotgun.

6 a) 'Say, listen, is he working on a case?' 'Yes' 'What case?'; THE THIN MAN, Myrna Loy b) 'Do you know that the guy said that machinery is going to take the place of every profession?'; DINNER AT EIGHT, Marie Dressler (to Jean Harlow) c) 'Goodness, what beautiful diamonds'; I'M NO ANGEL, Mae West d) 'You used to be big in silent pictures – used to be big'; SUNSET BOULEVARD, Gloria Swanson e) 'You will sit upon my left hand, and you will sit upon my right hand . . .'; AT THE CIRCUS, Groucho Marx

7 a) Goldenberg (his real surname) b) Henry Byron c) David Wark d) Friedrich Wilhelm e) Campbell

8 a) FREAKS, Wallace Ford b) DISHONORED, Marlene Dietrich c) GRAND HOTEL, Greta Garbo d) THE BANK DICK, W.C. Fields e) THE SHOP AROUND THE CORNER, James Stewart

9 a) Gene Wilder b) Elizabeth Taylor c) James Cagney and Joan Blondell d) Faye Dunaway e) Robert Redford f) Meryl Streep g) Woody Allen h) Grace Kelly i) Al Pacino j) Greer Garson

10 Greta Garbo standing at the prow of the ship at the end of Rouben Mamoulian's QUEEN CHRISTINA

11 a) William Pine and William Thomas of the Pine-Thomas production company b) Elissa Landi c) Louis B. Mayer d) W.S. Van Dyke e) William Wellman

12 THE WOMEN; Norma Shearer, Joan Crawford, Rosalind Russell; it had an all-woman cast (even the dog was a bitch)

13 a) THE THIEF b) A MAN ALONE c) QUEST FOR FIRE d) SILENT MOVIE e) SAVAGE INNOCENTS f) ONE MILLION YEARS B.C. (1966) (remake of ONE MILLION B.C., 1940) or THEMROC g) MODERN TIMES h) INCUBUS i) SEBASTIANE

14 a) Roberto Rossellini, Jean-Luc Godard, Pier-Paulo Pasolini, Gregoretti; Pasolini's was banned; Orson Welles b) QUARTET, TRIO, ENCORE; ten; Harold French c) John Landis, Steven Spielberg, Joe Dante, George Miller; Vic Morrow by a crashing helicopter; Rod Serling d) Five; Henry Hathaway, Henry King, Henry Koster, Howard Hawks, Jean Negulesco; Marilyn Monroe e) *Metzengerstein, William Wilson, Toby Dammit*; Peter Fonda, Alain Delon, Terence Stamp f) DEAD OF NIGHT i) Basil Rathbone and Naunton Wayne ii) Michael Redgrave iii) Mervyn Johns

15 a) THE AMERICAN SOLDIER b) ALL THAT HEAVEN ALLOWS c) DESPAIR, Dirk Bogarde d) EFFIE BRIEST, Fontane e) Hanna Schygulla, Margit Carstensen, Rosel Zech, Barbara Sukowa, Brad Davis

16 a) THE REVENGERS b) SON OF THE SHEIK c) GUESS WHO'S COMING TO DINNER? d) TROG e) BRAINSTORM f) TO BE OR NOT TO BE g) THE CARPETBAGGERS h) THE NAKED EDGE i) SARATOGA j) THE HARDER THEY FALL

17 a) All are characters played by Jeanette MacDonald b) All have played nuns c) All are directed by women (Elaine May, Vera Chytilova, Barbara Loden, Mai Zetterling, Ida Lupino) d) They were all child performers e) All starred Jane Fonda

18 a) NOW VOYAGER b) QUEEN KELLY c) THE BAD AND THE BEAUTIFUL d) THE MALTESE FALCON and CASABLANCA e) NIAGARA f) CAMILLE g) FRANKENSTEIN h) THE PASSION OF JOAN OF ARC i) BRIEF ENCOUNTER j) WHO KILLED COCK ROBIN? (Disney cartoon)

19 a) RAGTIME b) JUSTINE c) THE ADVENTURES OF ROBIN HOOD d) MERRY-GO-ROUND e) JOURNEY INTO FEAR f) TOSCA g) YOUNG CASSIDY h) SONG WITHOUT END i) MUTINY ON THE BOUNTY (1962) j) THE BOUNTY

20 a) Eugene Pallette; INTOLERANCE, THE BIG STREET, THE GHOST GOES WEST b) Hugh Herbert; DAMES, A MIDSUMMER NIGHT'S DREAM, THE BEAUTIFUL BLONDE FROM BASHFUL BEND c) Edward Everett Horton; THE MERRY WIDOW (1934), BLUEBEARD'S EIGHTH WIFE, LOST HORIZON (1937) d) Donald Meek; STAGE COACH, MRS WIGGS OF THE CABBAGE PATCH (1934), YOUNG MR LINCOLN e) Una Merkel; DESTRY RIDES AGAIN, ABRAHAM LINCOLN (1930), THE MERRY WIDOW (1934)

21 a) D.O.A., Edmond O'Brien b) JOLSON SINGS AGAIN, Larry Parks *as* Al Jolson meets Larry Parks who is to play him c) HOLD BACK THE DAWN, Charles Boyer to director Mitchell Leisen d) A CANTERBURY TALE, Eric Portman e) TURNABOUT, John Hubbard and Carole Landis

22 a) PARIS WHEN IT SIZZLES b) THE DANCE OF THE VAMPIRES (US: THE FEARLESS VAMPIRE KILLERS) c) EMPIRE OF THE ANTS d) THE GREEK TYCOON e) CHOSEN SURVIVORS

23 a) Elia Kazan b) Erich von Stroheim c) Sam Fuller and Nicholas Ray d) Fritz Lang e) John Schlesinger

24 a) JANE EYRE b) GREAT EXPECTATIONS c) MANHATTAN MELODRAMA d) THE GHOST AND MRS MUIR e) THE STORY OF THREE LOVES

25 a) Alan Schneider, Samuel Beckett, Buster Keaton b) Glen Hunter (1924), Red Skelton (1947), Harold Lloyd c) HELLZAPOPPIN, THE SMALLEST SHOW ON EARTH, SHERLOCK JUNIOR d) François Truffaut to Jean-Pierre Léaud in DAY FOR NIGHT (LA NUIT AMÉRICAINE)

SUPERBUFF!
Answers to Picture Questions

Page 167:

SCANNERS; extraordinary telepathic powers; Dick Smith; David Cronenberg; Patrick McGoohan; 'The Prisoner'; VIDEODROME; James Woods; Michael Lennick

Page 168:

MGM, 1936; (l to r) Clark Gable (SAN FRANCISCO – W.S. Van Dyke – USA), Robert Montgomery (TROUBLE FOR TWO – Walter Rubin – England), Lionel Barrymore (THE DEVIL DOLL – Tod Browning – France), Paul Muni (THE GOOD EARTH – Sydney Franklin – China)

Page 170:

a) DANGEROUS; Bette Davis and Franchot Tone b) Actress and architect c) Davis won her first Oscar d) SINGAPORE WOMAN; Brenda Marshall and David Bruce e) Alfred E. Green (1935), Jean Negulesco (1941)